RELUCTANT
PIONEER

Lake of Bays, July 29, 1875

RELUCTANT PIONEER

How I Survived Five Years in the Canadian Bush

THOMAS OSBORNE

Foreword by Roy MacGregor
Introduction by J. Patrick Boyer
Sketches by George Harlow White

DUNDURN
TORONTO

Printer: Webcom

Library and Archives Canada Cataloguing in Publication

Osborne, Thomas, 1859–1948
Reluctant pioneer : how I survived five years in the Canadian bush / Thomas Osborne ; foreword by Roy MacGregor; introduction by J. Patrick Boyer ; sketches by George Harlow White.

Originally publ.: Toronto : Stoddart, 1995, under title: The night the mice danced the quadrille.
Includes bibliographical references and index.
ISBN 978-1-92657-716-6

1. Osborne, Thomas, 1859–1948. 2. Frontier and pioneer life—Ontario—Muskoka (District municipality). 3. Muskoka (Ont. : District municipality)—History. 4. Pioneers—Ontario—Muskoka (District municipality)— Biography. I. Osborne, Thomas, 1859–1948. Night the mice danced the quadrille. II. Title.

FC3095.M88Z49 2011   971.3'1603'092   C2011-901285-5

1   2   3   4   5   17   16   15   14   13

 Conseil des Arts   Canada Council
du Canada   for the Arts   **ONTARIO ARTS COUNCIL**
CONSEIL DES ARTS DE L'ONTARIO

We acknowledge the support of the **Canada Council for the Arts** and the **Ontario Arts Council** for our publishing program. We also acknowledge the financial support of the **Government of Canada** through the **Canada Book Fund** and **Livres Canada Books**, and the **Government of Ontario** through the **Ontario Book Publishing Tax Credit** and the **Ontario Media Development Corporation**.

Care has been taken to trace the ownership of copyright material used in this book. The author and the publisher welcome any information enabling them to rectify any references or credits in subsequent editions.

J. Kirk Howard, President

Printed and bound in Canada.

Visit us at
Dundurn.com | Definingcanada.ca | @dundurnpress | Facebook.com/dundurnpress

Dundurn	Gazelle Book Services Limited	Dundurn
3 Church Street, Suite 500	White Cross Mills	2250 Military Road
Toronto, Ontario, Canada	High Town, Lancaster, England	Tonawanda, NY
M5E 1M2	LA1 4XS	U.S.A. 14150

The Drawings

The thirty-seven George Harlow White pencil sketches reproduced in this book were drawn in pencil by the artist at the same time Thomas Osborne was pioneering in Muskoka. These sketches are part of the John Ross Robertson collection at the Toronto Reference Library (part of the Toronto Public Library system). Dates are those written on the back of the sketches by White. The sketch location/subjects preceding the date for each are based on White's notations, but are not verbatim transcriptions. In a few instances the location was not given. Sketches are not cropped except for minor amounts on the edges to create a rectangle.

Before coming to Canada in 1871, White had been painting and drawing British Isles landscapes for some thirty years. He completed some seventy drawings in Muskoka depicting life and conditions around the time of Thomas Osborne's story. Among those reproduced in this book is one, on page 48, entitled "Osborne boys and their lean-to at the Portage," which shows Thomas and his brother Arthur Osborne at the entrance to a crude shelter they'd built, away from their cabin, to avoid its heavy infestation of fleas. It was drawn by White when he stayed with the Osbornes at the Portage in July 1875.

During his six-year stay in Canada, White made an invaluable contribution to the historical record, leaving behind a large body of drawings and watercolours, although he romantically softened scenes in the manner of English landscape artists of that era. After returning to England in 1877, he continued to paint and exhibit his art.

CONTENTS

FOREWORD

Discovering a Hidden Canadian Classic

Roy MacGregor

ROY MACGREGOR

THOMAS OSBORNE'S tale of pioneer life in the Lake of Bays region of Muskoka was written more than half a century after the events described. And yet, it is written in an elegant style with both a sense of immediacy and remarkable clarity. He is a fine writer, an excellent storyteller, and the tales told herein are, at times, mind-boggling in their starkness.

He is writing about my own stomping grounds—lakes I grew up on and, like Thomas, fished and hunted on—and yet my experiences pale in comparison to the tales he tells of poverty, starvation, bravery, endurance, and survival. He speaks of a time so far in our past that we have largely lost the ability even to imagine it. Just reading about the "fly dope" of the 1870s makes today's reader wonder if perhaps the bugs themselves would be preferable.

Osborne writes with authority on fishing, trapping, fear, injuries, the dark side of isolation, and the truly remarkable resilience of these early dwellers in a land where, today, city dwellers go to lay back and relax. Imagine a fifty-six-year-old man, Osborne's father, walking from Toronto to Portage through thick snow simply because he had not the price of a

Mouth of the Muskoka River at Fairy Lake, July 26, 1875

train fare. You may never experience the actual journey, but you will certainly feel what it was like in the pages of this remarkable book.

The author came from Philadelphia and, ultimately, returns to Philadelphia. Yet he has written about his years in the Canadian wilderness with something that is worth noting above and beyond the mere reporting of what he did and what he saw. And that is his love of life and optimism. It comes through in every chapter, no matter how harrowing the tale being told, no matter how dire the circumstances at times appear.

Lovers of Canadian pioneer literature owe publisher and historian Patrick Boyer a debt for finding Thomas Osborne's 1934 out-of-print gem, first published under the trivializing title *The Night the Mice Danced the Quadrille*, and giving it a new one, *Reluctant Pioneer*, that at least suggests the promises to be delivered between covers. It may now find the readers it missed in its previous incarnation. And readers will discover a book that should never have been passed over just because of a misleading title.

I have long been of the opinion that early Canadian literature has been badly served by the twin gods of First Scribblings—Susanna Moodie and Northrop Frye, Moodie the reporter and Frye the analyst. Moodie's spiteful *Roughing It in the Bush* stands, surely, as the most-quoted and most-studied of all early Canadian writings. She prayed that if her words were able to deter "one family from sinking their property and shipwrecking all their hopes, by going to reside in the backwoods of Canada, I shall consider myself amply repaid for revealing the secrets of the prison-house and feel that I have not toiled and suffered in the wilderness in vain."

This, sadly, was very much a "colonial" attitude. She had hoped to see British culture transplanted to this vast winter outpost and spent a lifetime trying to set herself and hapless husband, John, up as gentry. She ended up hating the country and the savage side of nature as she found it.

As for Frye, the Biblical scholar richly deserves international praise for his work on the Bible and William Blake—but not, please, when it comes to his own country's early writings. He himself was terrified of nature—a city-born and city-sworn academic who suffered from hay fever so severely that even a Sunday drive in the country could be a test.

He once wrote in his diary: "The Lord's work for me is sitting still in a comfortable chair and thinking beautiful thoughts, and occasionally writing them down."

Unfortunately, when it came to writing down his thoughts on early Canadian literature he seemed rather unaware of the beautiful and brave writings of such early explorers as David Thompson or Samuel Hearne. He seems, instead, to have read too much Moodie and too much of those outsiders who were writing for the lecture circuit as much as for the publishing house, often wildly embellishing their tales in order to heighten the dangers a soft, city audience in Britain or America might happily pay to be a part of, even if only vicariously.

It was Frye who coined the phrase "Garrison mentality" and claimed that within this northern imagination lurked "a tone of deep terror in regard to nature … It is not a terror of the dangers or discomforts or even the mysteries of nature, but a terror of the soul at something that these things manifest."

I remember thinking the first time that I read Frye on Canadian literature that all I had to do was substitute the word "city" for "nature" and the analysis would have held true for my own parents, my mother born in Algonquin Park to a ranger family, my father a life-long logger in the same vast park. A trip to the city for them, with its street lights, elevators, and clover leafs, was about as harrowing an experience as they could imagine. An isolated lake surrounded by dense, dark bush, on the other hand, was where they felt most comfortable, most at home.

And it is for this that I welcome the re-publication of Thomas Osborne's account of his years at Lake of Bays. He had his fears, of course, but he faced them. Rather than dread, he held hope. And though in the end he did not stay in North Muskoka—unlike his father and brother— he never for a moment felt he had "suffered in the wilderness in vain."

Roy MacGregor
Camp Lake

INTRODUCTION

A Reluctant Pioneer

J. Patrick Boyer

J. Patrick Boyer

Thomas Osborne's coming-of-age story from the 1870s is all about wilderness experience, but as a "back to the land" narrative it is paradoxical because of its ever-present counterpoint, the author's preference for city living.

Early in the saga, the author enters the Canadian bush in city clothes that soon enough are reduced to remnant rags. In the end, he returns to big city Philadelphia, getting his first shave in a year to help his mother recognize him, wearing new clothes, and keen for an indoor factory job. During the five years between, when others tried pairing him with young females in Muskoka, he spurned all local marriage prospects because he held out, not for a distant woman, but for a return to the city.

Thomas, and his younger brother Arthur who travelled with him into the bush and back in time, were not pulled to the rawest edge of the Canadian frontier by some atavistic urge to be at one with nature, only to obey William Osborne's call to join him in Muskoka. They were dutiful sons of a strong-willed father. Thomas never volunteered for pioneering.

His tentative excursion into untamed territory, his insistence that his mother and sisters flee back to the city to escape the privations of the family's primitive homestead, and his own resolute escape from Muskoka, infuse this true life story with its running tension. The recurring off-stage presence of a larger world beyond the district's scattered log cabins acutely deepens our understanding of what it really meant to be a pioneer.

Yet there is more. What makes Thomas Osborne's memoir so engaging is that these juxtapositions of urban and wilderness experience are not presented as solemn testament to hardship, but as a romping adventure story. This extra element sets his book apart from most reminiscences and reports by pioneers, giving it an intimacy and energy that leads Roy MacGregor to astutely identify the book, which Osborne himself called *Canada Pioneers*, as a classic. His boy's sense of irrepressible fun seems never too far below the surface, even in the most horrific situations, of which he experienced many.

After Thomas Osborne sojourned into unsettled Muskoka in 1875 at age sixteen, his ingenuity and determination helped him survive and, in certain ways, even thrive. This book might have been entitled, after another classic, *Tom Sawyer Strays into Pioneer Canada*. His adventures, like those of the youthful character Mark Twain introduced to readers in 1876, seem a model for those shrewd and adventurous boys on the Mississippi who skirted danger, stood strong when it counted, and enjoyed the fun in life. In place of Huck Finn, this Tom had his brother Arthur. The difference is, Thomas and Arthur were real, not fictitious.

Before he became a pioneer in the Canadian bush, Thomas Osborne had been formed by city conditions.

He started out in England's manufacturing city Nottingham, born May 3, 1859, the sixth child of textile workers Esther and William Osborne. His mother made caps and bonnets, his dad was a knitter, and at night the parents and their six youngsters crammed themselves into a squalid, small house on Factory Row. To escape his deadening routines and their grimy living, William relocated Esther and the children to the village of Mountsorrel, some dozen miles south. Here the Osborne's seventh child, Arthur, who would feature alongside Thomas in the family's pioneering drama, was born in February 1861.

Although his father's quest to sidestep industrial Britain's grimmest features brought Thomas to a smaller place, Mountsorrel was, all the same, an organized community with a structure that gave order to his formative years, more a city in miniature than any kind of training ground for Canada's waiting frontier.

That move from Nottingham epitomized William Osborne's willingness to try anything to get ahead, an early clue to the coming North American adventure. The man was a wily dreamer, pulsating with a deep urge to be more independent. In Mountsorrel he set himself up as village innkeeper, underwriting the venture by continuing his trade manufacturing stockings. For her part, Esther had no choice but to leave off cap-making to dutifully support her husband by keeping the inn while also raising seven children on the side.

As things panned out, an innkeeper's life was not as attractive as William had imagined. It placed him in service to others. Nor was it appealing to Esther. Her routine of piecework sewing caps in a textile mill had been replaced by unpredictable servitude to others in a village inn. As concerning was the fact her husband began displaying an inclination, like patrons at their inn, to escape life's disappointments with some help from the Osborne's handy inventory of intoxicants.

But William's true nature won out when, somewhere near the bottom of a bottle, he found the light and resolved to continue his quest to make himself a free man. It was a timely solution because Esther was about to check out of their inn and abandon its burdens herself. So together in 1864 the entire family, now ten in number because on top of everything else Esther had delivered more infant Osbornes while in Mountsorrel, sailed aboard the *Louisiana* over the Atlantic and into the New World's promise of something better.

Once again, Thomas found himself in a city.

Philadelphia's knitting mills had been like a magnet to his father, whose quest to improve the family's lot pulled him back to what he knew best, textiles. Here William Osborne's entrepreneurial qualities, his desire for independence, and the enterprising American atmosphere, all quickly combined. He acquired an ownership interest in the textile firm where he worked. He made several innovative adaptations to the company's textile machines. He improved efficiency.

On the Philadelphia home front Esther added two more offspring, bringing the Osborne's count of children to an even dozen, making Thomas a middle child in their growing brood, with the balancing and moderating attributes such placement produces. Attending school, working part-time, and getting around bustling Philadelphia's streets habituated Thomas to the rhythms and routines of city life. An energetic boy who worked hard and cheered street fighting, he liked where he was, who his friends were, and what he was doing. Engaged by the Philadelphia scene, he was learning, growing, and coming into his own. Thomas Osborne was home, in America, in the city.

Yet his father, after ten years of urban order and hard work had a sense of things closing in around him, felt a resurgence of the same restless rebellion that earlier propelled him from Nottingham to Mountsorrel. Now dissatisfied with life in textile manufacturing, because its routines enslaved more than liberated him, William Osborne resolved, once again, to seek something better.

A decade in the United States between 1864 and 1874, through the ending of the Civil War and the tumultuous era of "reconstruction" and further industrialization of northern cities, had been long enough for the exhilaration of the New World to solidly reinforce William's desire to be his own man. But it was sufficient time, too, for the tawdriness of American life to poke through the country's lustrous veneer. In his core, William remained an Englishman. Like others from the British Isles who'd made a fresh start in the United States, he was ineluctably drawn back to British ways. The magic, he realized, was that he could go home without leaving the New World. The best of both worlds beckoned just a short distance north, where the new country Canada had recently been formed in 1867 under its *British* North America constitution.

At age fifty-three William sold his business interests in Philadelphia and headed to Ontario, intent on relocating his family and starting anew. By this time the parade of surviving Osborne children had, one by one, reached early working age, left school, and followed their parents into the textile trade. Thomas's oldest brother, Owen, was already on the ascendant, envisaging for himself a prosperous future with his own textile factories. As strong-willed as all the Osborne men were, Owen refused to leave his bright prospects and was dismissive of his restless father's next plan, thinking it crazy and formed in too much alcoholic haze. The Osborne's first-born son vowed to stay in Pennsylvania. Owen did, however, undertake to settle up his father's business interests and send William money as proceeds from the sale of his interest in the textile operation, through a series of installment payments over several years, became available. He also accompanied his mother, sisters, and brothers over the U.S. border to see them safely reunited with his father, before returning to Philadelphia.

It is at this point in the family's nomadic adventure that Thomas himself takes up the narrative, beginning with how he found himself in yet another city, Toronto.

As for the head of the family himself, William Osborne found, after arriving in Ontario, that his business plans began shifting. Then he could not start a business, nor even get work. But true to form, upon discovering a man could get *free* land in Muskoka District, just 150 miles further north, he struck upon yet another plan.

William now envisaged himself as a large-scale land owner, self-sufficient in food, having no one to answer to but himself, free and unshackled, an independent man comforted by living in a British North American society. With newfound zeal he advanced into the Canadian bush to become a freehold farmer.

Once in Muskoka, William sent for two of his sons who were then still young enough to obey him but old enough for heavy work. Thus began life's transforming experience for Thomas and Arthur Osborne, both for the first time leaving organized society, trekking into Canada's unbroken wilderness.

The district in which William, Thomas, and Arthur Osborne began homesteading, barely a decade and a half into its pioneer settlement phase, had been traversed by aboriginal peoples for a least five thousand years, mapped by Canada's legendary David Thompson in 1837, and visited by fur traders and government surveyors through the early to mid-1800s. Muskoka first felt the modern age's harder edge in the 1850s, when logging began along its southern perimeter.

A decade later the district was opened to settlement for farming. At first a trickle of squatters, then additional hopefuls, traced their way along the crude Muskoka Colonization Road that government contractors were stubbornly pushing into the province's wild northern tracts. By 1868 Ontario's legislature, wanting to entice thousands more newcomers to fill and farm the still-empty district, enacted *The Free Grants and Homestead Act*. With that, a flood of homesteaders arrived. This created a land boom, with settlers pushing further north even into sections not yet surveyed, such as Franklin Township east of Huntsville, where the Osbornes ended up.

Those who came brought existing skills into a novel setting. Foresters felling virgin stands of immense trees had to adapt the known methods of their day to unprecedented challenges of rugged Canadian Shield typography. Road builders, used to softer and flatter southern terrain, had to scratch across rocky ridges, bridge over rivers and creeks, wind up stone-face canyons and down narrow valleys, skirt lakes and build up roads with logs through muddy swamplands. Settlers hoping to make productive farms like those they'd known around cities and villages elsewhere, hacked homes from the bush, put up crude log shanties, and cleared trees and stumps only to discover, in many cases, thin soil and bedrock outcroppings. As Thomas recounts, trying to turn up a field by ox-pulled plow was futile, because the blade caught in the underworld maze of roots. But poking out a hole in the ground with a pointed stick, working around stumps, opened space enough to drop in seeds.

Everyone arriving in Muskoka was in search of a vision that existed more inside their heads than was possible to achieve on the land. Their kitbag tools were, mostly, useless here. Much of their prior experience had been gained from a life that now seemed alien. Thomas's memoir, a chronicle of adaptation, shows how greatly humans vary in their ability to bend, change, and learn. The art was not in staying firm or being flexible, but in knowing when to be one, or the other. Pioneering was a human experiment in survival, with little margin for error. Death was a constant and close companion on the frontier, as Thomas writes with unvarnished honesty in recounting a number of somber examples.

The promise of free land and a fresh start was drawing many improbable candidates, like the Osbornes, to this unknown frontier of Muskoka, and later beyond it to Ontario's other "free grant" northern districts of Parry Sound and Nippissing. In addition to free land, some arrivals were attracted by the obscurity such a remote location offered, not only to make a fresh start, but to do so as a different person. In 1869, for instance, Isaac Jelfs left prominence in New York as a Broadway Avenue lawyer for "end-of-the-line" Muskoka where as an obscure homesteader he reinvented himself as "James Boyer," my great-grandfather.

Just a few years later, when William Osborne acquired squatter rights to his initial Muskoka property, it was in an even more remote northern section of the district, from a furtive Pole named Pokorny. In Pokorny's case, as Thomas makes clear, living in an out-of-the-way corner of wilderness was helpful if one had to escape the reach of the law. Pokorny had capped off his career of embezzlement by perpetrating a crime against Toronto's opera company, of which he was treasurer. He'd disappeared into the northern bush with a suitcase of cash, the box-office receipts from a Saturday night operatic performance. Pokorny would feature largely in the lives of the Osbornes, almost never to their benefit.

William Osborne and his sons joined a jumble of anxious characters who'd abandoned their problems — fleeing famine, war, flood, fire, diseases, poverty, boring jobs, poor housing, heartbreak, romantic entanglement, financial crisis, or some other personal hell — to start anew in the untamed Muskoka frontier. Most were hoping to cash in on the promise Ontario's government and its immigration agents were aggressively touting in American and British cities through glowing speeches, newspaper advertisements, and the widely distributed booklet *Emigration to Canada: The Province of Ontario*, to publicize the northern districts' pastoral prospects. This fantasy of agriculture on the Canadian Shield, so actively promoted by government and ardently embraced by adventurers and escapists seeking gift-wrapped opportunity, soon became, for many, a hardscrabble nightmare. Thomas's account shows exactly what this looked like, not from a government's overview perspective, but from the ground up.

Often conditions were insurmountable. Non-swimmer William Johnston, exhausted after another day chopping down trees in Muskoka's southern Morrison Township, drowned in the Severn River trying to catch fish to feed his hungry family. As he sank to the bottom, Johnson also went down in history as the first settler to die in Muskoka. His plucky widow, with two young boys to care for, pressed on alone, managing by valiant spirit and tears of determination in her eyes to somehow clear about nine more acres on the Johnston's lot, until she herself weakened, sickened, and died.

Thomas recounts many true tales of hardship and suffering, and of other bleak lives that expired in the unforgiving bush, where escape came neither by going back to a city nor out to California, but through the more convenient and certain route of death.

Between a homesteader and his or her hundred acres of "free" land stood years of backbreaking labour. Face to face with the bush, such settlers struggling to make their farm could be overwhelmed, and many were. The ancient wilderness had to be transformed into an agricultural operation in five years if one was to claim their chosen lot of land for free, much sooner if one hoped to eat. Learning from the never-ending toil of seasoned neighbours, new arrivals cleared their selected lots tree after tree, boulder by boulder. Not all the tips from neighbours helped. Homesteading clergyman Reverend Robert Norton Hill and others imparted incorrect instructions to Thomas about root cellar storage that contributed to the Osborne's near-starvation their first Muskoka winter, as their vegetables first froze, then rotted.

Some homesteaders perished, others fled the land, but persistent homesteaders adapted old ways and inherited practices to their pioneer reality, and learned new ways.

Thomas Osborne became one of the resourceful and determined pioneers who survived, not because he'd prepared for this life or even wanted it, but because after he'd dutifully answered his father's call to the

northern woods, this youth from the city, finding himself in a new setting where he had no choice but to work and survive, displayed true grit
overcoming adversity and real ingenuity adapting to primitive reality.

Often survival was not just of the fittest, but the luckiest. Thomas
was both fit and lucky — as becomes apparent through his many feats of
strength and endurance, and with many calamities avoided such as burning, falling trees, deep gashes, freezing weather, stormy lakes, unmarked
woods, and times without food. He was also fearless and determined,
and as a result was seldom hobbled by a sense of danger. While neighbours pitched in to help, others nearby posed a range of threats from
stealing land, logs, and chickens, to fighting and starting lawsuits.

Before long Thomas's tattered city clothes were replaced by simple,
durable coverings worn day after day until, threadbare, they all but vanished too. He never wore underwear, avoided the advances of females,
and bonded instead with nature, his brother Arthur, and Indian youths.
He was often happier cutting through the woods than following a road,
walked for dozens of miles at a stretch, and learned to carry heavy loads,
including his canoe and a heavy backpack of equipment and supplies,
over arduous portages.

He could discern his way up rivers and through forests in the dark
and seemed to intuitively know his position so he never got lost. He was
determined to eat rather than starve, and became such an adept cook
that others were in awe of. By illegally shooting deer while they swam in
the lake and catching fish out of season in nets, as well as lawfully picking
wild berries, he learned to live off the land. He also lived for five days
off nothing but muskrat, and for weeks on turnips alone. He became a
muscular "little giant" wielding an axe and lifting logs to clear land, even
managing to treat an axe blow to his father's knee and survive a glancing
cut to his own foot.

Thomas learned to load and shoot a musket. He killed partridges in the
trees, shot bear at dangerous close range, kept chickens, and slaughtered
pigs. In winter he survived plunges through the ice. In summer he paddled
a canoe, sometimes happily naked, and became a strong swimmer.

Thomas had not chosen this life. But with determination and a spirit
of optimistic realism, he prevailed as a homesteader. Daily he measured

survival by continuous small acts of successful adaptation: storing vegetables the second winter so they would not decompose, setting nets to
catch enough fish to barter for goods and supplies in Huntsville, using
bear grease when cooking bannock to give it a surprising sweet flavour.

Before getting to Muskoka, Thomas Osborne only knew an urban
way of life, but of necessity he reinvented himself as a true son of the
wilds. The city boy, despite his reluctance to be a pioneer at all, emerged
an iron-strong frontiersman.

1

A Risky Adventure Going to Canada

IN DECEMBER 1874 my father, William, who had been in Canada for several months, sent for us to meet him at Niagara Falls, Ontario. I left Philadelphia for Canada along with my mother, my five sisters, and three of my four brothers. I was fifteen and a half years old.

At Niagara Falls we had a layover of two hours for the train to Dundas, Ontario. We enjoyed a walk along the Canadian side of the river up to the Horseshoe Falls. At that time there was only a dirt walk and road from the railway station to the falls. There was no wall to keep people from falling over into the river below. I remember how my brother Arthur and I tried to throw stones out into the river but, try as we would, we could not do it. The stones seemed to draw back into the bank, which was very steep. We all enjoyed the walk and view of the falls as none of us except Pop had ever seen them.

At that time there were a few open saloons by the roadside; no cars, only cabs drawn by horses. As the cabbies were not trustworthy, it was a dangerous trip to take, especially at night. It was a well-known fact that men who had started the trip were never seen again. It was said that the cabbies would take men over from the American side to see the Horseshoe Falls. On the Canadian side they would be induced to enter one or other of the saloons where, treated to drinks until anything but sober, they would be robbed of their money and valuables. If they made a fuss about it, they were run out of the saloon and across the road. There

Lake Muskoka near Gravenhurst, August 14, 1875

they were pushed over the cliff into the river more than a hundred feet below, never to be heard of again.

One trick these cabbies would pull on their unsuspecting passengers was to induce them to take a sightseeing trip to the Horseshoe Falls from the American side at fifty cents a round trip. When they arrived near the falls, the cabby would stop and tell the passengers they could walk around and he would wait for their return. When they came back, he would tell them it would cost them five dollars to get back to the American side. To my knowledge, this practice was carried on up to and including 1900. I knew one young man personally who was treated in this manner; he was in my employ and told me of it himself.

Well, we boarded our train without any of that trouble, arriving at Dundas at dusk in the evening of December 4. At that time Dundas was a small village under a hill. I remember a ledge of rock projecting from the mountain that seemed to reach out over the village. A railway ran alongside the mountain about halfway up. It was the road we came in on, and we had to descend to the village by a flight of steps. As we entered the village below, we saw a sign hanging out over the door of a saloon. It said "The House of Ten Nations," and I believe it was the only hotel in Dundas at that time. We passed it by and went around into a side street where Pop had secured a small cottage. It was bare of furniture, cold and dreary; there were no street lights at that time. Pop and my brother Owen went to a regular country store not far away and bought a small stove and some candles. We found some wood and coal in a shed near the house, so we soon had light and a fire. While this was going on, Owen, who was quite a dancer, gave us all lessons in dancing to keep us warm.

The man for whom Pop worked had invited us to his house where his wife had prepared a good supper for us. This cheered us up very much; and so we passed our first night in Dundas. We did not sleep very much, I assure you. The next day, after seeing that we had some furniture and something to eat in the house, Owen left us to return to Philadelphia.

I won't go into the details of our four weeks in Dundas except to say that Arthur and I enjoyed a number of trips through the woods and up the mountain. On one of these, with some boys we had gotten to know, we climbed over the mountain and came to a sheer drop of some thirty feet straight down the flat face of the rock. Undaunted, we looked around and along the edge of the cliff until we found a tree growing up to just within reach. We all, one after the other, slid down the tree to the bottom of the ravine, which led down to a mill or stone crusher, then down to the village.

Arthur and I had another trip a day or two after Christmas. We went down the canal to the bay of Lake Ontario, not far from Hamilton. The canal and bay were frozen, so, with one pair of skates which we took turns using, we skated and walked the four miles down the canal and across to Hamilton. We sure ran a great risk of breaking through, as the ice was so thin we could see through it into the water below. The ice cracked as we skated and walked over it. However, we visited Hamilton and returned just at dark. I might add that Arthur and I, during our time together in Canada, ran many a chance, just as great, of losing our lives. We did not, apparently, have any fear.

At Christmas time, Arthur and I climbed up the side of the mountain and cut down a nice pine tree which our sisters trimmed with cotton and popcorn. That was all we had for our Christmas celebration. It was also the last time in Canada that we celebrated Christmas with a tree.

Pop's employer decided to move farther west to London, Ontario. My father said he would not go west. He was going north; and so we did. Between Christmas and New Year's we left Dundas for Toronto, where Pop secured a house on the outskirts of the city, the end house of four. The owners used the corner one for a saloon and the others for their living quarters and for lodgers. In the lower part of our house, ordinarily used for a kitchen, we kept some chickens we had bought in Dundas. I remember the weather was very cold, so cold we had to watch the chickens and gather the eggs as soon as laid, or they would freeze and crack open.

Our water supply was a well near the front of the house. It was a veritable oaken bucket, lowered and raised by a chain over a roller and turned by a crank of iron. I leave you to judge what a cold job it was to get water for cooking and drinking. There was city water too, but it was fit only for washing; even this was limited as the city would only let us have it twice a week; then everyone would fill up tubs and pans, etc.

This block of houses was at the corner of River and Don streets. Up River Street a little way was a butcher shop where they always had a big leg of beef on the meat block. If a customer wanted a slice, instead of cutting it with a knife, he would saw it off with a meat saw. The beef was always frozen solid.

At that time River Street ran down a grade for at least two blocks. Lots of sleighs passed to and fro over it, so it was smooth and hard. Arthur and I enjoyed coasting down it on a sled we built from old boards. It worked, is all I can say for it. Other boys made it of interest to us: they had from two to four dogs harnessed to their sleds to pull them to the top of the grade. There the boys would disconnect the dogs from the sleds and coast down to the bottom, the dogs running along behind. Then the boys would hitch the dogs on again, pile onto the sleds, and be hauled to the top. They would keep this up for hours.

We had lived in this house about six weeks when Pop secured employment for my three elder sisters, Arthur, and me in Simpson's knitting mill down near the bay. We moved into a nice cottage on Trinity Street. With a barn connected at the back of the cottage, we had lots of room and were fairly comfortable for a time.

Then Pop, unable to get into business or employment, decided to go up into Muskoka and take a free grant section. So, about the middle of February 1875, he left us to, as it were, seek his fortune.

We were doing well on our combined pay from the mill until the end of April when, due to lack of orders, Arthur and I were laid off. Annie, Marie, and Kate, my older sisters, were kept on to finish goods (it was an underwear mill). Arthur and I could not get into anything, so we spent our time fishing, mostly in the Don River, which entered the bay not far from our place. We brought home many a large string of catfish. Arthur and I would clean them, Mother would cook them, and we all ate them; they were of great help in feeding the bunch. Another source of food: Arthur and I would go to the freight yards and get enough corn from empty freight cars to feed the chickens, which were good layers.

We had been receiving an occasional letter from Pop. Finally, in the latter part of May 1875, a letter arrived to say he had found a location and bought a squatter's clearing and log cabin. Writing glowing accounts of it, he told Mother to send Arthur and me to him so we could plant the little clearing and raise all we could to help support the family for the next winter.

Muskoka Road north of Severn Bridge, September 14, 1873

2

Two Boys Push Deep into the Backwoods

I WILL NEVER FORGET the morning of May 25, 1875, when at seven in the morning we parted from Mother and sisters at the train station in Toronto. I leave the parting to your imagination: two boys going into the backwoods, I just past sixteen and Arthur a year and nine months younger.

We had for company a young man, about thirty years old, Frank St. John by name. He was on his way to take up a free grant section. He was a good sort. We rather enjoyed the trip to Severn Bridge, the end of the line. There we had to take a stage for eleven miles to Gravenhurst, a small town on the shore of Lake Muskoka where we boarded a nice little steamboat for Bracebridge, which we reached at midnight. (Frank left us at Gravenhurst. He went up into the Lake Rosseau district and we never saw him again, although we heard years afterwards that he had settled there and was doing well.) We enjoyed the trip on that boat up the lake and up the Muskoka River.

It was dark by the time we reached the river, which was not a wide stream. On account of floating logs, into which we frequently bumped, our progress was slow. On the way up we had a view of how the settlers cleared the land. It seems the underbrush is cut in the summer and fall, leaving the trees to be cut down in the winter months. The trunks of the trees are cut into fifteen-foot lengths, approximately, and in spring a fire is set to the brush as soon as the brush is dry enough to burn. The fire runs over the fields and burns all the brush, leaving the logs. These are rolled into great heaps and burned. It was one of these fires we saw as we slowly travelled up the river. There seemed to be at least a hundred of these great heaps of logs blazing up high into the air. It was a fine sight with the light reflecting down into the dark water below.

Finally we reached the landing at Bracebridge, a small town extending on both sides of the river. The landing was made of logs laid side-by-side in the water with a few boards on top of them. It was a rather ticklish job for us boys to keep on the boards; all the light we had came from lanterns used by men who had come down to meet the boat and take people to any of the hotels they might wish to go to. Pop had told us to listen for mention of the Dominion Hotel. We soon heard it and were driven to a nice small frame building.

Pop had told the proprietor of the Dominion Hotel to look out for us. He had us up in good time for breakfast and, after waiting some time and no sign of the stage, I asked him when the stage would be along. He said, "I'm sorry, boys, but the stage was full before it reached here, and there was no room for you. But never mind. You can stay here until Monday." It being Saturday, we would be two days behind in reaching Huntsville. To console us, he said, "Never mind. We'll go fishing tomorrow and have a good time."

I said, "No, sir. We must reach Huntsville tonight, even if we walk it. Isn't there a team of some kind going that way that will take us? We must get there tonight."

When he saw I was determined to go, he looked around, finally finding a man who was going as far as Utterson, a halfway place on the road to Huntsville. We were glad to get a ride in a wagon, a buckboard; so you can judge what a comfortable ride we had for fifteen miles over rough country road. We finally reached Utterson, had a good lunch, but no conveyance of any kind was to be had.

So we two city lads stepped out for an eleven-mile hike up hill and down, through dense woods, over a dirt road. For miles and miles we tramped along, meeting only one man, who was on his way to Utterson. It was all woods on each side of us, but there were frequent springs by the wayside, so we didn't suffer from thirst. When the sun set, it began to get gloomy; we could see nothing but the sky overhead and the dark woods on each side. So it was with great pleasure that we saw a clearing ahead of us. As we reached it, I saw a cabin at some distance from the road. As Arthur was all in and crying, I told him to sit down and I would go to the cabin and see if I could find out how far it was to Huntsville. As I approached the cabin, I realized people were around back, as I could hear voices. I went around to find the ones who were talking. I'll never forget the surprise I gave to a big family. The old granddad was the first to recover from the shock of having a city-dressed lad drop in on them so suddenly.

"How far to Huntsville?" I asked.

His answer, in a Scotch dialect, was, "Yo see yon ridge? Weel, wan ye get tae it, ye wull see it on tother side."

This good news cheered us up. We very soon reached the top of the ridge when, lo and behold, away down below us were a number of buildings. All we could find were ten, including barns and cowsheds—in fact everything looked like a house. Well, we headed for the largest, which proved to be Cann's Hotel.

We entered a room through a doorway at one side and, as we did so, an elderly man entered by a door at the opposite corner; this afterwards proved to be the entrance to the bar. Otherwise the room was empty, as far as we could see, with the only furniture a wooden bench on each of three sides.

As soon as Mr. Cann (as the elderly man proved to be) saw us, he stepped back to where he had come from, exclaiming, "Here they are." With that, Pop entered. He was overjoyed to see us for, when the stage came in without us, he did not know what to think. He was surprised to hear we had walked so far. He took us into the next room where a number of men were eating their evening meal. We sat with them and ate a big supper, all the while being stared at by all. They also had lots of questions to put to us. We retired early to a large room with two beds; one a stranger occupied and we the other. We all had a good night's sleep.

I was awakened at daylight by the tinkling of cow bells. The cows, it seemed, were allowed to roam around the village day and night. I lay for some time listening to what was music to me; I really enjoyed it and the sounds of people getting around. I simply enjoyed it. There seemed something soothing about it, so much so that I have never forgotten it.

Soon after, we turned out for breakfast, first having a wash-up in clear, cold water from a pump outside the kitchen door. Then we entered the breakfast room where a number of men were seated along each side of a long table with Mr. Cann at the head, serving the food.

Mr. Cann was assisted by a big, fine serving girl and by Mrs. Cann, his sister-in-law. Her husband had died, leaving her with three children, two boys and a girl. Up to that time, Mr. Cann had followed hunting and trapping through this district, but at his brother's death he settled on the north shore of that branch of the Muskoka River that runs through Huntsville. However, a man by the name of Hunt settled on the opposite bank and therefore the name was Huntsville. Mr. Cann built the only hotel, with the understanding that Mrs. Cann and her children make her home with him, she to be the housekeeper; a fine woman, always on the job. She seemed to like Arthur and me from the first, probably because we were about the same ages as her children. As long as I stayed in the country, she treated us the same as her own.

Soon after breakfast, Pop said we must be off for the Portage, as he called the place where he had bought the squatter off. It was about an eleven-mile hike east of Huntsville. A government road had been cut around through the woods almost to Pop's location. Pop spurned the road; he knew the general direction through the woods.

It was early in the morning when we set out. After walking about a mile south through the woods, we came to a bay of Fairy Lake where the north branch of the Muskoka River flows out, on its way down to Mary's Lake several miles below. There was a clearing on the bay side where a family had settled some years before. This was where we expected to get the settler to ferry us across the bay.

While waiting for the boat we were entertained by an old lady, the only member of the family I can recollect. She was a nice old lady, and I remember her saying to Pop, "It's a shame to take such nice lads from city life and ways to rough it in the woods."

Pop answered, "They'll get used to it."

Huntsville, July 23, 1875

Launching a boat on Fairy Lake, July 21, 1875

3

Some Slaving to Be Done Here

THE BOAT FINALLY CAME. Flat-bottomed, square at the stern with a pointed bow, it was propelled with oars to the opposite shore half a mile away. We enjoyed this part of the trip. As soon as we landed, Pop set his bearings so we would hit the government road at some distance from the Portage.

After tramping through the wild woods for a long time, we came to a meadow where all the trees had been killed years before by beavers. They had dammed up the stream, flooded the lowland, and so killed all the trees. Among the dead trees grass had grown up, forming a meadow, green at this time of year. As we walked through this meadow, Pop called our attention to a weatherbeaten, branchless tree, all white and dried like a telegraph pole. On one of his lonely trips through there, he said, he had seen a great bear near the top of this tree. He said he had felt his hair creep but, as he had no gun or other weapon of defence, he had turned to walk away. As he looked back, he saw the bear slip down the tree and make off in the opposite direction. I later found that bears will do this. Well, we didn't see any bears; nor, since we had no gun or anything to defend ourselves with, did we want to.

After Pop's story we resumed our tramp, eventually reaching the opening of the road, which was rough with second-growth brush. Soon after hitting this road we discovered a woods fire running ahead of us, so we had to walk several miles over burnt ground and charred logs. The stench of smoke, the ashes, and the smudge we kicked up almost choked us.

We finally left the burnt area. Still following the line through the woods cut by the road builders years before, we came to where the opening ended halfway across the Portage. Here there was a foot trail, formed by Indians over many years, now used by hunters and a few settlers who travelled across from Peninsula Lake to Trading Lake (or Lake of Bays). It was called Trading Lake because all trading by Indians, hunters and trappers was done with Chief Bigwin on an island away down the lake. The Indians had been sent to a reserve a number of years before we came.

The going was easier now. Soon we reached the clearing Pop had bought from the squatter. The sun had set by the time we reached the opening. As we came to the edge of the woods, Pop gazed out across the bay. It was so clear and calm it looked like a mirror, with the trees around the shores reflected in the water. With pride in his voice, Pop said, "There it is. Isn't that a nice sight?"

"Yes, over on the lake. But not so nice here," I said as I pointed down at the logs, stone, and burnt-over ground, which close by us showed more stone than ground. It was a forbidding sight. I said, "There is some slaving to be done here in clearing up this land of all its logs and stumps." My remark was my first impression and, as we afterwards found out, it proved only too true.

Over the logs and stones we could see a little log cabin about halfway between us and the bay. Here the former settler, Pokorny by name, a Polander, had lived with his wife and four children. Pop had bought the slashing and clearing from him with the understanding that they move clear away. But Captain, as he liked to be called, simply moved to another location on the next lot, just a short distance away on the side of the bay. We couldn't see them from where we were.

Finally we reached the log cabin, or hut. Arthur and I were about tired out and very hungry. It had been a hard tramp through virgin forest, up hill and down, through swamps and brush, and over smoky, burnt-over ground. But we still had work to do before we could eat or rest. We had to clear out the cabin. It was alive with fleas.

So we set to work by removing a makeshift table and a crib, a box-like place which Pop said the children had slept in. Mother, father, and baby had slept on a homemade bed raised on four forked poles about two feet off the ground. This rack, as I would call it, was first covered with small, round poles. Then fine balsam brush covered the poles six or eight inches deep; a blanket over all constituted the bed. A very comfortable bed it made too. We tore out all we could, flooring and all, spread the rubbish over the hard ground, and set fire to it, as Pop said, to kill the fleas. But it didn't!

While the fire smouldered we went out on the lake in a log canoe. It had been left on the Portage by the Indians when they had been ordered by the government to go onto a reserve and leave their old hunting grounds. This happened about twenty years before we came. After the Indians left, there came the government surveyors who pre-empted the canoe while surveying the land into as near 100-acre lots as the lake would permit. This land was in the Township of Franklin, Muskoka District, Province of Ontario, Canada. It was not open for location, so we became squatters. A squatter has the right to use the land as his own until opened for location by the government. Then a man with family can locate on 200 acres, or two lots. Pop, by buying the squatter's cabin and clearing, got a squatter's right to two lots, which took in the land more than halfway across the Portage.

Therefore he claimed this log canoe. We used it to get out to the night line, as we called it. We took several nice trout off the line and cleaned them in the little stream. We cooked them over an open fire near the cabin, made coffee in a can, and with crackers, of which Pop had a good supply, we sat down to our first meal. We were so hungry it tasted good, although the coffee was very smoky. This was the first of many meals just as bad or worse. After eating we scraped the ashes and fire out of the cabin, then made a bed of hemlock boughs and leaves on the clean, hard floor. It was very late when at last we lay down tired and miserable—at least Arthur and I were. We slept soundly, not waking until after sunup.

This was the morning of Monday, May 28, 1875. Soon we had repeated the meal of the night before but called it breakfast. Pop said he was going to a settler's, eight miles back down the road we had come over the day before. (It was called Brunel Road because it cut through the Township of Brunel.) He was going to get some seed peas, he said. Arthur and I could plant some beans while he was away.

He gave us about a peck of cranberry beans and two sticks about eight inches long and pointed at the end. He told us to make holes about eight inches apart wherever we could among the stones, roots, and stumps in a plot of cleared land at the back of the cabin. This was low land and moist, also close by the little stream. (I explain all this to show you what a fine place it was for black flies.)

Pop said to put two beans into each hole. He saw us get started then left us to it. We started to work. And so did the black flies. They had found something tender and juicy, and how they did bite! They swarmed around so thick we could hardly see the ground. But we fought them off as well as we could and finished planting the beans. We were in bad shape.

The flies had bitten us in back of the ears, around the neck—so badly that when we wiped them off, our hands were covered with blood. Although we felt like it, we didn't sit down and cry. When we got finished planting, we went down to the lake, took off our clothes, and jumped in. This cooled us off, so by the time Pop returned we were feeling all right. However, our necks, ears, faces, wrists, arms, and ankles were badly swollen.

The beans were only the beginning of our planting. We planted the peas that day on a plot on higher ground in front of the cabin; the flies were not so bad there, but bad enough. The first time he went to Huntsville, Pop got some mosquito netting and some fine wire, which he formed into frames that came over our heads and well around our necks. The netting kept some of the flies off and we could see through it; but this did not prevent the flies from creeping up our sleeves and down our necks. They would also creep up under the netting to the back of our ears. This not being satisfactory, he got a bottle of oil of tar, mixing it with pork fat and rubbing it on ears, neck, wrists, and arms; it helped some. We had a great time, what with the flies, oil of tar, pork fat, and the smoke from the fire in the cabin.

The cabin had a hole in the roof to carry the smoke off. The fire was built on the floor. Whoever had built the cabin had made the mistake of cutting the hole through the lower part of the roof. The smoke would rise to the higher part and circle round and round. We lived in a smoky atmosphere when indoors. So we were smoked, tanned by the sun, and swelled by the black flies. And that's not all: we were bitten by fleas at night. We were in sad plight; our clothes were in tatters too. So when we were invited to go to Huntsville to celebrate the First of July, we hesitated about going. Arthur and I had not been in Huntsville since coming through more than a month before. Pop, who had been there, said Mrs. Cann insisted he bring us down. So we went.

When Mrs. Cann saw us, she burst into tears, saying, "You poor lads! What has your father done to you?" It was no wonder she was shocked. We were like two ragamuffins, swelled up with fly bites, browned by the sun, the oil of tar, long hair, and our nice city clothes in tatters. I judge we presented a wild picture. However, she treated us fine, as did George and Mark, her two sons, and her daughter Julia, feeding us plenty.

The celebration was held on the bank of the river near and under the shadow of a very high bluff called Cann's Bluff, as it and the grounds were on the land owned by Mr. Cann. We had a good day of it.

But we left Huntsville early. We had about nine miles to go, mostly by water in the old flat-bottom boat. It was down the river and the length of Fairy Lake, then up a creek that was so shallow we had to step out in some places and drag the boat over bars and sunken logs. It was dark before we reached Peninsula Lake where we had to row about three miles to the north side of the Portage. From the north to the south side of the Portage was a walk of a mile and a quarter through the woods. That was the route every time we went to Huntsville. At first we rowed; then we paddled in a birchbark canoe, as Arthur and I soon became expert at it. We later enjoyed our trips to Huntsville.

Another view on Lake of Bays, July 29, 1875

4

We Start Our Homestead

ARTHUR AND I certainly enjoyed that day in Huntsville, especially for
the outing with other human beings, as we had seen but few. We had
met the Hill family across Pen Lake, and the family of the man Pop had
bought out, the Pokornys, who, as I told you earlier, had settled on land
adjoining the lots Pop had bought the rights to. Since they had agreed to
go clear away from this section, the matter was a sore spot to Pop. At first
they kept away from us and we from them. So we had lived practically all
the month of June without being with other human beings.

There was a man named Bill Green who would call on us at times. His
place was across Pen Lake near the north end. We figured it to be about
seven miles from the Portage on our side. He was brought up to this section by his father, Sam, when he was about five years of age. Like his
father, he followed the life of a trapper. Bill was married and had a little
daughter. His wife was a strong young woman. They had a clearing and
a log hut on it where they lived, and she worked like a man on the place.
His father was an old man and lived a long way down the Lake of Bays.

Bill took to me from the first. I remember one day when Pop and
Art had gone to Huntsville and I was alone. It was very hot, so I lay
down on some boards near the water and fell—no, not in the water, but
asleep. I was awakened by Bill, who said, "You shouldn't lie here; you
will be sun-struck."

During the month of June we planted corn and potatoes, the seed
for which we bought from the Reverend R.N. Hill, who lived on the far

side of Pen Lake, directly across from the North Portage. He had been there a number of years and had a large family and a large clearing. We had to bring the potatoes across in a boat, about two miles, then carry them across the Portage in bags for about a mile and a quarter. At first, Arthur and I could only carry fifteen pounds, but we soon got used to it and could carry twenty-five. It was hard work for us as we had to carry about fifty bushels in all. Pop cut the potatoes in pieces. We used the eyes for seed and the larger part for food. We also planted turnips, carrots, beets, and more beans until we had planted all the cleared land.

During all this time Pop, Arthur, and I would be up at daylight, get the fish off the night lines, clean and cook them for breakfast. We also ate soda bread and drank coffee. We made the soda bread by stirring and kneading the flour in the top of the bag, and baking the mixture in a tin plate in front of the open fire. We became quite expert at it. We enjoyed this menu for our breakfast almost every morning.

Then we would go off into the fields and plant and, later on, weed; the weeds grew faster than the crops. We worked from breakfast until sundown. Then Arthur and I would jump in the lake for a good swim while Pop would get supper. We never stopped for lunch. We got used to it and to all kinds of weather.

Pop decided it was time we started to build a house and have it ready by fall for Mother and the others. He decided upon digging into a hill opposite the front of the cabin and about two hundred feet away. We excavated into the bank far enough and wide enough for the foundation of the house. It was tough work.

For a change, we rafted lumber from a sawmill at Baysville, which was eleven miles down the lake, and two more down the south branch of the Muskoka River; in all, thirteen miles. We had to row the cumbersome raft up the river and out into the lake where, if fortunately we had a fair wind, we just drifted on up. In spring, the current in the river was so strong that on more than one occasion later on, when Art and I were coming from Baysville with quite a load of supplies, we were unable to paddle our canoe up. So we would have to fasten a rope to the canoe, go ashore, and pull it up after us for some distance.

As I remember it, we were four days and nights getting the raft of lumber up to the Portage landing where we piled it up to dry out and season. In stacking the lumber, Pop was nearly killed when a big stack gave way, burying him under the heavy green boards. Arthur and I worked like beavers to get him out. He was badly bruised, so he had to lay up for a few days; but, as he said, "It takes a lot to kill an old dog." He was past fifty-three years of age at this time.

Pop hired a man to come from Huntsville to hew timbers for the house, and to rive out shingles from a pine tree we cut near the house; it was an immense tree. The man's name was George Elliot, about fifty years of age and a carpenter by trade. He was a good worker and also good company. When we had a space large enough for the house, Pop engaged Mr. Tom Ware and his brother-in-law, Mr. George Cummings, to lay the stonework for it. Their land was at the southwest end of Peninsula Lake. George was a big, strong, good-natured fellow while Tom was small. Both were good workers—and good eaters.

At this time I had become cook for the crowd, and we got along very well while we had plenty of fish and potatoes. When these gave out, all we had was some flour. The fish had gone into deep water, so we were unable to catch any. Our potatoes, left from seed, were also gone. Pop had not received any money, so we couldn't buy anything. While waiting for Pop to return from Huntsville where he had gone expecting to get some money, we lived on flapjacks.

The flapjacks were made without soda or raising of any kind, just flour beaten up into dough with salt and water only, and baked in a frying pan over an open wood fire. They were so heavy that, after a few meals of them, poor George sat on a log with his arms folded over his stomach, groaning, "They're laying on my chest like a stone." It was only a few days before Pop returned, bringing lots of things necessary for better eats. One thing, among a lot of others, was a side of salt pork. While cooking this pork the odour from it was so strong it almost choked us. George said it was from a tough old gentleman pig. He was right again.

And so it went through the summer. We had good weather, but Arthur and I didn't like mixing the mortar for the stonework. The first storey was stone, the second was frame with a peaked roof which gave us an attic. The stone was picked up from the land, the mortar was mixed from clay and sand also from our land. The clay was tough and of a blueish colour, like piper's clay, and served well for holding the stones together. Into the back wall we built a fireplace with a large stone chimney running out from the house and up the hill at the back, giving a good draft to the fire.

I must tell you of some incidents that occurred while we occupied the log cabin. In the latter part of June, Pop told us some kind of animal was in the habit of getting on the roof at night, reaching down to a small window with what seemed to be a big paw, and scratching on the glass. We kept our hoes, rakes, and a pitchfork handy. So when it came, Pop woke me up. I could see a great big paw reaching down to the window; Pop said it might be a wildcat. We awakened Arthur and, without stopping to dress, rushed forth armed to the teeth, as it were, and in our shirttails.

We heard the animal drop off the roof into a small patch of potatoes growing at the side of the cabin. By the light of the moon, we could see an animal running away from us. We laid to with our farm tools. I think it was Pop who gave him the knock-out with the fork in the neck. It proved to be the largest porcupine I ever saw—he probably weighed thirty pounds. It was a great wonder we didn't get some quills in us. We came out of the battle to enjoy some fresh meat as well as some porcupine soup with vegetables. We thought it very good.

Another incident was the cabin catching on fire. Pop had gone to Huntsville the day before, leaving Arthur and me alone. Before we ate breakfast, we took the fish off the lines in the lake nearby. We started a fire on the cabin floor, which was usual, so it would be ready to cook breakfast. When we were nearly through cleaning the fish, I noticed the roof was on fire. We had a pail of water nearby to hold the refuse from the fish. I picked it up, fish refuse and all, and threw it on the roof. It put out the fire. Then, with some water from the little creek, we put out the fire inside.

But what a mess! We had to rebuild the pole bedstead on which we three slept. The fire had gotten under the pillow where Pop kept a good undervest. I think Pop was more concerned about the vest having a small hole in it than he was over the liability of the cabin being burned, or the danger to Arthur and me if it had occurred at night which, fortunately, it didn't.

I must tell you too of another thing that happened to me during that first summer before Mother and the girls came to the Portage. I had taken the flat-bottomed boat down to Huntsville to see if there was any mail and to get some provisions. There was no mail on my arrival, so I waited for the next stage to come in. Because it didn't arrive until five o'clock, I took dinner at Cann's Hotel.

For dinner we had my favourite pie, huckleberry, which was fine. I ate in their private dining room with the two boys, George and Mark, and their sister Julia, a bright, happy girl of twelve years. The hired girl waited on us, putting on the table for dessert big pies cut in quarters. They were so good that I ate piece after piece until Mark called to his mother in the adjoining kitchen, telling her, "Tom had eaten eight pieces!" "The hog," she said. "That's all right. Let him eat eight more if he wants to." That was the way she always treated me.

After eating, I left them to do an errand across the bridge. When I returned, Mrs. Cann hissed the big red spaniel on me, her idea of fun. He came with a loud barking, bringing most all the village dogs. There was a great black Newfoundland we called Doc because he belonged to Doc Howland. He stood almost up to my shoulders. I spoke to him. He was a good-natured dog and stood wagging his tail as I looked at him, barking like all the others. There must have been twenty dogs of all descriptions around me. I stood in the midst of them and talked to them until they became quiet. But not before a crowd of people collected to enjoy the sight, which was more enjoyable to them than to me.

I waited for the mail and received a letter from Mother in Toronto. I knew Pop would be glad to have it, so I decided to make for home; otherwise I would have been welcome to stay overnight with the Cann boys. As I was leaving, Mrs. Cann said so all could hear, "Don't let the bears get you when you cross the Portage."

I got up through the creek just at dusk, so it was dark when I crossed the Portage. I had a small pack on my back. At this time there was only a narrow footpath leading up through the brush and woods which, in many places, I couldn't see but could feel. I didn't see or hear anything or have any trouble until I reached a flat halfway up a high ridge. There I saw what looked like two eyes peering at me in the darkness among some second-growth bushes not more than six feet from me. At first I took them for the eyes of a bear; they were just high enough for a bear standing on its hind feet. Well, my hair seemed to creep up on the top of my head! But in a minute, I judged what it was (and proved it when I examined it later): it came from an old dead tree stump that had rotted, forming spots of phosphorous. But it really looked like two eyes.

Some days afterwards I had occasion to go to Huntsville again. I took dinner at Cann's in the regular dining room where they had one long table. Mr. Cann sat at the head, passing the plates of food to, as I remember, twenty-two men sitting at the table. I was the youngest, just past sixteen. When we got settled, Mr. Cann said to the crowd, "I know a boy who was scared the other night when he crossed the Portage." He and all the other men at the table looked at me as he said it.

I answered him by saying, "Yes, just for a minute." I told him of my experience.

"Yes," he said, "I know the spot. I've seen it a number of times, and I don't wonder at your being scared." He said that the first time he saw it he was sure it was a bear, and felt his hair creep, too.

He had been a hunter and trapper in those parts when the Indians were there and, as he said, he wondered if I had seen it that night. It seemed to be very amusing to the men. One man in the crowd said, "You don't mean to tell me you crossed the Portage in the dark!"

I crossed the Portage many times after that at all hours of the night both winter and summer, but I never saw the specks again. I think either Arthur or Pop demolished the stump.

It was a strange thing to me, but I could keep on the path, never straying to one side or the other. So it was always I who led the way; in some places is was so dark I couldn't see a thing.

Burnt land along the Muskoka Road, September 17, 1873

Osborne boys and their lean-to at the Portage

5

The Night the Mice Danced the Quadrille

I HAVE NEVER TOLD of the little lake we had on the place. It was only a short distance away from where we built the house and was about twenty-five feet higher than the Lake of Bays. The little creek I have mentioned several times flowed down from it and was our water supply for drinking, cooking, and cleaning. It was very good water. From the little lake it flowed down through a cut in the high land for about a hundred feet, then flowed gently through level ground for a short distance, making a turn near where we built the house. So, by digging a sort of basin at this point, we had a never-failing supply of good, clear, cold water, summer and winter. In winter, we had to cut through the ice every morning and often twice a day. As cold as it was, I frequently saw small minnows, as lively as could be, swimming around in the ice-cold water.

The stream continued on through the level land for another hundred feet, where it turned at the back of the old log cabin and on down through a pebbly bed. This was a great delight to Pop, as he liked to hear it ripple on and down the bay. There it widened out as it reached the bay and was very shallow for a short distance. At the mouth of the creek there was a nice sandy bottom which, in early spring, I have seen black with minnows. We would scoop up these minnows in a dip net and use them for bait on our lay-out lines.

These lay-out lines, or night lines, were made of heavy mason twine about fifty feet long. We usually tied the lines to a snag or small tree hanging out from the shore over the edge of the lake. The hooks were tied to this line with an extension of about eight inches, so with the minnow on the hook it hung down from the main. The minnows were always alive. They would wiggle around and attract the big trout and other kinds of fish.

The hooks were tied on at intervals of three feet. At the outer end of the line we would tie a heavy stone as a sinker. This we would drop into the water where it would sink, sometimes to a depth of twenty feet. The hooks, bait, and line would sink near to the bottom. We would put these lines out at night mostly, and soon after daylight next morning we would take them up into a canoe or boat, starting at the end of the line nearest the shore.

In the spring of the year we would get mostly salmon, brook and speckled trout, and other varieties of fish. The trout would run from two to eight pounds. One time we caught a trout that would have weighed twenty pounds. It seems a small dogfish had swallowed a minnow and the big trout swallowed it, so we found the minnow and dogfish inside the trout. He was a fine big fish!

The little lake was a nice body of water. We never reached the bottom of it, even with a hundred-foot line. Several times we put out night lines there but never caught a fish. The hooks would be torn off even with wire tofts, but we never found out what did it.

To return to the cabin and the fleas: they became so bad we had to move out. We built wigwams of young trees and brush out in the woods, but after a few days the fleas would find us out, becoming so bad we would have to move to other ground.

About this time we had George and Mark Cann come up from Huntsville bringing a Mr. White, an artist, with them. We built a large tent of brush and poles in which we all slept. Mr. White was always up at sunrise, drawing pictures. I wish you could see the picture he drew of our camp and us boys. You could see us as we lay there in the brush, with two of us raised up and looking at him as he sat on a log in front of the camp. It was sure a good drawing of a camp in the woods.

We did not get rid of the fleas until we had the floor laid in the house. It being two feet off the ground, we were never troubled with anything of the kind. But I must tell you of how persistent the fleas were.

We hadn't been inside the cabin for several weeks when one day Bill Green came over to get something he had left with us in the cabin. So

Arthur and I went with Bill into the cabin to get it. I remember the cabin looked nice and clean when we entered, so we sat down for a talk. Bill sat on a bench at our old board table, Arthur on a block of wood, and I on our old cot, both of us facing Bill. We had been there only a few minutes when I saw the fleas chasing up the outside of Bill's trouser legs. He saw them at the same time and, with a yell that would have made a banshee jealous, he rushed out of the cabin and down into the lake. Arthur and I did the same as we were in the same condition. (These were not small fleas by any means.) We went into the lake up to our necks, where we gave the fleas time to drown. When we came ashore we removed all our clothes. It took us about an hour to pick all the fleas off. Bill was fit to be tied. Needless to say, it was a long time before we entered the cabin again; in fact, we didn't venture in until the weather froze the fleas out.

By September 1st we had the house enclosed with half the roof shingled, doors on, and sash but no glass in the windows. We let Elliot go; Cummings and Ware had left us some days before. As Pop had a very sore toe from dropping a log on it, we persuaded him to go to Mother in Toronto to recuperate and then bring the others back with him.

While he was away, Arthur and I, who were alone, built a place to sleep in the corner of the big room on the first floor. Between the fireplace and the end wall we arranged two carpenter's horses with pine boards as springs. We used balsam brush for bedding, with a blanket thrown over that and a blanket to cover us; we thought we were fixed fine and comfortable. I do know we slept well. Also, we didn't have to open the windows for air as there was no glass to keep the night air out. However, it gets very cold in September. I have seen ice a half-inch thick on the 11th of September, but we did not suffer from the cold.

One rainy day, some days after Pop left us, I decided to make a paddle by chipping down a piece of ironwood like a fence rail. To chip it down thin enough, I laid it down on the floor, holding it down with my foot while I chipped it with a carpenter's adze that Elliot had left with us. Anyone who knows what an adze is knows it is an awkward tool to work with; this proved only too true in my case.

I had been using it only a few minutes when it missed cutting the wood and slipped. It cut through my heavy shoe and into my instep, narrowly missing the large vein. My shoe was full of blood before I could get it off. Arthur was badly frightened. I told him to go over to some men who were building a house about half a mile away for a new settler and get one of the men to come over.

As he left me, I put my foot into a pail of cold water which we always kept handy. Arthur returned with a Mr. Young who, as soon as Arthur told him how bad the cut was, had put a big piece of tobacco in his mouth. He chewed all the way over. When he reached the house he had a good, big wad of fresh, juicy tobacco ready, as he thought, to place on the cut to stop the bleeding. But he did not need it as the cold water had stopped the bleeding, and I was sitting by the fire with a coarse towel wrapped around my foot. On removing the towel, we saw it was a clean cut, one and a quarter inches long.

We had some Egyptian salve which, when rubbed or spread on strips of cloth, was a very good adhesive plaster. With some of this, Mr. Young drew the edges of the cut together, binding my foot with strips of cloth. He told me to lie around for three days and then redress it the same way. This I did, but I was lame for some time.

I must tell you of a little circumstance that occurred one night as Arthur and I lay asleep on our improvised bed. I was awakened some time in the night to see the moonlight streaming in through the empty sash onto the floor. It was as clear as daylight, and in the bright light from the moon on the floor were a number of large field mice dancing a quadrille. It is a fact, although some say I must have been dreaming. Not so!

I managed to awaken Arthur, who was a sound sleeper. We lay there watching these mice for some time. It is a fact that those mice danced back and forth just as if they were human. They danced on their hind feet with their front paws extended, going towards each other until their paws would meet, just as human beings do. We watched them for some time until they dropped on all fours and scampered away. I never saw it occur again.

Fairy Lake, July 31, 1875

North Falls, Muskoka River, October 16, 1872

6

The Others Arrive and So Does Winter

I WAS LAID UP with my cut foot for some days; Arthur had to do the cooking and get the firewood, in fact take care of everything. Previous to my mishap we had harvested the peas, beans, turnips, and carrots. The corn and potatoes weren't ready for cutting and digging, but we did have plenty of green corn and potatoes, so with some fish and game we had plenty to eat. We worked on the house and grounds, grading in front. We also dug from the back of the house into the bank for a sort of root cellar and, along with our work, we did some fishing.

A new settler, Mr. Brown, had taken up lots adjoining ours to the east and built a nice, large log house. Later, from Pike County, New York, he brought his wife, little daughter, and his brother-in-law. Dense woods shut them off from the lake and from our clearing. They were very nice people but not cut out for the backwoods.

One evening after I was fit enough to limp around, Arthur and I were sitting after sunset in front of the house. We always had a long twilight. Just as it was growing dark, we heard someone at the top of our clearing on a road that had just been cut through. They were whistling a familiar tune that we both knew, and we also knew the whistler to be our little brother Sam. He was leading the way for Mother and our sisters Kate, Emma, and Lidie. (Sisters Annie and Marie had not come with them; they wisely preferred to return to Philadelphia.) Mother and the others had walked all the way from Bracebridge, at that time a distance of upwards of thirty miles.

It seems Pop had engaged two men with a big wagon to haul the goods and family from Bracebridge to South Portage. The wagon was drawn by two big horses, but some short distance from Bracebridge it turned over and dumped out the goods and passengers. There was no one hurt, but a crate of chickens broke open, letting them loose. As it would take some time to make repairs, Mother decided to come through by foot, bringing the children with her. How she and the children did it, I don't know; it was a feat to try the strength of a strong man. However, they came through in good shape, reaching us just at twilight.

Mother and all were very tired but glad to meet us again and find us alive and well after four months' separation. While glad to see us looking so well and strong, she was alarmed at my limping. I assured her I was fine; but in my running over the rough ground to meet them, the bandage came loose, which did not add to my foot's appearance.

I had gotten so I could make good coffee without that smoky taste, so I made them some and fixed them a good feed. After they had eaten and felt rested, Mother had a good look at my foot. As the strain had opened the cut and disturbed the plasters and bandage, it really looked bad. We bathed it in warm water and drew the cut together again with our homemade adhesive plasters and bound it up. I had no more trouble with it, and it came along all right; but it was several weeks before I could walk without a limp.

Pop did not come for several days. He was very much put out at losing most of the chickens, all but four out of twenty. As they were a choice lot, Pop always claimed the men upset the truck so they could get possession of the chickens. We never recovered any of the others.

Now our troubles became worse. It was only a few days after they came that Kate showed signs of having caught a cold. She became, as we thought, delirious. Mother had me get Mrs. Pokorny, wife of the man Pop bought the place from. He claimed to have been a doctor, so we thought she might know what was best to do for Kate. All that was done did not improve her condition, so Pop had Dr. Howland come from Huntsville. He said Kate was temporarily out of her mind. That proved only too true. She became very wild, that condition lasting about two weeks; then she would become normal and apparently as well as ever.

After a week or two she would lose control of herself and again become almost unmanageable by us. This continued all through the winter. It seemed strange to us: she would be as nice as could be at times, then suddenly become wild.

Well, we worked on the shingling and putting glass in the window sashes and fixing as best we could for the winter. We also harvested the corn and potatoes, pitting them in the ground. We did this from instructions given us by the Reverend R.N. Hill and others. We scraped a hollow place on the ground, making a layer of leaves and dry grass to form the bed, then heaped the potatoes on that, about twenty bushels to each pit, covering them with more leaves and dry grass. We covered this with earth to a thickness of two feet. This was thought sufficient to keep them from freezing during the winter. We had about a hundred bushels of potatoes, turnips, and carrots which we pitted in this way. We thought we'd have plenty for winter use. During this time we had some heavy frosts, but not heavy enough to freeze the ground.

We cut a lot of wood for winter use, and made all the preparations for winter that we could. Our fireplace worked well, so we could keep warm for the months of October and November. The weather, while cold, was not freezing the lake; we were able to catch some fish. With potatoes, turnips, carrots, peas, beans, flour, tea, and coffee (no milk, butter, or sugar), we got along very well until December 3rd.

That day was nice. The lake was open with just a little ice around the shore. Pop had gone to Huntsville and would not return until the next day, so Arthur and I decided to draw our firewood to the house. We had what we thought a big lot of cut wood on top of the hill back of the house. We drew it down on a hand sled. About three o'clock I noticed a change in the weather; it was growing cold very fast. I said to Arthur, "We must get all the wood we can and put it in the house."

We had a small room which was intended to be used as a kitchen. Well, we almost filled this room with all the wood we had cut. Then we drew in all the wood we could get from limbs that had fallen from the trees during stormy weather. We continued until it became dark, when it had grown so cold our hands and fingers were numb. Kate, who happened to be having a good spell, helped. Emma helped us too. They all depended on me and did as I suggested. They seemed to think I knew what was best to do, although I really think it was all intuition with me.

By the time we stopped work the lake was freezing over. We all realized we were in for a cold night. Mother asked me what we had better do, and I said, "You will have to take the girls in your bed with you in this room"—meaning the room the fireplace was in—"and bring Arthur and Sam down from upstairs into the girls' room." This was a small room with a one-inch board partition dividing it off from the room with the fireplace. This being settled, she wanted to know what I was going to do. I said, "Sit right here by the fire and keep it going all night."

While this change was being made, we had something to eat with plenty of hot tea. It was growing colder and colder.

I got two big pails of water and stood them on the edge of the hearth, about two feet from the fire. We all sat around in front of the fire until we got sleepy. Then Arthur and Sam retired to their room and to bed. I went in to see that they were well covered with heavy bed covers; I had advised Mother and the girls to do this with themselves. When I returned to the big room, Mother, Kate, Emma, and Lidie were in bed. I saw to it that they were well covered so, as I thought, they wouldn't be cold. I then sat down by the fire.

Every little while I would go into the back room for more wood. I would open the outer door to look and listen. It was clear, with the sky full of stars. As the night passed, the timbers in the house would crack and groan, sounding like gunshots. The trees in the woods were cracking, sounding as if there were a lot of men chopping. Then, too, as the lake froze, the water underneath seemed to evaporate and the ice would settle and crack with loud report like the clap of thunder. The crack would run from shore to shore. It was a weird sound and continued all night long.

At one time during the night, Mother complained of being cold. They had on them all the bedclothes we had. I thought of the rag carpets on the floor and took them up, folding them in half to make them double thick and heavy. I put two of these over Mother and the girls, and did the same for Arthur and Sam. This was better and they seemed more comfortable. I then sat by the fire listening to the lake cracking. The noise resounded through the hills. I wondered if it would ever stop freezing.

I sat by the fire, at intervals going for more wood and heaping it on the flames. I was sure glad we had gotten in so much. If we hadn't, I believe we would have frozen to death, the cold was so intense.

It was a big relief when daylight began to break. I found the water in the pails frozen on the side away from the fire. The house was of stone at the back and ends but only wood in front. The front, not being lined inside, made the cold seem worse from that direction. I believe that was the reason for the water freezing towards the front of the pails.

We were very glad to see the sun come up. Even then it was so cold we had to keep turning in front of the fire to keep warm while getting breakfast, after which we felt better. That was one time when hot coffee was good and we drank freely of it.

The lake was frozen over and looked nice, it was so white. Pop came home at noon and was glad to find us all alive. He said he had crossed Fairy Lake in a boat on his way down the day before. He walked across on the ice on his way back, following a yoke of oxen and a load of hay. He said the ice must have been ten inches thick, all frozen in one night. He said it must have been down to sixty below zero. I know it was the coldest I experienced in all the five winters I spent in Canada.

It had frozen through our pits of potatoes clear down and into the ground below. The turnips and carrots, too, were frozen. The potatoes we could use as long as they stayed frozen. We would put them in cold water, stir them well to remove all dirt, then put them into boiling water to cook. When cooked this way with the skins on they were good but had a sweet taste. We could eat them until they thawed in a warm spell in February when a great many went bad and were unfit to eat. By April all that were left had spoiled. We had depended on our roots, with our peas and beans, to see us through the winter.

We had laid in a supply of flour in the fall, buying it from a grist mill at the north end of Peninsula Lake, a place named Grassmere. There a Scotchman had found good water power and was grinding grain for the settlers from miles around.

Arthur and I had started for this place in a boat with meagre instructions and, not being able to locate it, went ashore on a point of land which, we found, hid a small bay from our view. After reaching the high land we found our destination. As we turned to go back to the boat, I spied what I thought was a branch of a tree floating in the water; but it proved to be a good-sized buck deer. We gave chase, but could not keep it from going ashore. I don't know what we would have done with it had we overtaken it; we had no gun or any instrument to kill it with.

When we rounded the point, we could see a small clearing, which we found belonged to Bill Green. We told him of the deer, and he took his gun and canoe in hopes he might see it. He did not find it, but I thought what a great help it would have been to us if we could have killed it. It was the first deer we had seen.

Along in March I thought I might catch some fish through the ice. I took an axe and a spade to cut a hole about a hundred feet from shore. I first cut the ice as far down as I could and then finished by chipping with a spade. When I finally reached the water, the top of the spade was level with the ice, which was fully three feet thick. I did not get any fish.

At this time there was a mild spell which softened the snow so that a muskrat made its way down the little lake across the clearing. When we saw its tracks in the soft snow, we all gave chase and finally caught and killed it. So we had muskrat stew. It was good. We had not been able to kill any game during the winter (except for the occasional squirrel). Partridges and other birds, rabbits too, all seemed to have burrowed in during the severe weather.

And so we lived through the winter. I have wondered that Pop didn't lose his mind because of all the privations. As Mother had contracted inflammatory rheumatism in her hands, her finger joints swelled up badly and were very painful. Then, too, Kate would have her bad spells, which, with the cold and insufficient food, were great worries to us all, especially Pop.

To help out, while waiting for money that Pop expected to come from Philadelphia in settlement of his business affairs there, I went over to the Reverend R.N. Hill, knowing he had plenty of flour and cornmeal. Talk about drawing blood from a stone! I finally got a little by saying that if my father didn't pay for it by spring, I would work it off. Pop paid.

7

Escaping a Stormy Lake Catastrophe

ONE MILD DAY IN MARCH, Kate, in one of her spells, eluded us, and got away from the house. We soon found her tracks in the snow. Pop, Arthur, and I followed the tracks up to the little lake and around and about in a zigzag course for fully a mile, covering the full length of the lake. Kate had walked close to some air holes in the ice, a few of them large enough to allow a person to slip and fall through, but had passed them by and entered the woods. Pop, who had out-distanced Arthur and me, found her sitting on a fallen tree almost at the top of a very high hill. As she refused to walk, he carried her down on his back. She seemed to enjoy it, continuing to laugh all the way back to the house.

Well, it was misery in the extreme. But when the ice broke up on the lakes and we could put out our lines and catch lots of fish, we all felt better. Mother and the girls enjoyed sitting in front of the house. There they could plainly see the floats on our lay-out lines bob up and down as the fish would strike and pull the floats under. The edge of the bay was about a hundred feet from the house. The floats were made of pieces of split cedar about a foot long and three inches thick. The fish we caught were mostly trout, and fighters, and could be easily seen as the lines were run diagonally and about thirty feet from shore. There were three lines, each about fifty feet long. At times, it kept one of us busy taking the fish off and re-baiting the hooks. It was quite interesting to see the big floats bob up and down.

That was mild until a loon got itself hooked in the neck as it dove to pass the line. With the loon plunging, the floats bobbed up, down,

Peninsula Lake, July 26, 1875

and around until Arthur and I went out in a canoe and killed it. For the benefit of those who do not know what a loon is, I will say it is a wild waterfowl between a full-grown duck and a goose in size, with a long bill coming to a stubby point. It is black on the back from billpoint to tailend, while the underbody is white, well spotted with black dots. It is a nicely shaped bird and is to be admired for its smooth, heavy, close-fitting body of feathers. It is very quick at diving.

I have shot at them many times but never killed one. I have been quite close to them as they floated very quietly on the smooth water, and have seen a good load of birdshot hit the water at the very spot where the loon was when I fired, only to hear it give the laugh as it came up some distance away. This shows you it must be very quick of eye as well as a quick diver. The laugh is something like this: "Loo-oo-loo-oo." When they make this call, it reverberates over the water and around the hills. On a quiet night, it can be heard for miles; it's a weird sound to the lone boatman or camper. Its meat is tough and very hard to eat. Mother, for instance, boiled this one for twenty-four hours, then threw it away. It was so tough we could not get our teeth into it. The next bird in toughness was an old crow I later tried to boil so we could eat it. It was as tough as the loon.

The only meat we had outside of fish was an occasional porcupine. This is good eating and looks like nice chicken; it is just as juicy and tender. We found it very good for a change and, lots of times, were glad to get it.

As the fish stopped biting, we fell back on the mussels that grew to a good size near enough to shore to wade in and pick them alive. After washing them thoroughly, Mother would place them in a baking pan, place the pan on some hot coals with the heat of the fire over the top, similar to putting them in an oven. The mussels were covered with just a little water, and in a few minutes the shells would open, allowing us to dig out the meat with a fork. A little salt made it palatable. A tender green that Pop called "fat hen" went well with the mussels, and cornbread, too. As there was nothing better to be had, we enjoyed it. For tea we used a plant called prince's pine which grew in abundance among the pine trees; after being dried, it made a substitute.

While we were getting plenty of fish, we would take some down to Huntsville and trade for cornmeal, flour, salt, a little sugar, tea, and coffee. The few hens we had foraged for themselves and laid a few eggs that helped out for food and were a nice change. And so we survived.

The berries helped too. We all enjoyed oatmeal pudding well filled with red raspberries or huckleberries. We mostly boiled the berries in the oatmeal and, when cooked, poured into bowls and left until set and cooled, it made a nice pudding. I mention this to show you how we lived during the only spring and summer Mother was with us on the Portage. There were some pleasures attached to it, such as boating and swimming, for all of us.

About the first of May the doctor said that Kate should go to a hospital in Toronto, Pop to take her. She was away until, in June, the doctors pronounced her well. It was arranged that Mother should go to Toronto to bring her back. Arthur and I took her to Huntsville in the flat-bottomed punt, or rowboat. We left home early in the morning of a nice July day. We started early so we could catch the stage at Huntsville for Bracebridge, then a steamboat to Gravenhurst, and then the train to Toronto.

We were delayed on the way to Huntsville. The creek between Peninsula Lake and Fairy Lake was so shallow we had to drag the boat over it in several places. Then, too, a large tree had fallen across it in such a way that we could not get over or under; we had to chop a section out of the tree so we could pass through. The tree being about a foot and a half through, it took us some time to cut it in two places. Fortunately we had the axe with us. But we were late reaching Huntsville.

To save time, we landed below the bridge; this saved us pulling up against the current, very strong at that time. We ran the point of the boat onto the shore. I told Mother not to get up until we pulled the boat alongside.

I had just stepped ashore when I heard her scream. I turned in time to see her literally sitting in the water. She threw up her hands and I could just reach her wrists so, with sufficient presence of mind, I grasped them and pulled her out, a very wet woman. I ran up to Cann's Hotel where Mrs. Cann took her in hand. I saw her late in the afternoon when she had fully recovered. She seemed to be enjoying herself in some of Mrs. Cann's clothes while getting her own in shape to wear. Arthur and I left her there to take the stage the next day.

It was quite late when Arthur and I started for home, and it was dark when we reached the creek. We had quite a time getting the boat through, having to wade and pull the boat over the shallows in the total darkness. We didn't mind. We had gotten used to roughing it, taking things as they came. At that time there was only a narrow footpath across the Portage and, owing to the darkness, we had to feel our way with our feet. We had become very good at that way of travelling, and arrived home some time in the early hours of the night. Pop and all were shocked to hear of Mother's narrow escape from drowning. But, as Pop said, "All's well that ends well."

So we settled down to fishing and taking care of our small planting. We were very short of seed. Because so many potatoes were spoiled by the freezing, we had very few seed potatoes to plant. We did have corn, so we planted quite a field of it; and peas, beans, turnips, beets, and carrots. So we devoted the greater part of our time in May and June to fishing. We managed to sell and trade enough fish in Huntsville to buy potatoes, flour, and other necessities to live. I say "live" because that was about all we did, especially after the fish stopped biting.

Mother and Kate visited in Toronto with some old neighbours by the name of Hendry until early in July. Arthur and I met them in Huntsville, bringing them up to the Portage in a rowboat. Kate was very quiet. She seemed to be in her right mind but sort of melancholy. However, she remained well and enjoyed trips in the canoe and boat, and picking berries which grew in quantities.

Red raspberries grew fine and big all over the clearing. They grew up of themselves, as did small wild cherries as soon as the ground had been burned over in clearing the land. Huckleberries grew naturally and in abundance. They were very plentiful on some points of land down the lake.

One day we took our big flat boat and rowed several miles down the Lake of Bays to one of these points where the berries grew aplenty. In the boat were Pop, Arthur, Kate, Emma, Lidie, and I. We left Mother and Sam at home. We took some bread for lunch and a tin kettle so we could boil water for tea. We had one pair of oars to propel the boat. Arthur used one and I the other. We sat on separate seats, one on each side of the boat, while Pop sat in the stern with a paddle to steer. You can imagine it was a big boat to hold six of us, all the paraphernalia, and a big shotgun.

We made good time reaching the point. We all commenced picking the huckleberries, which grew very large and plentiful. We did not stop for lunch until we had filled the receptacles. We had shot two squirrels which, after making tea, we boiled in the same tin pan. With bread, the meat and juice of the squirrels, and all the berries we could eat, we made a good lunch.

While eating lunch, we noticed that a storm was coming. We hastily loaded the boat and started for home. As the storm was coming up the lake, it meant a fair wind and wave for us; but we hoped to beat it up the lake. We had gone half the way to the narrows when the storm caught us. The wind was strong and the waves were big, but being in our favour we did not mind. It rained in torrents, and the thunder and lightning were terrible.

In spite of the waves being in our favour, Pop swerved the boat towards the nearest land. As he did so, the boat swung almost into the trough of the waves. It looked for a few seconds as if we were going to turn over. I called to Arthur to pull hard, and at the same time I back paddled. Between us we righted the boat. It sure looked bad, for the boat was careening over on the wave. But all kept very still, except Lidie, who was then just past seven years of age—she only gave a little squeal. I think Emma and Kate were badly frightened, while Pop looked very serious. Arthur and I were too busy rowing to be scared.

It stopped raining soon after. The wind also abated but the waves continued to run high. We were in the middle of the lake. It was fully three miles ahead to the narrows, which Pop steered for but missed. We landed on a sandy beach to the left, between where Owen's cottage now stands and where they've since built a large hotel. We were all wet through; our matches were wet, too.

We tried to start a fire by shooting powder from the gun into leaves and sticks, but everything was too wet to burn. We walked or sat around for some time, waiting for the waves to go down so we could pull the boat out and around the narrows, the entrance to the bay and Portage.

It was almost dark when we finally reached home. Mother and Sam were glad to see us; they knew we must have been out in the storm. When we told her how near we had been to turning over, she seemed, I think, to be more frightened than we were who had been in the boat. This was the nearest to a catastrophe we had while they were with us. Suffice it to say, we didn't take so many with us on our next trip.

I well remember one day. Emma, then a little girl of eleven, took our only boat out for a ride. When about a hundred yards from shore, she got mixed up. In spite of all we could tell her, she kept turning the boat around and around. In the end, to keep her from jumping overboard in her excitement, Arthur and I swam out to her, bringing her and the boat to shore. Needless to say, she never tried that again, nor did any of the others—they all learned to manage a boat.

There was no road up to the little lake at that time, so Arthur, Pop, and I cut one through the trees and around on the north side to the point of a ravine. We cleared the brush from among the pines, leaving a nice bed of dry pine needles like a carpet. It was sure a nice place. We also built a large raft so we could all go out on the water. Mother and the girls liked it up there.

One Sunday afternoon we had all gone up. I took the big old muzzle-loading shotgun along with us. Later, as the sun began to go down, I shouldered the gun for a walk to see if I could get a squirrel. I walked to the ravine where the land was boggy and wet; but the grass grew strong and rank, so it was not bad to walk on. I had gotten about halfway across the bog when a nice big buck deer jumped up, almost at my feet. As I always walked very quietly, I was almost on him as he slept in the dry grass. He gave me a look then started on a run for the lake. I knew it was no use shooting, as there was only fine birdshot in my gun, so I called to the others to see the deer swimming across the lake. They all enjoyed the sight—the first wild deer they had seen.

It was soon after this that Bill Green and I started on our first trapping expedition.

Boater crossing Lake of Bays, July 27, 1875

8

Surviving My First Trapping Expedition

WE SETTLED DOWN to weeding and hoeing the potatoes, which along with the corn, peas, and beans had grown so well we could pick and eat them. So, with some fresh fish to eat, we lived through the summer. By winter there wouldn't be much left of the vegetables, just a few peas, beans, turnips, carrots, and beets.

In the fall, when Bill Green was getting ready to go on a trapping expedition, he asked me to go with him and, before going, to work around his clearing, to live with them while harvesting his crop of hay from a beaver meadow near his clearing, and to help with harvesting his crops of barley, oats, corn, potatoes, turnips, and more.

They had a cow, so we had lots of milk. Mrs. Green, a good cook, made up some great meals. One thing I remember was real shortcake in long biscuits. We would split them lengthwise, spread them thick with cream or curdled milk about half an inch thick, then cover them with a thick layer of maple sugar. Were they good? I guess yes! So good I have never forgotten them.

We worked around Bill's place about three weeks, bringing us to the middle of October. Then we started out for the trapping grounds he claimed as his territory because he had been trapping there for a good many years— an unwritten law among trappers in the wilds anywhere. It would have gone hard for anyone who invaded his routes if he caught them trapping.

Our first trip was to a small lake which Bill declared was twenty-five miles beyond the next nearest human being. We passed through several

Beaver meadow near Huntsville, July 29, 1875

small lakes to reach it, over carries between lakes. The first carry was one and a half miles; others were shorter until we reached the last one which, Bill said, was three miles long. There was no path to follow on any of the carries, so when we reached the last one Bill said, "I will lead the way. If I get out of your sight, just watch for the broken twigs and blaze marks on the trees."

Bill had made these blaze marks a number of years before; the twigs were old. The blaze marks were made by chipping a piece or sliver out of the bark and wood of trees with a tomahawk or axe. The marks become almost obliterated as the trees grow. The bark grows over the nick made by the axe and are not easy to see by one not accustomed to looking for them. I could follow them easily.

We each carried a canoe balanced over our heads and made to rest on our shoulders by placing paddles lengthwise on the braces or seats. By a quick turn with hands gripping the paddles and sides of the canoe, it was over our heads with it, upside down. Then we would adjust the paddles so they rested on our shoulders, our heads up inside the canoe. In this way we could balance the canoe and tip the bow up or down as we wished. We had good control, even with a light load such as cooking utensils, gun, axe, blanket, and traps in each canoe. Bill had the larger canoe and also carried the provisions. He took the lead and I followed as best I could.

Bill was a big, strong, long-legged Indian-like fellow. He could step over fallen trees whereas I would have to go around them. He was at least ten years older. I was only sixteen and a half and not long in the woods, whereas he had been brought up to it from five years of age. He was used to travelling through rough woods. The result was that he was soon out of sight.

I followed his instructions for a long time, never losing sight of the blaze marks on the trees, or so I thought, until I had gone more than three miles.

I came to a nice stream in a sort of valley where the scattered trees formed an open space; there I rested the forward end of the canoe on a fallen tree and crawled out from under it. After taking a long drink from the cold stream, I sat on a log to think. My conclusions were that I must have turned off onto a line of old marks made, as I judged, by surveyors whom I knew had been through, surveying the country and laying it out into 100-acre lots for homesteaders.

After sizing up the time and distance, I concluded from the direction of the blaze marks that I had travelled at an angle, veering to the left of the route taken by Bill and not so very far from him. I concluded he had reached the lake, so I gave our call, like that of a screech owl, and soon got an answer. I remained where I was until he reached me. He came through the dense woods and underbrush to the sound of my call. Bill was satisfied that it was easy for me to have gotten lost or led astray, for he had not given a thought to the old surveyors' marks when he had given me my instructions.

We soon reached the lake. We prepared a camp for two weeks. Bill did not have a cabin on this lake, so we found a nice hollow place in the ground where we could build a fire. We tipped our canoes on edge with the upper edge resting in forked sticks, a canoe on each side of the fire. In this way the fire would supply heat up into the canoe. After covering a portion of the ground under the canoes with fine twigs from balsam branches and placing a blanket over them, we made a nice place to sleep. With another blanket to roll up in, we were quite comfortable as long as we kept the fire going. This we did by putting more wood on it every time we woke up feeling cold.

We had fixed everything for the night, cut a big lot of wood, eaten our bread, drank a lot of hot coffee, then laid down to rest. It had been a long, hard day's trip paddling our canoes and crossing the carries. I wondered if I could find my way back if anything happened to Bill, never dreaming the time would come when that would be necessary.

Well, we remained a week just living and trapping. The lake seemed to be the home of muskrats, there were so many. After eating our first lunch, we took the canoe for a ride. We also took our gun with us. I knelt in the stern, paddling and steering, with Bill in the bow shooting the muskrats. The surface of the water seemed to be alive with them. It was all nice to me; it was so quiet in the moonlight—no human beings but ourselves. We remained out on the lake for some time, finally returning to camp to build up a roaring fire and settle down in our beds for the night, rousing once or twice during the night to replenish the fire.

We were up by the peep of day. After a breakfast of muskrat, bread, and coffee, I took lessons in the scientific way of skinning the muskrats we had killed the night before. Bill was a professional at that job. We would pull the skins over a stretcher, wrong side out, and hang them up in the smoke of the fire to dry. After that, at this time of year, they would keep for weeks. The fur was on the inside; as they dried they formed a bag that you could put your hand into and feel the nice, soft fur.

Each morning we would go the rounds of the traps and remove the animals—mostly muskrat, the occasional mink or otter, and one morning a duck. We would always reset the traps and lightly cover them with grass. They were set on sunken logs or on the ground just at the edge of the water.

Sometimes we would place a small piece of parsnip near the traps. The muskrats liked the smell of parsnips. When they came to eat, they would step into the trap, get caught by the leg, jump into the water, and drown. The traps were attached to three feet of chain with a ring and a wedge on the end. In setting them on logs, we would drive the wedge into the log; in setting them at the edge of the water, we would drive the stake into the bank and slip the ring over it, making it impossible for the animal to escape. Once in a while one would twist its foot off and get away. If one happened to be alive, it would usually show fight and we would kill it with a paddle.

Every day we spent some time cutting grass in beaver meadows near our camp and lake. Bill expected to draw the hay out during the winter when the lakes were frozen and the ground was covered with snow.

We had been in camp a week when Bill had to return home to carry the mail between Huntsville and Grassmere. He had the contract to carry the mail once a week. He left me just before sunset, saying he would return the next night and bring some grub back with him. All I had when he left me was one piece of bread the size and thickness of my hand, some salt, and coffee. As he left me, he said, "Get plenty of wood cut for the night. And don't let the wolves get you." I wasn't at all afraid.

Well, I did not see him for four days and five nights, and you might wonder how I survived after the one piece of bread was gone.

I followed up the traps, catching a good many muskrats. I would get up at daylight, make the rounds of the traps, reset them, return to camp, and skin the rats and stretch their skins. Then I would select a nice meaty one, cut off the hind quarters, clean it thoroughly, scatter salt over the meat, put it on the end of a long stick like a skewer, and hold it over the fire to broil. They were nice and juicy, and with lots of black coffee, I managed to get along until the afternoon of the fifth day.

You may wonder at my staying. I was only a boy and had never been in that part of the country except going through with Bill, so I hesitated in taking a chance. I feared if I got lost I would surely starve to death. So I remained, day after day hoping Bill would return. I was not afraid, however. Bill had left me his double-barrelled twelve-gauge shotgun with two cartridges, all he had. And I knew how to use it. But I didn't have to.

As the weather was cold, I had to replenish the fire several times during the night. An inch of snow fell one night. I usually sat by the fire until the fresh wood got into a good blaze. There was one animal a long way off that barked and yelped very much like a dog, keeping that up most of the night. I judged it to be a lone wolf. Other animals, such as porcupine, deer, and bear, would come around the camp at night. When they ventured too close, I would stir up the fire and they would rush back into the woods.

I enjoyed going the rounds of the traps. One morning I decided to move one of the traps which had not caught anything. It was one where the ring was passed over the stake and the stake driven so tight into the bark that I could not move it. While kneeling in the canoe, I gave it an extra pull. When it came loose I went over into the water headfirst and backwards. Fortunately, the canoe did not turn over, so I grasped it with one hand and paddled with the other to the shore. The water was deep and I knew the bottom was of a deep, soft sediment. I dared not touch bottom. I recovered the trap, reset it, went the rest of the rounds, then returned to camp where I removed all my clothes. While they were drying, I flung a blanket over me, Indian fashion, and went on skinning and stretching the skins.

In the middle of each day I would go to the meadow and make hay while the sun shone. In the early evening I would cut enough wood to see me through the night, and just before dark would go around the lake to see if the traps were all right. On one of these trips, as I was slowly drifting close to the shore near an inlet where beavers had thinned out the trees, I saw two nice big black beavers cutting down a tree. It was a good-sized tree about a foot thick, and they were working one on each side, biting into it as a woodsman would do and much the same shape, slanting the cuts up and down. For some time I watched them make the chips fly. I didn't want to waste my precious cartridges, so I slapped the brush with my paddle and they disappeared instantly.

The next day I set a trap for beaver and caught one. I never knew if it was one of the two or not; however, I had beaver tail for supper. The tail is long and wide and, broiled over hot coals, it is just like butter or jelly, it is so fat and juicy. I enjoyed the change from muskrat meat. It would have been a good meal had I had some bread with it.

And so the time passed until noon of the fifth day when I decided to take a chance on finding my way out. But I went to the meadow first to see if the hay was all right; we had mowed down about an acre or more.

At the far side tall grass stood as high as a man's head. I climbed on a fallen tree where I could see where we had mowed and to the opposite side of the meadow. As I looked, I saw something coming towards me through the tall grass. I couldn't see what it was, but from the waving of the grass I knew it was some animal. I waited with my gun ready to shoot as soon as it reached the clearing we had mowed. As it broke out into the open space, I was overjoyed to see Bill's black collie dog spring out. I think it was just as glad to see me. At the same time I heard Bill call from the woods beyond the meadow, and we soon got together.

It developed that he had been showing two lumbermen the timber through the woods. They had come on foot all the way from his home. They had brought lots of food with them, so I soon had some coffee made. I had to broil some muskrat meat; after they heard my story they wanted to try it. They declared it fine. Suffice it to say, they would not have liked it as a regular diet for five days and nights without something more than salt and coffee to go with it.

During the meal I told Bill I had decided to find my way out. He said, "All right. You might as well, as I am going to show these men through the woods around the north section. We'll reach home the day after tomorrow." As they had not brought any extra food, I asked Bill to give me some pointers on how to reach his place. He told me to follow the broken brush and blaze marks to the first lake and between all other lakes. "When you get out from shore, look to your left to the end of the lake. You will see two high points of land. Aim between them, then look along the shore for broken brush and blaze marks, then go ashore and follow the marks until you reach the next lake. When you get out from shore, look straight ahead and you will see a tree standing up above the others. Aim for it and then do the same as you did on the first lake."

I did all right on the first lake, but by the time I reached the second it was quite dark. However, I could see my way well enough while out on the lake, as the sky was clear and I could make out the point of land to aim for. When I reached the shore, alas, it was so much in dark shadow that I had to make a torch from birchbark, which we always carried with us, so I could see where to land. I crossed the portages between lakes by balancing the canoe over my head with one hand while I carried the lighted torch in the other. Besides the canoe and gun, I had an axe, some cooking utensils, two blankets, and a good-sized bundle of dried skins. It made quite a load to carry through the woods even in daytime. Here I was in the dark and dense woods at night—but I was determined to get through.

Well, I found my way to Bill's cabin. I remember the stars were shining bright, but I had no idea what time it was. I rapped on the door, and Mrs. Green asked who it was. When I told her, she said, "Come in. You will find Ben and Hughie on the floor by the range. Have you your blankets with you?" When I told her I had, she said, "Then roll down alongside the boys." (Ben and Hughie were her brothers.) I did and was asleep instantly.

How I ever made my way alone all those miles by water and through the woods and never went astray, I never could tell. If I had gone astray in the least, I believe I never would have lived to tell this tale. It was enough to test the nerve of a grown man in that position. Yet I was only a boy not yet eighteen, and only one and a half years from a big city, Toronto. However, I did not falter once on the trip.

Bill returned in a couple of days. We continued working on his little clearing. Then he said, "You better go see your folks, as we will go on another trip farther away in a couple of days."

I went over to find things in such bad shape that I called Mother outside for a talk. I wound up saying, "You have got to leave here, or we will be having you underground before spring."

Her answer was, "How can I go? We have no money."

I said, "Write to Owen and Marie, also to Annie. Tell them the truth about conditions here. Don't mince matters in the least. Owen has the money, so between them they will send you enough that you can take Kate, Emma, Sam, and Lidie back with you to Philadelphia. But before you go, have it understood with Pop that he sell out at the first chance. Then we will all return to the States. Arthur and I will stick by him. Mr. and Mrs. Brown have thrown over their place and have gone back to Pike County, New York. So there isn't anyone here now that you could call on if you should be taken sick or unable to help yourself. There is no one near except the Pokorny family, and Pop would never consent to fraternize with them."

I did all I could to persuade her, and she finally decided to take my advice. Then I told her that Bill and I would be away for some time, and I hoped she would be all ready to go, if not gone, by the time we returned. I went over to Bill's the same night. This was about the end of October 1876.

Mary Lake, August 9, 1875

9

Tricky Ways to Catch Fish

BILL AND I LEFT the next morning at daylight for a two-week trip up north. Later in the day we passed our old camp, going on through lake after lake and carry after carry until we reached what Bill called the Little Sand and the Big Sand. There was a narrows between these two lakes, Bella and Rebecca, which we could paddle through; we had to cross the Big Sand to reach the cabin Bill said he had there.

It was sunset when we reached Little Sand. It was dull, cloudy, and cold as we set out for the narrows about half a mile away. We paddled along side by side, he in his canoe and I in mine. There was very little wind as we reached the narrows. We could easily see any ripple on the water. We had gone about halfway to the narrows when I noticed a rippling close to shore on my right. Bill was at my left. As I turned to him, he said, "Well, what do you make of it?"

"Fish," I said.

"Yes, and big ones too," he said.

We were paddling very slowly along side by side. Bill said, "Stay where you are, but work in sideways. I'll go ahead and go ashore, and come down to where the fish are and shoot into them. You watch me. When I shoot, be ready to grab any that come to the top."

All worked out as planned. I was close in as he shot into the shoal of fish. One big fellow jumped clear out of the water and over the front of my canoe. Two others lay on top of the water and I pulled them in. They were big fine salmon or lake trout. When we examined them later, we

Settler's shanty on Lake Vernon, July 1875

found the bullet had passed through the cheek of one and across the back of the neck of the other, leaving a clean gutter, as it were, in each and not damaging the body in the least. Bill soon joined me and we headed for his camp. On the way he said the fish would weigh twenty to twenty-two pounds each.

His camp was a small hut formed of split logs, built upright and close together. The roof was the same, with hemlock bark laid on top to drain the water off when it rained. The fire was built on the floor, and there was a hole in the roof to carry out the smoke. A lot of wood lay already cut to build a fire. He always left his camp so that, if he returned after dark, he could make a fire at once. Bill said, "You get a fire going and water boiling while I clean the fish." There was a nice stream that entered the lake close by the camp.

It was dark and we had to make torches of birchbark so we could see our way around. By the time I had the fire going, the water boiling, and a pot of coffee made, Bill came with the fish. He had cut and split the fish down the back after first removing the heads. After first scattering salt over them, he then hung the two fish up over the fire. This smoke-dried them and preserved them from flies; they would keep for a long time. He put one of the heads into the pot of boiling water, adding some salt. When this one head had boiled long enough, we drained the water off. There was enough meat on it that, with bread and coffee, we had a good meal. The cheeks alone were solid meat and as large and thick as the palm of my hand. There was a lot of edible jelly and meat in the head. Altogether we had a good meal.

While Bill smoked a pipe of homegrown tobacco, we built our bed of balsam brush inside the cabin and finally lay down for a well-earned rest. It had been a long hard day. When not paddling our canoes, we were carrying them. Bill said we were fifty miles from the nearest human being.

It may be interesting to my readers to learn how Bill made his tobacco. He grew tobacco, of a sort, on his clearing. In the fall he would pull the plants up with the roots still on and hang them up in his barn to dry. When thoroughly ripened, he would strip the roots off and then the leaves. He moistened the leaves and packed them into a hole in a block of wood previously bored for the purpose; this hole was bored with a one-inch bit or auger. He packed the moist leaves down using a round peg and driving it in with a hammer or axe head. The hole would sometimes be ten inches deep. He would let it age in the wood press, as it were, sometimes for weeks or months. Then, as he wanted tobacco, he would split the block and out would come a nice, big plug of tobacco, just dry enough to smoke. He would shave off enough with his hunting knife to fill his pipe, rub it between his hands, pack it in his pipe, and light up. I did not smoke, but I enjoyed the fumes from his pipe.

We were up at daylight the next morning, boiled the other fish head, and so, with bread and coffee, had breakfast. We did not come here to trap, as the game was very scarce. But the lakes were full of salmon trout which were running up on the shallows along the stony shores. It was the custom of the trout to do this in the fall of the year. As Bill said, "The fish are worth more to me as food for my family." Besides winter food for his family, he would sell the fish in Huntsville and trade them for clothing and other necessities.

He had a long-handled spear to catch the fish. We had also brought an iron grate which was on the end of an iron pedestal. When in place at the front end of the canoe, the grate extended over the front, making what is called a grating, or jack-light. When fired up with burning pine knots or chips, this throws light down into the water. It lets you see objects easily to a depth of twenty feet or more, and any fish that come into the rays of the light.

After tidying up, our first job was to find dead pine trees. From them we would cut out knots and chips that were saturated with pine gum. We found these at the base of all limbs of dead trees, no matter how old and rotted the trees might be. But it was no easy task. It took both of us hours to find and cut enough to last us from dark until about two in the morning.

After cutting enough the first day, we lashed the two canoes together side by side using strips of inner basswood bark as a rope. This formed a sort of raft and, because the canoes were only partly covered by the crosspieces, left sufficient room for any fish we caught. The next thing was to fasten the jack-light in the front end of one canoe. It had to be firm and rigid and extend far enough forward to prevent sparks from falling into the canoe.

It was dark by the time all was secure. After a meal of bread and coffee, we pushed the double canoe out into the water. The jack-light was in the left-hand canoe, and I in the stern to steer and paddle the canoes as Bill directed. Bill, with his long spear, took his place in the front end of the right-hand canoe.

When all was in place, Bill lit the pine knots by holding a birch torch underneath the jack. The knots were soon in a nice bright blaze, throwing light up and down and all around. As I looked at Bill, tall and grim, standing with spear in hand in the bright light, he looked like the picture of Mephistopheles in quest of souls. But there were no "Soul au Lafate" here, so we just drifted along the shallows.

I would see trout a long distance down in the water, coming towards us. Bill would wait until they came within reach of his spear; then he would drive the spear at them, never missing, and almost always spearing the fish at the back of the head. In this way, it killed the fish instantly and, at the same time, didn't damage the body.

So we drifted around these two combined lakes without a sound of anything except the continuous dropping of big trout into the canoes. About two o'clock in the morning, we ran the canoes into the mouth of the creek near the camp and threw ourselves down on our balsam bed, clothing and all, not even removing our boots; then up at daylight, to clean and cook a fish for breakfast. Afterwards, we cleaned, salted, and hung up to smoke all the split fish. We built a smudge fire under them as they hung from poles fastened to trees. One day and one night was sufficient to dry and smoke them so they would keep well for winter use.

This fishing continued for two weeks until Bill thought it time to return home. He suggested that I remain there alone for a week, but I refused to stay; I was thinking of my experience on our first trip. We had a large amount of fish. So I knew it would take him at least three days to reach his home; there would be so many trips to make across the portages between the lakes. About fifty miles, as he said. He would return with provisions, he said as before. When I still refused to stay, he seemed very angry at first, but he finally decided it might be as well for me to go with him.

I suggested we make a detour that would bring us down by Colebridge (now Dorset) to the Lake of Bays, or Trading Lake as it was called by the early settlers. It got this name from trading done with the Indians when they made their homes around its shores and on the islands. Now there is a large resort and hotel located on the island, called Bigwin Inn after Chief Bigwin, chief of all the Indians in this section, who made his home on this island. I have seen the ruins of his log houses.

By coming this way around, we could call on Bill's father. Known as Old Sam Green, he lived alone in a log hut on the peninsula at the back of where Bigwin Inn now stands. Bill thought this a good idea. I did, too. Taking this route would bring us to the Portage, so I would know if Mother had gone.

It proved to be good for Old Sam Green and Bill too. We found the old man in critical condition, almost starved to death and with a large abscess between his shoulders. He said he had thrown all the bread he had to his five dogs. They looked as if they were ready to devour the old man himself. We soon satisfied the hounds by throwing each a large piece of fish. We also made a pot of tea for Sam, who soon revived. We bathed and poulticed the abscess, which had not broken. It must have been very painful, as he said he had been nauseated and unable to get on his feet.

Well, we fixed Sam up so we could lay him in my canoe with the hounds after we had transferred all my load into Bill's canoe. Then we paddled to a settler's place five miles away, around the end of the penin-sula, and across the main body of the lake; there we left the dogs. Next we pointed our canoes for the Portage, taking Sam along in my canoe. We reached the Portage at dusk. Mother was all ready to leave the next morning. It had been four weeks since I had talked her into leaving, and I had not expected to see her again, so we spent some time visiting, then soon said goodbye. She left the following day to return to Philadelphia. It lacked only a few days of being two years from the time she had left the city. It was now November 1876, and we had departed on December 4, 1874. It was to be three years before I saw her again.

Arthur helped Old Sam across the Portage and between us, Pop helping, we carried our things to Peninsula Lake. There we placed Sam in my canoe, as before, so Bill could go on to his home with all the fish and camping utensils in his canoe. I continued on down to Huntsville to place Sam in a room at Cann's Hotel, leaving him there in the care of Dr. Howland.

I was expecting to return to Bill's place that night, a paddle of about seven miles. I had been on the go since daylight, paddling and carrying until about ten at night, and had to come down through the creek in the dark, with only a clear, starry sky overhead to guide the way. Since I would have had to return the same way, with the current against me through a mile of creek, I decided to remain in Huntsville overnight. I was influenced in this by Mr. and Mrs. Cann asking me to stay, saying I could sleep with George and Mark, their boys. They were happy to have me stay and to have breakfast with them. I was only too glad to accept.

The next morning I left them early. I was back at Bill's before noon and started to work on a patch of barley. It had to be reaped with a sickle because it was mostly lying on the ground. This and digging potatoes kept me busy for a week. Then Sam came back to stay while recuperating. So, as there was no room for me, Bill told me I might as well go, saying, "You would not stay and fish up at the lakes, so I have no more use for you."

What a good thing it was that I had refused to stay up there. Under the circumstances, I might have been there a long time; I believe I never would have found my way out.

He was to have paid me three dollars a week. But when I asked for it, he said he didn't have any money but would give me potatoes and corn. I accepted, getting quite a lot of each, the balance to be paid in cash. I never received any. When I asked him for it a long time afterwards, he said he had given it to Pop when he met him in Huntsville. If Pop got it, he never told me.

Pop held on to any money coming to any of us. In fact, neither Arthur nor I ever had a dollar all the time I was in Muskoka. Pop would use it to pay his expenses on frequent trips to Huntsville or Bracebridge. If he didn't have any money, they would trust him at any of the hotels. So Pop was always owing something.

Fallen bridge near Huntsville, July 25, 1875

1 0

I Look for Paying Work

WHEN I RETURNED to the Portage in late November 1876 we formed a compact or partnership. It was agreed that I would act as cook, Arthur would look after firewood, and Pop would do washing and mending. This settled, we took stock of all we had.

First was a little black spaniel the Browns had left with us when they moved on, then a white-and-yellow cat, and six hens. We housed the hens in a cavern-like place we had dug in the bank close to the stone wall of the house, running it back to the big chimney which we thought might keep the place warm. This place was four by twelve feet and nine feet high, with a hemlock bark cover and a board floor at the front end. It seemed a nice place for the chickens. We fixed a den in the back room of the house for the dog and cat, but during the coldest weather they lay by the fireplace at night. Both were faithful animals and good company. For ourselves, we had the big bed in the room with the fireplace. We three slept together, the bed being large enough. Sleeping together, it made it much warmer for all of us.

Our stock of food consisted of some oatmeal, cornmeal, a little flour, some beans, turnips, peas, and the potatoes I had received from Bill Green. All the potatoes we grew ourselves had been eaten as fast as they became large enough. We also had a small amount of fish, salted and dried. And so we started the long winter. We did have salt, coffee and tea, and baking soda. The baking soda we used not only in corn cakes and bread but as a medicine for the heartburn we were troubled with. I've seen Pop take it by the spoonful, and dry too.

Winter soon set in. It was a short time until the lakes were frozen over and the ground covered deep with snow. By Christmas we were snowed in. Pop said, "How nice it would be if we could den up for the winter like the bears."

While we had food, and to clear up the land for planting, we worked at chopping down trees and cutting them into lengths so we could roll them into big heaps in the spring. We cleared the land from the bay, quite a wide swathe, up over the hill, down to the level, and a much wider space through to the shore of the little lake, cleaning it up along the shore and down to the ice. This opened up several acres of land.

We had not been able to increase our supply of food except for an occasional rabbit, squirrel, or partridge. So at Christmas we had a meagre celebration on corn cakes, beans, and turnips. Our potatoes were all gone, so we had a poor set-out for Christmas dinner. We didn't worry about it.

After breakfast we went up the side of the hill to cut more trees. The wind was blowing strong, and I was cutting a tree near the top of the hill. Arthur was working a short distance to one side of me. Pop was down below me trimming branches from a tree he had felled. The tree I was cutting leaned uphill, so I chopped so that it would fall that way. Just as it was about to fall, the wind caught the bushy top and swung the tree backwards. As soon as I saw it going I called to Pop, who was in the direction of its fall. He saw it and jumped and tumbled over logs and rolled through or over the loose branches, getting just far enough away so that only the ends of the branches whipped him. It was a close call. If he hadn't been quick, it surely would have killed him. Was he mad! And how he did call me for letting the tree fall his way!

By the end of January 1877 we had cut down the trees over several acres, I should judge. We had to stop then because we didn't have snowshoes. The snow had become so deep we couldn't struggle through it; nor stand on it, it was so light and dry. That it reached a depth of seven feet on the level was proved later on when we needed some dry wood to help burn the frozen green wood. I made snowshoes for Arthur and myself out of soapbox boards, good enough to let us shuffle over and stand on top of the snow. Arthur and I cut down a dead tree for its dry wood. Ordinarily the stump would have been three feet off the ground, but when the snow had gone in the spring, this stump was ten feet high.

We were now shut in the house most of the day and all of the night. To pass the time, we worked at making axe handles and paddles. We had nothing to read. None of us smoked, so for a lot of the daytime we just sat and looked in the fire. We would go to bed soon after dark to keep warm. On cold nights we would have to keep turning to the fire, first one side and then the other, to keep warm. Nobody knows how cold it was.

We couldn't go to Huntsville, the only place we had hope of getting something to eat, without money. Neither could we get any game; everything had burrowed under the snow. There the animals could find warmth and subsist on grass and roots, for the snow was so soft near the ground that they could live there during the period of cold weather. We could not do this, so we soon ate up all but some dried peas and turnips, which we lived on for two weeks. I would soak the peas overnight, boil turnips, and we'd have them with salt and tea. And so we existed until the peas were gone. Then we had nothing but turnips. We lived on mashed turnips until the end of February.

At that time the snow melted during the day and froze again at night, forming a crust on top. So with my improvised snowshoes, I got across the Portage to Peninsula Lake, which was solid ice and snow. Thus I had no trouble crossing the lakes and making my way to Huntsville, where I received a letter containing five dollars from the folks in Philadelphia. This was the first letter we received that winter. In fact, we had received only one letter since Mother returned to Philadelphia; that was to tell us she'd arrived safely. This one said that Annie and Marie had rented a house for them all to live in, so they were quite comfortable. Annie and Marie had sent the money—they little knew how badly it was needed.

I invested in a small cloth sack of flour, the same of cornmeal and oatmeal, salt, and some tea and coffee. I made a pack and carried it to the Portage, about ten miles over lakes Fairy and Peninsula, cutting across the land between them. I snowshoed over the Portage from north side to south side, so I had covered twenty miles in all. It was dark when I reached the house, but Arthur and Pop were glad to relieve me of my load and see the provisions I had brought. By rationing, it relieved us until we could hike around and get rabbits, squirrels, and partridge. So we pulled through the winter.

The poor cat didn't pull through as we had. Without anything it could eat, it starved to death. One very cold morning when I entered the den to give the chickens some corn nubbins, I noticed they were all huddled together in the far end. They seemed to be very much excited, and acted as if they were talking to one another. I saw that the straw was bunched in a heap in the middle of the floor. When I examined the heap I found the poor cat, stiff and lifeless. It certainly looked as if the chickens had buried it: the straws had been laid over the cat piece by piece, crisscross, as though each straw had been placed one at a time until the cat was covered from sight. Why the chickens should do it I could not say, unless it was out of sympathy. I do know that those chickens watched me while I uncovered the cat, remaining in the back end of the den until after I removed it. All the chickens survived the winter. I believe the above is worth noting for its peculiarity.

The lakes opened up the last week in April and we began to catch nice trout to eat and sell or trade in Huntsville. We did well in trading for potatoes. Pop cut the large ones for seed and we had a good supply to eat. With these and the fish, we lived pretty well. Then, too, as time went on we had some fine, long, thick stems of rhubarb from plants Pop had put in the year before. Some of these I sold in Huntsville at two stalks for ten cents. They were fine thick stalks, sweet and juicy; I had no trouble selling all I could take to Huntsville.

We burned over and cleared up the land where we had cut the trees during the winter. We could get all the seed we wanted and we worked hard. By the end of June we had planted quite a field of potatoes, turnips, peas, beans, a large field of corn, and more. By the time we had our planting done, we were again in poor shape for food. We had just a little flour and oatmeal, some fish—really not enough for three.

At this time we received another five dollars. We invested in food, but I couldn't stay and help eat it up. I decided to leave it for Arthur and Pop. We figured it would last them a month with care not to indulge too freely.

I had heard they were cutting a road through the locks to strike Brunel Road. A gang of men were at work chopping the trees down and grading through the woods. This work was about eight miles from the Portage. I cut through the woods, saving a mile or two by not following the road part way. I found Mr. Young in charge, the same man who had fixed up my foot. He couldn't give me a job. But if I was hungry, he said, I would find some boiled pork in a kettle, and a half-loaf of bread, at a certain place back on the road. I found the kettle but no pork or bread, but there was a lot of thick pork fat in the kettle. I had a cake of bread with me, so with my knife I split it into two slices and spread them an inch thick with pork fat. So I had a good lunch.

Feeling better, I struck off through the woods to hit Brunel Road. It ran to Port Sydney, at the foot of Mary's Lake where the north branch of the Muskoka River runs out. After descending a steep grade, Brunel Road crossed the river by a wooden bridge. I was about to cross over when I noticed two men coming towards me from the opposite side. I waited for them to reach me.

I asked them if they knew where I could get a job of any kind. The older one asked the other how he was fixed. He said he had all the help he could use, but added, pointing to a large white building across the road on the top of the grade, "That house is a general store. Their hired man has just left them this morning. You might get his place."

It was now dark, but I went on and into the store. A woman was at the back of the counter. I told her what I was after, and she asked me if I could take care of and drive a team of horses. I said I could. She asked me a lot of questions and seemed satisfied I could fill the bill. She said her husband had gone to Bracebridge for supplies and would not be home until late; so I had better come in the morning, to be there by six o'clock. She did not ask me where I would stay overnight or if I was hungry. Yet, I had told her where I had come from; in all, I believe I had walked at least thirty miles. I left her, saying I would be on time.

I felt she was favourably impressed by me, but why, I could never fathom—unless it was my face or my straightforward way of speaking. I was poorly dressed and almost on my uppers for shoes, and no socks. She could not see all of that, of course, in the dim light of the kerosene lamp, the only light in the store. However, I was pleased that I had a chance for a job. I had a twenty-five-cent piece and two little silver three-cent pieces in my pocket. I could have gotten a bed at Morgan's Hotel for twenty-five cents, but I was hungry. I spent the quarter for something to eat. Later, I'll tell what became of the three-cent pieces.

I walked up through the very small village of Port Sydney. It extended partly along the river and shore of Mary's Lake. As I returned from the lake, I noticed there was something doing at the new frame building some distance from and above the road. It was built among rocks and large boulders, with a wooden walk spanning the rocky way up to the house. It afterwards proved to be the village hall. I joined the people going up. About halfway there I was stopped by an elderly man who said, "The admission is twenty-five cents to see the entertainment." I couldn't take it in, of course, and told him so. His answer was, "A little nonsense now and then is relished by the wisest man." I have often thought since that it was an absurd thing to say to a man with only two three-cent pieces to his name. Of course, he didn't know that, so I forgave him.

I didn't have a place to lay my weary head, and weary it was, too. I was tired in general. I had noticed a hollow between two rocks with a grass bottom that I thought would make a good place to sleep. I walked around looking for a barn or some better place to spend the night but could not find any. I waited until the concert was over and everything was quiet. It was the night of June 23, 1877. I crawled under the rock and laid myself down. The grass was dry and comfortable. I soon went to sleep, having nothing on me except shirt, pants, and knit jacket.

I had been asleep a long time, so I thought, when I awoke shaking with cold. I got out of there and went back to the store, where there was a big barn. But it was locked. Then I remembered an empty house I had passed, away over on top of the grade across the river. There was a stable at the back and I thought there might be some hay or straw in it. I went back to it, first going through the two-storey house. I went through each room; there were no blinds on the windows and the sky was clear and full of stars shedding enough light to see my way. Finding nothing to cover myself with, I repaired to the stable and discovered just a little hay in a long manger. This looked good to me, so I rolled in; but it was too cold to sleep. I concluded that it was the woods for me.

Along the road about a mile from the house was a nice pine and hemlock woods. I walked to it and in a short distance found some dry leaves and small sticks. Fortunately, I had some matches. After getting a blaze going, I stood over it until I felt warm. I collected more wood and piled it on the fire. Then I laid myself down on the pine needles alongside the fire. Soon I was asleep, awakening at times to build up the fire, thinking each time it must be near daylight.

As I have remarked before, everything hath an end, as did this, the longest night I have ever passed. I was up and around by the first streaks of day, but sat by the fire until I could look across to the village and see it waking up. Then I went down to the river where, without soap or towel or comb, I had a bath in the cool water; I just let the water dry up on me, then dressed, smoothing my clothes and steadying my nerves.

I went to the store where I met Mr. and Mrs. Fawcett. He was a tall man, rugged and strong, and I liked him at the time. He seemed to think I was all right, so we made a deal whereby I was to be their hired man at ten dollars per month and board. This being settled, they said, "Come in to breakfast."

As we entered the dining room, I noticed the family and all were waiting for me. There were Mr. and Mrs. Fawcett, their daughter Lizzie, about fifteen; two sons nine and ten, the hired woman about twenty, then two able-bodied men who had been working for Mr. Fawcett for a few days. We all sat down. As I looked over the table which was all set for the crowd, I was satisfied that I could eat all that was on it for the nine of us and then ask for more. If it was a sample of the meals to come, I was afraid I would not get enough to eat.

After we ate, the two men picked up their kit bags and left for their homes back in the woods. The boss said to me, "I have a lot of lumber to haul to a settler about four miles east and a mile back off the Brunel Road, up in the woods. So we might as well hitch up the team and get going." I went with him to the barn where I found two big Canadian horses, one white and called Bill, fat, round, and, as I found, lazy. The other, an iron grey named Nancy, was a little taller than Bill. Strange to say, I liked them and they liked me; for four months I took care of them and drove them, but never once did I have any trouble with them.

I helped harness the horses and hitch them to the big wagon. It had a good spring seat where we sat to drive. Mr. Fawcett took the reins and drove out of the barn, down the grade, across the bridge, and turned into the sawmill and lumberyard. There I was surprised to meet the two gentlemen I had met the night before. They proved to be brothers. They and their father had been there a long time. They gave me a smile of recognition. I got to know them well afterwards. They were both fine in every way, never seeing me without speaking a good word. We loaded the wagon with sawed lumber, boards, and scantling, as well as joists and timber; it made a big heavy load. Mr. Fawcett drove. We got up the long, high grade from the bridge by giving the horses a rest halfway up. We drove along the road for two miles then turned into the woods road; it was rough going. At one place we had to climb a steep hill where there was a slanting, smooth-faced rock which, being covered with moss and fresh earth, we could not see. The horses could not get a good footing with such a load to pull. We both got down. I scotched the wheels and at a third try, I with the whip and he with the reins, we got over it.

We finally reached the farm, unloaded, and drove back to the lumber mill where we loaded a second time. Then Mr. Fawcett said, "Now you drive on to the same place, deliver the load, and return to the house for dinner. I'm going over to Utterson and will be back by the time you are." It was then about ten o'clock and I was feeling weak. In fact, I had been working all morning on my nerve. I kept myself at it by repeating these words, "If you want to live, you must work." So I took up the reins and drove out as he stood looking at me.

I made good time until I reached that rocky ledge where the horses could not get a footing. After trying several times to get up, as we had done before, I decided to take off half the load. The horses were then able to pull it up and on to the settler's. I told the man I would go back for the other half, but he said, "No, I'll pull the rest of it in." He no doubt realized that I was all in.

I wasn't long getting back as the horses were just as hungry as I was. We reached the barn at 2 p.m., long after dinner. The boss took charge of the team while I went in to dinner. Martha, the hired girl, waited on me. She gave me the laugh when she heard how and where I had been stuck on the rocky hillside. But she sure gave me a good feed and told me the reason for having such a poor breakfast. The two men were leaving, and Mr. Fawcett would not give them a good meal because they were leaving. She told me I would get plenty to eat, and I did. She was good to me all the four months I was there.

Brunel Road approaching Mary Lake, August 9, 1875

11

Six Cents Over

I COULD FILL a good-sized book in telling all my experiences in my four months with the Fawcetts of doing all kinds of farm work and taking care of the horses and barn. There was half an acre of truck garden to look after. It was all planted, so all I had to do was keep the weeds down and hoe between the plants. He had a large bed of strawberries planted in hills. This was where I learned how to grow strawberries and gained a lot of knowledge of gardening. He also had a large farm about a mile and a half west along the road; in fact, the road ran through it. There was a nice one-room frame house on it where we could take shelter and eat our dinner; we spent a good many days at the farm.

The night before I was to leave on my first trip to Bracebridge for supplies for the store, Mr. and Mrs. Fawcett gave me full instructions and $150 in cash. I was to pay for everything and enter the amount I paid for each. I was to go to a certain hotel, put up the horses, see they were watered and fed, get my dinner while they were eating, then go to the various stores and place my orders. At three o'clock I was to harness up the team, collect the goods, and pack them as close as possible in the wagon. At five o'clock I was to drive down to the boat landing and pick up two cases of goods for a Mr. John Smith, a neighbour, who expected them in on the boat.

Up at four the next morning, I fed and curried the horses, giving them a good feed of oats and plenty of hay while I, at Martha's call, went in to a good, big breakfast. After eating, I gave the horses a drink and hitched them to the big wagon. But this time the whole family were out; so with more advice, I started on my first drive of twenty miles to Bracebridge.

The first three miles were hard going. At one place there was a corduroy bridge (a bridge built of logs laid side by side to make swampy land passable). After passing over that, the road led through a clearing covered with stumps of trees and logs; here the fire had been run, burning up all the small brush and trees, leaving the logs to be rolled into big heaps and burned, the usual way of clearing the land. As I came to this place, the people (all help in doing this work) were piling the logs onto the side of the space that had been cleared for the road. It was quite a trick for me to drive in and out between log piles and standing tree stumps, but I had to drive through to reach the main road.

I had travelled several miles when a young man hailed me from a cabin some distance from the road. When I pulled up, he said, "I have a trunk I want to get to the boat landing. Will you take it for me?"

"Yes," I said. "But you will have to get it out here as I cannot leave the horses."

He dragged the trunk out and we got it in the wagon. He climbed up beside me on the high spring seat. He said he had been staying with an uncle for a year but had decided to return to his old home in Philadelphia.

I said, "Yes, I know where it is." And when I asked him his name, he said, "James Peacock."

"Yes, and you live in the Kensington section," I said. He looked at me as I said this.

He said, "Yes. How did you know?"

"I was on the lot at Amber and Adams streets when you and Jimmie Devine had a fight. You were taller than Devine, but he was a fighter. You both fought until you couldn't stand up."

"Who are you?" he asked.

"You would not remember me, as I am some years younger than you," I said. "I was only ten at the time, but I was always with boys older than myself, and I was on the side hurrahing for Jimmie Devine at that fight."

We both thought it strange for us to meet as we did, and so far from home. I left him at the boat landing and never saw him again. But here was the rub for me: I had $150 in my pocket. He was going to my old home. So it ran through my mind how easy it would be for me to take the boat with him. By the time my bosses could find out where I was, I would be in the U.S.A. The temptation was there. Here I was in rags, as it were, and no prospect for the future but a hard life for the years to come. Then I thought, "Honesty is the best policy. These people have put their trust in me and I won't break their trust." So I left him and drove to the hotel, put up the team, and had a good dinner; then I went out and placed the orders to be made up for me to pick up later in the day.

After settling at the hotel, I hitched up the team and collected a wagonload of groceries: two barrels of flour, one each of oatmeal, sugar, salt, dried apples, currants, and a number of boxes and bags. Then I drove down to the boat landing where I found the two cases were big ones, so I had to get the boatman to help me. I packed my other goods closer together to make room in the bottom of the wagon for the larger case. The other had to be put on the high seat, leaving just enough room for me to sit on the right side.

As I started away, they said, "Look out, boy. You have over two ton on that wagon." They knew where I was going and how late it was to start with such a load. It was after five o'clock, but it being the last week of June, I knew I would have about three hours before it became really dark, as we always had a long twilight. They knew I would be in the dark over the tail end of the eighteen miles and, at best, it was not a good road.

I waved them goodbye, picked up the reins, and with a "giddap there," started for Port Sydney. I went along for several miles until I came to a stretch of lowland which had been filled in while I was away. When near the end of it, I met a team coming towards me; I swung over to let them pass. As I did so, I noticed the men watching me, so I naturally looked back at the tracks I had made in the soft ground. It made me shiver to see I had been within a foot of going over into a deep ditch. Lucky for me, I cleared it.

I had no trouble until I turned off the main road. It was now dark. I drove along until I came to the place where they had been piling up the logs when I last went through. The heaps of logs had been burned and the ashes had spread across the road; I could not see the road. All I could do was drive for the opening that showed where the road entered the woods, driving to avoid the stumps and the embers of logs that were still burning. At one place I thought I was clear of the smouldering fire, but one end of a long piece stuck out. It caught in the spokes of the left rear wheel, causing the log to turn upright, sending sparks in all directions. But my team, being tired, did not plunge away; I also had a tight rein on them as it was a down grade.

When I reached the opening through the woods the horses kept pulling to the right. I tried to pull to the left to get, as I thought, on the corduroy bridge. It was so dark I couldn't see that, while I was away, the bridge had been moved to the opposite side of the road. The horses could see, and if I had let them have their way we would have been all right. As it was, they got the front wheels and right rear wheel on, but the left rear wheel was off. I stopped, got down, and felt where the trouble was. Fortunately, close by the wheel that was down there was a log that had been cut on the usual slant by the woodsman. I took the reins and guided the horses along until the wheel came to the sloping end of the log. When I urged the horses ahead, the wheel came up on the corduroy. I jumped up on the seat, fastened the reins to it and said, "Go to it, horses. You can see better than I can."

And so we reached home about one in the morning. Mr. and Mrs. Fawcett met us with lanterns. They had heard us coming and evidently were glad to see us; they couldn't imagine why we were so late. It was all right when I explained about leaving Bracebridge so late with such a heavy load, and having to let the horses walk all the way.

Mr. Fawcett took charge of the horses. I went in to get something to eat and to give Mrs. Fawcett my account, and the change that was left. She figured them up. Mr. Fawcett came as I finished eating and said to her, "How is it?"

"Did you have any money of your own?" she asked.

"No," I said.

She said, "Everything is all right, except there is six cents over."

Then it came to me that I did have the two three-cent bits, but I couldn't correct myself. So that was the last I ever heard of them. It was also my last bit of money. I made that trip a number of times, but was never again so late returning.

It was now time to harvest the hay, oats, and wheat, one following the other in quick succession and in that order. Mr. Fawcett engaged a man to work with me on the mowing, all of it done with scythes. He was a big, strong fellow named Collingwood Seely. He and his people had quite a farm back on Brunel Road. I found him a fine fellow, but being twice my age and a strong, good worker with a scythe, he could lead me around the field mowing a wider swathe than I could. He worked with me about six weeks. We cut and drew in the hay, oats, and wheat, storing the hay in the barn at the back of the store, and stacking the oats and wheat in the field. His strength and experience made the mowing, stacking, and storing hard for me.

He let me load the wagon while he pitched it up to me to spread out. He would pitch up such big forkfuls that it made it hard for me; but for all that, he gave me the easiest part of the work. I was sure put to the test in all the work while he was with us. He always treated me fine, and for that I grew to like him very much. We worked, ate, and slept together.

I gained a lot of knowledge from Collingwood Seely, especially the care of horses. He had a nice medium-sized mare which he could do anything with. It was a sight to see him spring on its bare back, no reins, and fly or gallop down the hill, across the bridge, up the opposite side, and over the top as he waved to us, disappearing on his way home.

When I was not on a trip to Bracebridge, I put in my time on the half-acre garden, or at the farm I told you about, about a mile from the store and barn. It had a one-room bunk house where we ate our lunches. The farm was all fenced, and the main road ran through. After the hay was taken off, we turned it into a pasture for the horses, leaving them out all night. The black flies were very bad, so it was hard on the horses. I would take a bottle of Yellow Indian Oil with me every morning to rub in their ears and up under their throats. My hand would come away filled with black flies and blood. As I approached the barn, they would run to the fence and stretch out their necks for me to rub them with oil. At times I would take them down to the river and, taking an old broom, jump in myself, take them into deep water, and give them a good brushing. They liked that.

On the first day of July 1877, Canada's Dominion Day, Seely was off for the day, so I was sent to hill up potatoes down on the farm, not far from the road. About nine o'clock, as I was busy working along, I heard singing away off on the main road and through the woods. As the singing came nearer, I could hear the old familiar "Old Black Joe." It was a party of young people on their way to a picnic on an island in Mary's Lake. They passed close by but did not speak. I felt a little homesick; it was such a reminder of Philadelphia.

Everyone had a big time celebrating the day and evening because there was a dance on the deck of the first steamboat on Mary's Lake. It was open to the public. I went aboard early in the evening. Afterwards we could see the people dancing; they seemed to be having a good time. Captain Denton was in command, with Mr. Smiley to assist him. Captain Denton, I think, was part owner of the boat. It ran up to, and through the locks in the river above the head of Mary's Lake, through Fairy Lake, then around and under Cann's Bluff, entering the river which came down through Huntsville from Lake Vernon. The boat was unable to get any farther into Huntsville than just below the bridge; at that time quite a strong current ran under the bridge.

It was a great time. All enjoyed celebrating that day and night, with the boat taking people for a ride out on the lake. The people of Port Sydney enjoyed being ahead of Huntsville in getting the first steamboat; and I sure enjoyed the change and seeing so many people.

There was pleasure as well as hard work. One pleasure was taking Martha, Lizzie, and the two boys boating to an island in the lake where huckleberries grew aplenty. Martha always packed a big basket of eats. We would go into the bunkhouse at the farm, eat our lunch and have a good time. We spent a number of days in this way in late July and early August. It was a relief from the regular routine. I don't suppose any of them ever forgot them; even the two boys had a good time. I was detailed to accompany them as there was no one else who could.

There was, however, a cloud. It was quite evident that Mrs. Fawcett wanted me to take up with Lizzie. Martha, too, did all she could to bring Lizzie and me together. But I would have none of it: my thoughts were for Philadelphia, and I was determined not to take up with anyone. Mrs. Fawcett grew cool and fault-finding, but I never let on I noticed.

So time went on. One Saturday I borrowed Billie the horse, with a riding saddle, to take a trip to the Portage. I left late Saturday afternoon for the seventeen-mile trip from Port Sydney. I got along very well for about fourteen miles until the sun began to set—and so did Billie; he seemed to sense he was going away from home.

I rode him to within three miles of the Portage where we entered a dense part of the woods, swampy with black muck in the road. Billie stopped. I couldn't move him. I got off and led him to the Portage where we tied him to a post with the only piece of rope we could find. In the morning we found he had broken loose. We found him in the corn field, which was in tassel, but he hadn't trampled down any of the stalks. Pop, however, was mad. I was only too glad Billie hadn't gone for his home.

I left the Portage late Sunday. Pop came across the Portage with me, he walking and I riding. Pop gave me a lot of instructions in riding and that came in good. Billie was anxious to go. Pop said, "You won't have any trouble getting him home. Just hang on. Don't let him throw you." Good advice: I no sooner left Pop than Billie, sensing he was going home, started to run, then canter, then gallop. I could hardly hold him and keep my seat. We made good time. In fact, I might say double-quick time. I was sore but glad to reach home.

Soon after my trip the time came for planting. Mr. Fawcett and I took the horses to the farm where he plowed around the field to show me how to do it; I followed in his footsteps. The field was covered with pine stumps; they don't rot out very quickly, nor do the roots. Therefore the plow-point caught a number of times. If he swore, I didn't hear him; but he looked like he did. After a second round, he said, "Here. See what you can do."

I took the reins guiding the horses and gripped each handle of the plow. With a "giddap," we started and almost immediately dug the point under a root. This was repeated every few feet for halfway around the field. I was disgusted, and evidently he was too. He said, "It's no use. You can't handle a plow."

"No," I said. "And it will take a better man than you to plow this field."

He said, "I will get a man to do it, and you can go. I can't keep two men." And so ended three months or more.

I asked him for the balance of my pay. There was about seventeen dollars due me. I had bought some clothing from him. Then, too, Pop had been down several times. I had bought him some provisions. That reduced my pay from thirty dollars to seventeen and something. He gave me ten, and I accepted an order on Mr. White, the government agent at the locks between Mary's Lake and Fairy Lake, at the sawmill. I accepted the order as I had met Mr. White and his wife several times. They had been to the Portage on fishing trips. One time they spent three nights and days. (This was before I left the Portage in the spring. They were very nice people and thoroughly enjoyed the fishing.) But he was of a violent temperament, big and strong. He would go into tantrums.

One morning we were outside the house; Mr. and Mrs. White had been talking. When Pop, Art, and I came out, he swung around from her and said, for no reason I ever knew, "I can lick any one of you!" His sleeves were rolled up, and he had his fists up for a fight. We were taken by surprise and didn't say a word. Then he said, "I can take all three of you."

"It isn't necessary, as you know," I said. "Either one of us could knock you out, and you know it. So shut up, or I will take you first."

I put up my fists and looked him in the eye. He calmed down at once. I think he feared we might all join in. His wife stood looking at us with a smile as he said, "I guess we'll call it off." He was a good fellow otherwise.

So, by accepting Fawcett's order on him, I felt he would make it good. He owed for a bill of goods brought from Fawcett.

I spent the night in Port Sydney with a man and his wife I had made friends with. It may be interesting to know how it came about. One morning in July he brought his yoke of oxen to the store and asked Mr. Fawcett to let me take his place at the last minute at a barn-raising where he was expected with his oxen. He appealed to my boss, saying his wife was very bad and that the doctor told him not to leave her. Mr. Fawcett asked me if I could handle the oxen. I said I could.

Now, I had had no experience but had seen others handle them, so I felt sure I could. The boss said, "All right." The man gave me his whip and said, "Bring them out." They were standing in the comer of a fence at the roadside. I turned them out and around so well, he said, "You are all right. But look out for the black one. Keep close to him."

I drove them with "haw, gee, and whoa" for about four miles out Brunel Road to where they were raising the barn. A man met me, and I told him whose place I was taking and why. "All right," he said. "Drive in the woods road. You will meet other teams. The boss will tell you what to do." About a half-mile in I met two yoke of oxen fastened tandem, both pulling on a long timber that had caught between trees in such a way that they couldn't move it.

So it was up to me to chain my oxen to the yoke of the other. I did, and we pulled it clear. Then I went forward, unfastened the chain, and let it drop. I don't know if it was the rattle of the chain as it struck the ground, but my oxen sprang away before I could get to their heads. They ran out to the main road and turned for home. About a mile from where they ran away, they turned into the woods. There I found them browsing on the leaves of a fallen tree. The black one gave me a look I didn't like, so I gave him the whip. They were in such a position that they couldn't get away. I think I whipped some sense into the black brute, because after the whipping he let me pick up the chain and wrap it around the yoke beam. I then drove them out and back to the barn-raising where the men were just sitting down to a big feed called dinner. And what a dinner! I gave the oxen a lot of hay and joined the others. Did I fill up? Well, I guess!

I had no more trouble with the oxen and returned them to the owner. He was all smiles as he said, "I have a little son, born one hour after you left." We were good friends ever after, but I'm sorry to say the baby lived only a few days.

I helped him with his work, so I was welcome to stay with them any time and as long as I wanted. But as I was anxious to get to the Portage, I stayed with them only one night, leaving the next morning. As I came by the store, Martha, Lizzie, and the boys were outside to see me go by. I just waved to them. That was the last I ever saw of them. Port Sydney was out of my line of travels.

I must have walked thirty miles that day. I was tired and glad to reach the Portage and what we called home. Arthur and Pop were glad to see me. There was a lot to do.

Mary Lake, August 9, 1875

12

Killing Deer Out of Season

THE CROPS HAD DONE WELL and the potatoes were ready to dig. But before doing this, we dug a space out of the sand bank up towards the lake yet close to the house. On the space, twelve by fourteen by two feet deep, we built a double-walled cabin. We filled the space between the walls with leaves, packing them in good and hard. We built a roof with the sand we had dug out. In front we built a double door; and the double walls in front were much farther apart than the others, so when filled in it was thick enough to keep severe freezing out. This made a fine root cellar for our potatoes, turnips, carrots, and beets. We had built well, so we lost none of them by freezing. I can remember it was always nice and warm inside in the coldest weather. We filled it full, so we were well fixed for winter in that respect.

At that time a gang of men was cutting the road through from where Brunel Road had stopped, about a mile from us across the Portage, to Cain's Corners. They didn't come straight through and down by the house to our corner of the bay but climbed up and over a ridge, swinging east. This brought them down and through where Brown had built.

There was quite a gang of workers. A man by the name of Baxter was in charge. They had a cook and a regular camp built not far from us. We visited them a number of times and were treated to some good meals. I enjoyed visiting the cook. He knew his job and could turn out the biggest loaves of bread, baked in a tin Dutch oven in front of an open fire.

Inside a settler's cabin

Mr. Baxter and I became quite friendly. One day he asked if he could come along with me on a trip to Huntsville in the birch canoe. We had been in Huntsville some time. I had left him to go wherever he wanted, and I went to Coburn's to get a lot of groceries on my order. When I was ready to leave, I found Mr. Baxter at Cann's Hotel with his right arm and shoulder all bound up. It seems he was fooling with some men on the high stoop in front of the post office when one of them pushed him over on his head and shoulders, breaking his collar bone. He was a sick man, moaning and groaning all the way to the Portage as he lay in the canoe.

I got him to the road camp, saw he was all right, and left him. But there was no one to do anything for him but me. So I visited him every day for a long time, fixing him up and rewinding the bandages. He sure appreciated my help. But the job was only a short one. He left, and I never saw him again.

Early in September, only a few days after my return to the Portage from Port Sydney, Mr. Pokorny came over and asked Pop in a very conciliatory way, "We want some fresh meat. What do you say to joining Louis and me and my hound Fannie to see if we can get a deer. You and the two boys (meaning Arthur and me) with your canoes. We can go out on the peninsula where we won't be seen by any strangers." He meant it was out of season; it was six weeks before the opening. We agreed. He told Pop afterwards he was afraid that if he went alone and got a deer, Pop would report him. Pop would not have done that.

Early the next morning we started, Captain and Louis each in a canoe and Louis with the dog; he was to put the dog ashore about halfway up the peninsula, and to take his stand farther south near Bigwin Island, on which Bigwin Inn is now located. We expected the deer might swim out there. I was shown over the island one time by Old Sam Green. He showed me the ruins of what had been Chief Bigwin's home and trading place before the government ordered the Indians onto a reserve a number of years before we came to the lake.

On the peninsula there is a narrow, low place we called the Neck where we often crossed into Three Mile Creek Bay. We would carry our canoes over. This bay was supposed to be three miles deep from the main part of the lake.

To come back to our hunting: Pop and Art were stationed in their canoes near the Neck. I was to cross over into Three Mile Creek Bay and remain in my canoe near the land close to the Neck where I could look clear to the main part of the lake. The bay varied from a half to one and a half miles wide. With the sun shining bright on the quiet water, it looked like an immense mirror.

I had not been at my station very long when I heard Fannie baying a way back on the peninsula. The sound was coming towards me, so I expected the deer to take to the water near me. I was all set, paddle in hand and in water, gun close at hand, when I noticed the baying of the dog was going away from me, towards the other end where Captain was.

I had about given up hope when I espied a small black speck on the water a long way down the bay. It came to mind that Sam Green had told me that was how a deer looked at a distance when swimming across the lake when the lake was quiet.

As these thoughts raced through my mind, I was watching the black speck and getting my canoe underway. I could see the black speck moving towards the opposite shore. Now this happened to be the widest part of the bay. I pointed my canoe so I could get to the opposite shore ahead of it. As I drew nearer, I could see by its horns that it was a buck.

Well, I did my best. My canoe was a poor one. The bottom was rough and uneven; it retarded my progress so much the deer beat me to the shore. When it landed, the distance was too far for me to shoot. As I stopped, I looked back to where it came from and saw Fannie swimming after it. I waited for her and urged her on; she landed just where the deer had been and took up the trail, all the while baying.

Around a point of land, not far from where the deer had gone ashore, there was a small bay where I felt sure the deer would take to the water again; so I paddled for the point. When I was near it, close to shore, I could hear the deer coming down through the woods, apparently making for the point which, I could now see, ended in a flat rock. I stopped, remaining like a statue. The deer, a big fine buck with horns in velvet, came out on the flat rock point not fifty feet from me.

(As a deer's horns grow, they are covered with a thin fur resembling velvet, shiny like silver. The horns are soft, just like gristle or soft bone that is easily broken. They remain this way until winter, then they shed the fur and the horns become very hard, clean bone. The deer sheds these every spring, growing new ones each year.)

It was a pretty sight. Imagine, if you can, me kneeling in my canoe, paddle in hand and in the water ready to push ahead, as still as I could be; the deer standing out in full view with the sun shining on him, and the clear smooth lake all around us. He turned his head for a look both ways, then plunged into the lake. I was ready. I pushed my canoe between him and the point, driving him ahead of me near to where I had been stationed on the opposite shore. When near enough to shore, I took careful aim and shot him just behind the right ear. His head went down, then came up. He was as lively as ever. I had hit him all right; there was blood running down his neck. (Afterwards we decided we didn't have enough powder in the gun and only number six birdshot; so it was not sufficient to kill him.)

It was up to me to get around him and keep him from getting ashore; this I did. I recollected Sam Green had told me how he had a deer in the lake and how he chased it down so he could kill it with his knife. I didn't have a knife large enough, but I chased him around and got him not far from where I wanted him. I reached down, grabbed his tail, and as my paddle was a hard, heavy wooden one, I used it to club him on the head. My first and second blows broke two inside prongs; my third came down edgewise on the top of his head, killing him instantly.

I had to hold him so he wouldn't sink, as they do this time of year. Sam Green had told me this; to me he was an authority on a great many of the hunters' tricks. While holding him with one hand, I took off my belt and fastened it to his horns and the thwart, or seat, of my canoe. Then I pulled him to shore, managing to pull him up the sloping bank with his head downwards. I cut his throat to bleed him, then fired off twice, the agreed-upon signal if any of us got a deer.

I sat down to wait and noticed Fannie coming along the shore. She had come around the upper end of the bay from the point where the deer had jumped in, at least two miles. She lay down alongside the body of the deer. She must have been played out: chasing the deer up and down the peninsula for some miles, swimming across the bay, chasing the deer again, then walking back to me. I thought she was fine.

The others, after waiting for some time, came looking for me; they hadn't heard my signal. I leave you to judge their surprise when they saw the body of such a big deer. They estimated it would weigh at least 200 pounds. Captain slapped me on the back, saying "Goot, goot for you." Fannie came in for an extra pat.

We butchered it there. We got half the meat, Captain the other half. The hide and all the rest went to Captain as owner of the dog; this was the usual or unwritten law of hunters. The meat we really could use. The nights were so cold we could keep it until we ate it. We sure enjoyed that meat with our corn cakes.

That was the beginning of a better feeling between the Pokornys and ourselves. A number of times after the hunt I visited at their cabin in the evenings. He was a well-educated man, claiming he could talk in seven languages. I don't doubt that he could.

One evening while I was visiting them he brought up the subject of why people said he was lazy and would not work. He said he was all right when moving to the woods; but lifting a large kitchen range they brought by boat to North Portage, taking it over to the south side, he strained the muscles of his heart. To verify his story, he would have me listen to his heart action. To me it sounded like two big gear wheels running with a grinding noise. This satisfied me there was something wrong. He showed me a certificate that proved either he or his father had been a colonel in the Polish army. He was a wonderful man to say the least; but not to be trusted. He and his family would take anything they could lay their hands on, or beat anyone in a deal, regardless of honour.

He also told me he practised medicine in Philadelphia for a number of years, said he had a big clientele of mostly young women from the elite of Philadelphia who came to him with headaches or minor troubles. He would give them some advice and a package of oatmeal tablets prepared by himself, and receive five dollars for a visit to his office for each one. He said he made a pile of money, but he was not satisfied. He came to Toronto and, after a few years, came up to the woods.

He never told me the "whys," but I was interested enough to find out. He had embezzled a lot of money and had come to Canada. In Toronto he married an Irish woman. After some years, he became a member and treasurer of an opera company in Toronto. One night, so the story goes, they had a big house. As treasurer, he packed the receipts into a suitcase for deposit in the bank on Monday. Instead of going home, he slipped out and afterwards had his wife and children join him. He finally drifted up to the Portage, squatting on the south side where my father found him with his wife and five children. The eldest was about fourteen and the youngest a baby.

They lived in a one-room log cabin, eking out a living by fishing and what they could raise on a small clearing they had managed to cut out of the woods. I judged Mrs. Pokorny was the one who did the work. She was a large, strong woman and could handle an axe or hoe as well as most men. Their cleared land was but a very small piece clear of logs, but they planted between stumps as best they could. I don't know how long they existed there (I say existed, as that is all that could be said of it). He had been only too glad to sell his squatter's rights and get off the Portage, going on to another lot farther down the bay.

In the fall of that year, 1877, two brothers, Ed and Archie Gouldie, would come to where Dwight now is. They came every fall to fish the lakes and trap up the river. We had several deer-hunting expeditions with them. I well remember one outing we had, not long after the hunting expedition with Pokorny.

We took three hounds and our camping outfit, blankets, axes, and guns, but no tent or any shelter, other than our canoes. We made a camp on the far side of Ten Mile Creek Bay on a sloping stretch of land near the narrows entering Colebridge. For eats for five of us for three days and nights, we had about seventy big ears of corn, a big lot of potatoes, bread, salt, and coffee. We sure had a great time.

After we had placed the canoes, made balsam beds, and had a fire going, we filled a big gypsy or camp kettle with ears of corn, hung it over the fire to boil, and had coffee underway too. A couple of the fellows came in from fishing, so with all the rest we had broiled fish to go with the potatoes, bread, and coffee. It was dark by the time we sat down to eat.

We were a lively bunch. There were the two Gouldies, David Dickie, and Arthur and I. And we sure got away with a lot of eats! The corn especially was good, and how it disappeared! I think we ate forty ears of corn that night; it was good and juicy. Dickie was a lively fellow and full of jokes. He could sing fine. So we passed the first evening.

Bright and early the next morning, before eating, we started out for deer. The Gouldies took the dogs around in the narrows and turned them loose to drive the deer into the lake. Archie Gouldie was stationed in his canoe around in the bay beyond the narrows, Ed Gouldie in the narrows, Dickie at the point facing the big lake, Arthur halfway between Ed and the camp, where I was stationed. We were all in canoes with our guns. Soon we heard the baying of the hounds as they took up the scent. At first they came towards me, then turned towards the narrows, driving a two-year-old spike deer into the water near Archie. He shot it. I heard the report of the gun and started for the narrows when I saw Arthur and Dickie paddling towards each other. They were a long way from me, so I didn't hear them shout; but I saw them lift something into their canoes.

When I reached them, I saw they had caught two fawns alive. My, but they looked nice! Light brown with white spots. It was agreed that we keep them alive, so we made a nice bed of leaves, brush, and grass; then we tied them up so they could lay on the bed while we went for another drive. We were away about three hours; on our return, we found the fawns dead. Evidently they had killed themselves by beating their heads on the ground in their struggles to get free. I believe all of us felt bad to see them lying there. To me it seemed as if they were dead babies. We remained there three days but did not get another deer.

13

The Perils of Porcupine Soup

OPENING OR EXTENDING the road brought a number of new settlers. At first we had only the Pokorny family half a mile away on the bay. The next nearest was a man by the name of James Humphrey, about three miles back on Brunel Road. Then came a one-eyed man who settled in the woods four miles at the back of our place. We knew him as Tom Steele. The Buchanan family came next, settling on a lot between Brunel Road and Pen Lake. In this family were Mr. and Mrs. Buchanan, elderly people, and Bill and Alec, their two sons. Next came William and Eliza McKeown with their little daughter, Maggie, eight years old. They settled near North Portage on Brunel Road, about a mile and a half from us. Mrs. McKeown was a daughter of the Buchanans. They all hailed from Conshohocken, Pennsylvania, so we became good neighbours. Then Bill Thompson came with his wife and three children, two boys about the age of Arthur and me, and a small girl. They settled Browns' abandoned place. He got a good thing of it too. Brown had left a small clearing with a very good, substantial Norway pine log house. Their lot was next to ours but back from the bay. The Thompsons were used to backwoods farming; and how those boys could swing an axe surprised us. We at first became quite friendly. Along with the Pokornys, who had shown friendly feelings, Art and I had good times boating and swimming. We gave them lessons in both; the Pokorny children were Louis, Agnes, Francis, Maximillienne, Ida, and Bertha.

Log shanty near Huntsville, August 3, 1875

So, with the Thompson boys, who could swing an axe to perfection, and Lou Pokorny, who was expert at paddling a canoe (he had a very good birch canoe; we had the one we built, and also the little one Arthur built), Art and I had a great time. We learned a lot about canoes from Lou and chopping trees from the Thompson boys.

With the money I had earned, Pop bought a large birch canoe. Afterwards he had extension outriggers put on it so he could use it himself, as he did not care to paddle. He also rigged up the old canoe for rowing, but we used both canoes with paddles too.

With visits from Old Sam Green, who told us many tales of his experiences in the woods and on the lake, we had lots of company from all our new neighbours. Tom Steele often called to see us. Then we would have the Cann boys come to visit us. Across Peninsula Lake there was a family by the name of Fraser. Mr. and Mrs. were elderly people, their son John about thirty, two young women, and a boy about twelve. They were nice people.

Just beyond the Frasers in the bay were the oldest settlers, Reverend Hill and family of several children, who had come settled there twenty years before we came. At quite a distance from us and in a deep bay was Bill Green and his wife and child. Then came the Ballantine family, Scotch people who developed a water-powered grist mill and established a post office which came to be known as Grassmere. About two miles west of North Portage lived Solomon Casselman, his wife, and son. A little older than I, he was quite a husky boy who was also good company for Arthur and me.

With all these people around us, it seemed more like a settled country. Then there was William Casselman, brother to Sol. He had a farm about one and a half miles from his brother's. There were several children; but as they were better off than we and carried themselves as being superior, we had little to do with them. They were on the Fairy Lake side at the end of the creek. Later came the Hood family on the west side of Pen Lake at the entrance to the creek. They were very friendly. Opposite the Hoods was a family named Ware. Inland from the Wares were the Cummings, a big family of girls. We didn't have much to do with them, although he was a brother-in-law of Tom Ware's. They had both worked for us building the house.

One day Ware and Cummings came to see us, bringing a man whom Ware introduced as his father. He was a big man with bushy black hair and about forty years of age. His name was Thornton. It took me by surprise because Ware was an old man. But it developed that Thornton had married Ware's widowed mother, a woman in her sixties but as wily and strong as a great many women of forty-five. She was a worker. I became well acquainted with them later on. They were close neighbours to the Hoods.

When I worked for Thornton afterwards on his place, I found both Mr. and Mrs. Thornton to be good hard workers.

Thornton told a great joke on himself and wife. They had been troubled with bears stealing their corn, so for several evenings Thornton had lain in wait for them. He didn't see any bears, so he gave up. A night or two afterwards, they were awakened by the report of a gun. Thornton, thinking someone was after the bears, grabbed his gun and went out to see who it was. After tramping around the clearing and the woods but not finding anyone, he returned home. A day or two afterwards, Mrs. Thornton went to her cupboard to see how her preserved gooseberries were keeping. She saw that three of the jars had burst. This, it was decided, was what they had taken for reports of a gun.

In the early spring of 1877, Pop and Arthur had found a white birch tree large enough for a good-sized canoe and a small one. We all worked on building the large one, while Arthur and I built the small one. We succeeded in getting the bark off the tree in good shape. It was very pliable, so we had no trouble getting it staked to shape, or in getting material for lining ribs, bow, and stern blocks; or in getting long strips for the gunwales and thwarts (cross-pieces) used for shoulder rests when portaging and seats when paddling. We had lots of straight-grain cedar which we cut into proper lengths for the various parts. These we soaked in the lake for a few days; then we had no trouble riving the thin lining which goes inside between ribs and bark.

The bark is laid inside out and shaped by driving stakes into the ground to form the shape of the canoe. Apart from the bark, every part was made from split cedar. Not a nail was used in building; everything was sewn using roots from cedar and hemlock trees. To sew the gunwales together, we bored holes through the cedar blocks in the bow and stern and along the sides. We split or cut the bark at intervals so we could level the bottom up from the centre to each end. The thwarts, or seats, were all sewn the same way. When all was complete, we had a canoe twelve feet in length by two and a half across at centre, nicely balanced, but not as smooth on the bottom as it should have been. This was the canoe I chased my first deer in, finally killing it.

Arthur's canoe was only eight feet by one and a half. It was a smooth-running canoe but too small for general use. But Arthur and I used it for trapping along the shore of the little lake. I did take a trip to Huntsville in it once, but it was too much of a risk. I had good weather and kept close to shore where I could; going up the river from Fairy Lake to Huntsville, I kept close to the east side. The river is not over a hundred feet wide on average but very deep. At a clearing on the opposite side of the river, I saw three men watching me glide along at a good clip. I sure could make that little canoe go in the quiet water. They were evidently interested to see a man paddling such a small canoe.

When I landed below and in front of the post office, the same three men I had seen watching me hurried around. One of them was Dr. Howland. He called to me to bring the canoe up so he could see and weigh it. It weighed only thirty-three pounds—heavy for its size. It was quite a curiosity to a number of village people who came to see it.

I didn't carry any load in it; I had gone down merely to see if there was any mail. After getting the mail, I returned to the Portage. Fortunately there was no wind, so I had no trouble. Arthur and I used it lots of times but never upset it.

We bought a good birch canoe, large enough so Pop could use it. However, he liked the punt best and also the old log canoe. He had outriggers made so he could use oars on both the log canoe and the big one, as I've mentioned. We now had two flat-bottomed rowboats, or punts. We kept one of them on Pen Lake.

Pop rigged up one canoe with a straight sail by stepping a light mast through the forward seat, with a loose pulley at the top. The sail was about three feet square and rigged up like a house curtain with a cord running through the loose pulley and long enough to reach back to the person steering. We could use it only when the wind was fair or at our back. We would pull the sail up, holding the cord in our teeth so we could drop it quickly in case the wind blew too strong. It sure worked fine; Arthur and I used it a lot. The sail was not large, but I have held it up at times until I thought it would lift the canoe out of the water. The canoe seemed to fly with the wind.

Pop also got a large clinker-built boat, eighteen feet long by four overall. It was rigged up with a large mutton-chop sail. Arthur and I had great times with it. We took one trip around the lake looking for our log canoe, which had disappeared in a strong wind off shore. We never knew if it had drifted away or was set adrift. However, Arthur and I covered a good many miles in our big sailboat. We followed the drift of wind as far as Colebridge (Dorset), along the shore near the outlet at Baysville, and around various islands by tacking and drifting over, across and down in the trough of the big waves where the wind had twenty and more miles of drift. Neither of us had any fear. I believe we had become like the Irish—not enough fear to know the danger. It was so wherever we went or whatever we undertook. On this trip we were away all day, returning in the evening to find Pop more worked up than we were. He could see how rough the lake was, and he thought we had upset.

In the latter part of August while I was in Port Sydney, Pop and Arthur had Dr. Howland, Postmaster Kinton, and a friend come over from Huntsville to spend the day with them. Pop decided to play a good joke on them, especially on Kinton who was inclined to be fussy in his eating. They did not have any lunch with them, so Pop told Arthur to take them out for a ride down the lake in the big sailboat. It was a nice day with just a good breeze. They were glad to go.

As soon as they were gone, Pop took his old muzzle-loading shotgun and hiked off into the woods in quest of some kind of meat. All he could find was a nice fat porcupine. With the porcupine and a lot of vegetables, he made a big pot of soup. They all returned good and hungry. When they got a whiff of the soup, it made them even hungrier, so Pop dished out a big bowl for each one. Without asking what it was, they said, "You shouldn't have killed a chicken for us." This was a cue for Pop, so he passed it off as chicken soup. They all ate hearty except Doc, who pretended to eat. He talked all the time about how good different wild animals were for eating. Kinton said, "Yes, but deliver me from eating porcupine!"

Doc said, "That's because you never had any that was cooked properly. Why, it's just like chicken. I don't believe you would know the difference."

"Oh, yes I would," Kinton said.

As soon as they drew back from the table, Doc says to them all, "And how did you like the porcupine soup you have just eaten?"

"What?" Kinton says.

"Yes," Doc says, "it was porcupine soup you have just eaten."

It was too much for Kinton. He ran out the door and vomited it all up. It was a jar to him.

It is all imagination. The porcupine is strictly vegetarian, living on roots and twigs. Its meat has a gamey smell and taste, but putting a piece of charcoal in a thin cloth bag into the soup while it's boiling takes all the gamey odour from it; then it turns out as sweet as can be. We often ate it cooked this way. Except in cold weather, we could always get a porcupine. I have knocked over lots of them with my axe as I passed through the woods.

They are bad for dogs. When the dog chases one, it will burrow its head in a corner between small rocks, leaving its tail out and up. When the dog goes at the porcupine, it slashes the dog with its tail, filling the dog's mouth with quills. If not extracted quickly, the quills work up into the dog's head, penetrating the brain. The dog soon goes out of its mind. The first hound we had, and a nice one, too, got so loony we had to shoot him. The red spaniel, Shot, got a mouthful, but we got all the quills out without his losing what little brains he had. An old female we had would never go near a porcupine. We called her Vick. She was never much good, but smart enough to avoid quills.

Later on in September 1877 we had a Toronto neighbour, John Hendry, come to visit us. He had moved to Bracebridge with his wife and two small boys. A carpenter by trade, he was getting all the work he could do. We had a good time. He seemed to enjoy boating, fishing, gunning on long hikes through the woods, and roughing it with us. He was a good fellow, jolly, full of fun, a good singer of comic songs and a real comedian. We sure enjoyed listening to his singing and hearing his jokes. At night, as he was leaving, he made me promise to spend a week with them during the winter.

North Bay shoreline, Lake of Bays, July 27, 1875

14

Empty Cabins

AFTER HENDRY'S VISIT, we settled down to harvesting the crops, which turned out very well. We filled the root cellar with potatoes, turnips, and carrots. The peas, beans, corn, and some of our wheat in the sheaf we stored in the big attic of the house where it would keep dry. As soon as the corn was dry enough, we scraped off each end, leaving the middle for seed.

After getting the corn off, it had to be cleaned of hulls and chaff. To do this, we chose a windy day that was just right. We spread a sheet on the ground to catch the corn as we poured it from the pail, held high enough so the wind passing through it would blow the chaff away, leaving the corn clean and ready for grinding.

Art and I took a boat load over to the mill at Grassmere and had it ground into nice cornmeal. We paid the toll for grinding the corn. We also took a hundred-pound bag of wheat; but it was awful, a mixture of flour, hulls, and some chaff all mixed together. Your imagination will tell you what kind of bread it made. We used it by mixing it with a small quantity of cornmeal to make corn cakes. That way we could eat it. As Pop said, he could digest anything up to a horseshoe nail. We used a lot of baking soda to overcome heartburn. However, we had lots of good corn cakes and cornbread made from two-thirds cornmeal and one-third white flour. We thought they were good.

I also made good bread from all flour with yeast for raising. I started the yeast with Smith Brothers dry yeast cakes. I would soak the cakes in warm water, mixing it into mashed potatoes and warm water. Then I set the mixture in a bread bowl, the old way of setting the rising for making bread. When the leaven had formed a nice light foam like yeast, I would take half a pint of it, putting it away in a tight fruit jar. When I would set another batch, I would use that in place of a yeast cake. In this way, I always had yeast. I used it this way for years, never having to buy a yeast cake. It worked fine. After the leaven had worked, I would mix it with flour and knead it into a firm dough. Then I baked it in front of the fire in round tin pie plates. Pop always said I could make bread as good as any he ever had.

All three of us were big eaters when we had anything to eat. I have seen us do away with a half-gallon of oatmeal pudding, a lot of potatoes, a dish of mashed turnip, and, sometimes, a three-pound trout or a big venison steak broiled over the fire, and a big heaping plate of corn cakes or a lot of bread washed down with lots of black coffee. We had no milk, sugar, or butter—just salt. When we could get it, we ate a lot of pork or other fats, especially in winter. All the people here were big eaters.

Mr. and Mrs. Ruthven, just the man and woman, settled on land about two miles back of us in the woods. I ran across them one day when going through the woods to visit Tom Steele. He was four miles from us, farther west and in a direct line beyond the Ruthvens. I happened to get to Ruthvens' at noon. They would have me "sit up," as they called it, and have something to eat. I never refused an invitation. Mrs. Ruthven was a large woman and a large eater. It is a fact that she kept on eating until she groaned and fell asleep at the table. After a nap, she woke up as well as ever. This was a habit of the people who had plenty. Then again, it was surprising what little we could live on when necessary.

After leaving Ruthvens', I continued on my way through the woods to Tom Steele's. I had quite a scare on the way. I had climbed up and over a steep hill and down into a dense cedar swamp. I couldn't see any way around it so entered to cross through. I had gone but a short distance, climbing over fallen trees and through dense brush, when something whizzed by my head. I looked up to find half a dozen of the largest grey owls I ever saw. One after the other they swirled down close to my head with an awful screech and a hizzing sound. I fired off my gun, but it didn't seem to do any good. It sure sent the shivers through me as I worked my way across the swamp. Then they left me; not one of them had hit me. It was a weird experience.

I continued on to Tom Steele's where I remained until the sun had set. I followed the woods road from his place out to Brunel Road; that saved me crossing the swamp again. As I started down a steep grade, approaching a dark place in the woods, and at a black muddy place in the road, I could see ahead of me a number of white specks bobbing up and down over the mud. It was another weird sight, with the blackness at the back of them. At first it startled me; then, as I approached, I could see it was several deer playing in the soft mud. It was their white tails that showed as they danced and sprung up and down. As I had only birdshot in my gun, I didn't shoot at them. When they heard me, they ran off into the woods. I stood and watched the white dots bobbing up and down as they ran away, all I could see of them in the dark. I reached home without any other adventure.

We often took trips through the woods, mostly on Sunday. Pop always prided himself on how he could make his way and not go astray. I well remember a trip we took soon after we came to the woods. We were living hard at the time and in the old log cabin. Pop was anxious to show Arthur and me the Wolf Bay Bluff and the view from it over Pen Lake. We reached the bluff without mishap and took in the view and the land. We left it, as Pop said, to return to the cabin in a roundabout way. I know we passed around a couple of knolls when I judged we should be near home. But to my surprise, we came out on the bluff again—just where we started from. In going around the knolls, we had missed the proper course. When we did the same thing again, I suggested we follow the lakeshore around to North Portage. Pop very reluctantly consented. I said, "The longest way round is the shortest way home." It was a long hard tramp.

When we reached the Portage, Arthur complained he was hungry. Since we all were, Pop said, "You will have to boil an extra lot of dumplings when we get home." I soon had the pot on and a dozen dumplings in place of six, the usual number. The dumplings, made of white flour, salt, water, and a little baking soda, were made into balls as large and round as a small baseball. We used them instead of bread with boiled fish. We didn't have any vegetables at this time.

For a change from dumplings, I would make up big cakes from the same kind of dough. To form them, I would roll the flour sack down and form a basin in the flour, pour in some water, add salt and soda, then mix it in the hundred-pound sack with a spoon into a firm piece of dough, working it by hand to a dry cake, one at a time, as large as a common pie plate. Then I would place it on hot coals and ashes, tipped up before a good hot fire, turning it frequently until nicely baked. We enjoyed this soda bread, as we called it. It was the only kind of bread we had for months.

Another trip was away off to where Dwight is now located. At quite a distance from the northwest corner of the bay and on top of a hill, we came across several black cherry trees about forty feet high. The cherries were nice and ripe. We had not seen any black cherries on any of our other travels. In sizing up the trees for some distance around and about, we decided that many years before it must have been an Indian settlement. Later, we proved this to be so.

On another trip, on the opposite side of North Bay near Bobcaygeon Road, we found a small clearing and a nearly new log cabin. There was no one around. After waiting some time, we entered the cabin to find cooking utensils, a big loaf of bread, and a big pan of oatmeal pudding. We made a fire, warmed up the pudding, made some coffee, and had a good feed. We were sorry there was nobody to thank for it. We never found out who owned the place. Everything was cold but quite fresh. We judged the owner must have gone away the day before. We never knew.

Another time, I was storm-bound down the lake, away over on what is now Bigwin Island. I took shelter on the shore opposite the Three Mile Creek Bay to wait for the wind and waves to calm down. For a pastime I walked into the woods, climbed a high bank, and walked into the woods beyond. I found a small clearing and a log cabin. There was nobody about, so I entered to find it empty of occupants. There was nothing to eat, and the fire looked as though it had not been used for several days. On opening a small cupboard, I was surprised to find several pieces of silverware. I remember a cake tray with a handle over it, a teapot, sugar bowl, a covered butter dish, and a creamer. All were badly tarnished. What a strange thing to find, I thought, in such an out-of-the-way place, miles from anyone or a road. Strange to say, there was no blanket or other bed clothing; no clothing of any kind or cooking utensils. I decided the owner had gone on a long trip.

Sometime afterwards, I returned to find the silverware gone. I judged either the owner had returned for it, or someone like myself but not as particular as I had run across it and had taken it. I never found the solution. It is just possible that the owner had gone off in his canoe with his main possessions and had been swamped and drowned. If out in deep water, his body would sink, never to rise again, as the Lake of Bays was considered treacherous. There were so many bays and turns; and the winds would come from so many directions they would form a choppy sea. That made it difficult for one not used to riding waves to keep right side up, especially in a canoe. Then too, the winds would come up very suddenly and in strong gusts. If a person were not an expert canoeist, he was liable to upset.

Three men once left Baysville for Colebridge (now Dwight) in one canoe, usually a heavy load. It was late in the fall. The following spring, a man making the same trip was forced into a bay by a strong side wind. He saw a canoe upside down near shore. He found the body of a man strapped underneath; it proved to be one of the three. The others were never found.

Old Sam Green told us of a sad experience he had. He and a brother were living together. They started out to cross the wide part of the lake to where the Wa-Wa Hotel was later built. They were going to a beaver meadow to cut the very luxurious grass that grew there. They had their scythes, rakes, hay forks, and other tools with them in one canoe. When in about the deepest part they saw a deer. Sam said he told his brother to remain quiet and not try to hit the deer, as he was afraid his brother might do. Never having seen a deer in the water, he was very much excited. Sam told him to let him handle it but, when close to the deer, in his excitement, his brother raised a fork and struck the deer. He missed it, and the force of the blow upset the canoe. The brother could not swim and, like all people who cannot swim, he grabbed for anything he could reach. He grabbed Sam around the waist, causing them both to sink. Sam, knowing they would both drown, managed to get his feet up on his brother's shoulders and pushed him off. He never saw his brother again; he sank at once.

Sam managed to reach the canoe and save himself. He lost all the tools. Drifting ashore on his upturned canoe, he found one paddle caught in the thwarts. With this he paddled back to the place where they had upset, but there was no sign of the body; for days he followed the shore where it might have drifted. No one seemed to know the depth of the lake. Sam told us this years afterwards with tears rolling down his face. He was a tough old fellow, but I always found him to be good-hearted. He had lived alone a number of years before I met him.

To get back to my story: After we had all our crops put away for the winter, we cut up and piled a big lot of firewood in and near the house for winter use. By the time we had done all this, winter was on us. I remember the morning of the 11th of September. There was ice on the water a quarter-inch thick. It was growing colder, although we did have a spell of nice Indian summer. It grew very cold later, so by early December the lakes were frozen over.

We settled down for the winter, Pop making fish nets, I knitting socks and mitts, Arthur making axe handles or paddles at night and on rainy days by the fireside. On all days that were fit, we would go to the woods and cut down trees. We cut a wide section on opposite sides of the low ground, around the knoll at the end of the little lake, and on both sides of the creek. We opened up a space for a road through to the new road to shorten the distance from the corner of the bay in crossing the Portage.

In spring we graded this section of road from the bay up close to the house and on between the knoll and lake. This saved a long grade up from the bay and was also a shorter way in crossing the Portage.

While we were cutting the big hemlock trees, one lodged on top of a large dead silver birch. To get it free, we cut three other big hemlocks to fall on it, our idea being to break it loose from the birch; we didn't want to risk cutting the birch from under it. As this didn't loosen the other tree, we three went up to the birch to see what could be done. We had just gotten close to it when all but the birch began to fall. I said to Pop, since he was nearest to it, "Throw your arms around the birch. Arthur, yours around Pop." I did the same with Arthur. As it happened, we were on the side of the birch opposite the hemlocks, which slid down the birch, spreading apart as they fell, thereby missing us. We didn't get a scratch, but it was a narrow escape from injury or death for all three of us.

About this time we received a letter from Mother in which Owen had evidently been consoling her about how much better Arthur and I were to be away from city life and its dangers of accidents. Little did they realize we were in danger and taking chances every day and sometimes at night. I guess we never realized it.

Log cabin with sloping roof, July 28, 1875

15

Frozen into My Boots and Socks

CHRISTMAS AND NEW YEARS passed like other days with us, and so began 1878. In the last week of January, we had a mild spell with rains. This melted the snow to water on top of the ice on the lake; when it turned cold, it froze, making good ice for walking and skating. On a Sunday morning it was just right, so Pop said to me, "Now is the time for you to pay your visit to John Hendry in Bracebridge."

I put up a little lunch which I could carry in my pocket and fastened on Arthur's old wood skates (yes, they had steel runners, straps, and a screw to fasten them into your boot heels—a sure way to keep them on).

So I started on a twenty-four-mile skate straight away to Baysville, with a good strong wind at my back and a clear, cold, bright sun in my face. I spread my coat out to act as a sail. Did I go? Well, yes! I sailed down the river too; building the dam had raised the water, so there was no current to keep it from freezing. I believe I made far better time than I ever did in my canoe in summer. I have often paddled a canoe from South Portage to Baysville and back in one day and enjoyed it, too.

I reached Baysville before noon and started over the hard, frozen road on foot for Bracebridge. It seemed colder on land than on the lake. I tramped along for about two hours when, feeling a little weary and hungry, I asked permission to sit in a house at the roadside. The man of the house grudgingly consented. I remember there was a woman and three children who sat and watched me eat my bit of lunch while the man drilled me with questions as to who I was, where from, where going, how

I got so far, how I expected to get to Bracebridge, and so on and so forth. They didn't offer me a hot drink as we would have done. As I was leaving him I said, "Thank you. If you ever come to the Portage we will surely treat you to a hot cup of coffee. Goodbye."

From there I walked a long time without meeting anyone. Then I passed by a school where they had held Sunday services. The people were coming out as I passed. I had not gone far when a horse and sleigh caught up with me. Two men were in it, the driver and the minister. They pulled up, asking me to ride if I was going on to Bracebridge. I saw the sleigh had a democrat body, so I tumbled in. It was now getting dark and very cold; in fact, I was nearly frozen by the time we reached Bracebridge. They let me off near John Hendry's place.

The Hendrys gave me welcome and soon a cup of tea which I drank down with a piece of bread. It at least warmed me up. We had a nice visit but it was soon bedtime. They fixed me up comfortable for the night.

After breakfast, Mr. Hendry and I got in some firewood for the day's use and did some chores. I had caught cold riding in the sleigh the night before. I was quite hoarse, so they gave me a dose of cough medicine. Then we went quite a distance from his home to his shop. I helped him all day sawing and planing on sash, joists, and doors. This we did each day, returning to the house at night for supper. We had two meals a day. Mornings I would stay, get in the firewood and do up the chores. I enjoyed it for four days.

I had noticed Mrs. Hendry was very economical. All went well until breakfast Friday when she noticed the sugar bowl was empty. She grabbed it up, remarking, "First one thing runs out, then another. By and by we'll be out of everything." As she said this, I imagined she looked at me harder than usual. It was enough for me. During the day, I told him I was leaving for home the next morning. He pressed me to stay on but I wouldn't. We parted next morning soon after breakfast. She put up a lunch for me. It was very good of her to do that much. It consisted of two thick slices of bread with some small pieces of beef shirts, fat and skinny, cut into small pieces and fried. I thought it was good. I didn't eat it until I was near Huntsville, at that time said to be forty-two miles from Bracebridge. The weather was moderately cold all the way to Huntsville.

I rested in Huntsville. This time I should have laid over, but for some reason I didn't. I walked over the road to Knox's where I turned to walk about five miles over the length of Fairy Lake to William Casselman's. I was all in by this time; so, seeing some stems of dry hay sticking up through the snow alongside a stump, I collected a mouthful, chewing it as I walked along. I have never forgotten how chewing that dry, dead grass revived my lagging body. From here it was a mile and a half through clearing and woods on a rough farm road to Pen Lake and Sol Casselman's. It was a clear starry night.

When I reached Sol Casselman's house, seeing a light, I knocked and was told to enter. I found Sol and his wife sitting by their kitchen range. I sat with them and told them where I had walked from. When I was rested, I started to go and she asked me if she could make me a cup of tea. "No," I said. "It's only three or four miles farther. I'll make it to the Portage."

Leaving them, I ran down a steep bank and out into the snow, a foot deep. It would not have been so bad, but the snow was on top of thin ice. That was caused by the main ice settling and water rising on top of it and freezing. This made a thin crust of ice on top of the water which gave way under my weight. My feet went kerplunk into the water and the snow went onto the tops of my boots. It was a hard, cold trip across to the Portage; but it was only a short distance through the snow and water to solid ice where the walking was better. The ice was cracking as it froze and sank as the water evaporated underneath. Once, almost at my feet, it cracked with a report like a clap of thunder from one side of the lake to the other. It was all so quiet; no one was near me, or any sign of life. It was a weird but glorious night.

I was very tired when I reached North Portage. I sat down for a minute, then went on, reaching a place where I could see our clearing through the woods. A fallen log projecting out looked inviting. I kicked the snow off and sat down. Almost instantly I felt myself going to sleep. I realized if I did, I would never awaken. With that thought, I jumped to my feet. Even then I could appreciate what a starry night it was and how peaceful it seemed. Just a nice place to die, but not quite! So I called as loud as I could in hope that Pop or Arthur might hear me. I struggled on to the house. The door wasn't fastened. I pushed it open and stumbled in. That was the last I knew for a few minutes.

When I came to, Pop was slitting my bootlegs down to the ankle. I was sitting on a chair and Arthur was poking the fire into a blaze. I told Pop as quick as I could that my feet were frozen into my boots and socks. He said, "They have got to come off." With that, he pulled them off, socks and all, frozen together with a lot of skin off my toes, too. They got a tub of snow and pushed my feet into it. At the same time, Arthur made some tea. I drank a lot of it, and as my feet began to thaw out I felt more comfortable. I told them of my experiences, then undressed, rolled in a blanket, and lay down by the fire.

I had some sleep during the night, waking early and all choked up. We didn't have anything in the house good for it. Arthur went out and collected some cedar leaves and made a tea. It's fine for making you sweat. I drank a lot of it and perspired freely; this eased me some. I didn't leave the house for four weeks. Meantime, Pop wrote to Mother about my condition. She wrote back to say, "Put a teaspoon of cayenne pepper in a glass of boiling water and drink it as hot as possible." I did, but oh my! It took my breath. I danced around some time before I could breathe at all comfortable. It fixed it, so I began to improve, finally getting better.

During the winter we found a nice lot of Norway pine, good-sized trees, at the outlet of the narrows. We cut a lot of them into logs to have sawn into lumber at the mill in Baysville once the lake opened up in spring. We got them out onto the ice just within the narrows. We made a raft of them with a boom of logs securely fastened around it with ropes made of the inner bark of basswood.

In February and March, the sun has great power, bringing the maple sap up; so that spring we went in for making maple syrup. We got a thirty-gallon boiler, round, and to catch the sap we chipped out bowls like little log troughs from basswood. We used Arthur's little canoe for a reservoir to hold the surplus sap. We hung the boiler from a crossbar over the fire, and we had two deep buckets for collecting the sap.

At first, we had to wade through snow up to our knees when going from tree to tree. One trouble we had: the sun would melt the snow under our troughs, causing them to tip and spill the sap. However, we got a lot of syrup for our labour. One or the other of us would keep the fire and boiler going night and day, boiling the surplus sap down to syrup. I enjoyed being with it all night when all was quiet.

In the spring and while the ice could bear our weight, we went out to see how our raft of timber was. We found the ice had melted away from it; it was all floating as if in a pond of water surrounded by ice. We saw to it that it was well secured to the shore so it couldn't drift away, and so left it. One night soon afterwards the ice broke up in a strong wind blowing down the lake. The raft held good. There were no other people on the water, so we felt it quite safe to leave it for a few days.

Arthur was out strolling one evening soon after and saw Captain and son Louis coming in their canoe from the narrows. He thought nothing of it at the time. The next morning we rowed out to see if the raft was all right but found it was gone. Evidently it had been cut loose, as we found some pieces of our basswood rope had all the appearance of having been cut. Then Arthur remembered having seen Captain and Louis in their canoe coming from the narrows. Pop concluded they had cut it loose, and the strong wind had scattered the logs into and down the lake.

Pop was so sure of it that he had Captain up before Doc Howland and the Reverend R.N. Hill, justices of the peace in Huntsville who heard the case. On Captain's refutation and Arthur's evidence, they decided it was a case for the provincial court to hear in Barrie in June. Arthur, Captain, Louis, and Pop were ordered to appear, Arthur as a witness, Captain and Louis as defendants, Pop as complainant. The upshot of it was that the case was thrown out for lack of evidence. Naturally, Captain was jubilant. We were sure he was guilty.

Arthur had quite a story to tell of his experience. First, Captain, claiming to be an atheist, refused to take the oath on the Bible. The judge allowed him to affirm by holding up his right hand. What Arthur enjoyed most was sleeping in a nice soft bed, something he had not done for a long time. Then the eats, too. My, how he did splurge on the pork chops for supper and the ham and eggs for breakfast, with all the nice fixings. In telling of it, he said, "Yum, yum, but it was good!" He sure enjoyed it all. All witness's expenses were paid, since the case was tried as a provincial offence.

As I approached my eighteenth birthday, when I could lay claim to a section of land, I secured at Pop's dictation the next two lots to the east of his. Together the two were marked on the map as 193 acres. A single man was entitled to 100 acres of tillable land. Since there was so much untillable land on the two lots, I claimed both of them. But I had to take two men over the lots who, with myself, made affidavit to the effect that there was only 100 acres of tillable land in the two lots, the balance being rock and swamp. They took in Wolf Bay Bluff on the north. Going south from the bluff there was a long grade of good land ending in an almost level tract of about five acres, extending to Baxter Road. Then came a cedar swamp and a beaver meadow with a little lake on it. All this was caused by beavers damming up a creek which entered Rat Bay; it killed off a large section of land and woods, forming the lake, meadow, and swamp.

When Baxter and his men cut the road through, they opened up a nice spring on the edge of the swamp. This spring was open and free of ice in the coldest weather; the water was cold in the hottest weather. I had many a drink from it in both extremes. It came in good for us since, after securing the lots, we started cutting the trees down.

By spring we had cut down about five acres of almost level land. It proved to be good: after clearing it up in the spring, we planted it in wheat that grew well, with fine, long heads. It was a heavy crop. In the fall, we stacked most of it by building a log platform; therefore, the stack was close to the ground. We didn't build well because the snows and rains of winter got into it. Then, the next spring, the Thompsons drove their pigs into it. The pigs burrowed a big hole into the wheat before we became aware of it. I lay in wait for them early one morning only to see one of the boys driving the pigs down the road to it. As soon as he saw me he turned and ran back home. I stepped out, turned the pigs back, and, when far enough away, gave them a charge of birdshot, shooting at their legs. Their being far enough away, the shot scattered, so it did no permanent injury. They never came again.

When summer came, it got hot and dry very quickly. The trees we had cut down were dry enough to burn. The fallow fire burnt up all the small stuff, then we rolled the logs into heaps and burned them. Next, we picked up the bits which are always left after a big fire is over and put them on the burning embers. When all was consumed, we would shovel all the ashes over the ground—anything but a nice job; in fact, it was all nasty, dirty work. Then, too, when the sun shone it would become really hot. You can imagine how nice it was to be in a cloud of fine ashes and wet with sweat.

We cleared and planted a big piece of land. Then, since we were nearly out of eats, I left.

Homestead on Fairy Lake, July 25, 1875

16

The Ups and Downs of Net Fishing

I LEFT ARTHUR AND POP to look after the growing crops and to ration what was left to eat. I went to Huntsville where I got a job with a one-legged man who had charge of the telegraph office. He also had to keep the wires between Huntsville and Utterson in order.

He engaged me to climb the poles wherever we found the wires in bad condition. I would climb to the crossbar, loosen the wire from brackets, let it down to him, get down and help him take out or put in a piece, then climb back up by digging the sharp prongs into the poles. My ankles got very sore from the steel leg braces; the strain was all on the ankles. But it was either work again or no eats. We had a horse and buggy to travel by. His wife would put up a big basket of food for noon lunches. We had other good food at the store. Taken all in all, it wasn't bad. Then, too, as he had a general store, Pop and Arthur could get anything they needed, to apply on my pay.

After the day's work was done and the horse put up for the night, I would meet with the Cann boys and their sister in the house part of the hotel or out in the canoe. We sure had some good times. It didn't last long; about three weeks. So I took a job with the Fetterleys at their saw-mill down the river by the locks.

This was a tough job, hauling the sawdust away in a big hopper on a car. It filled itself, the sawdust running from the buzz saw down a chute into a box. While the box was filling, I would collect and carry the strips and slabs away from the saw, which was on the upper floor. At times I would run down and out on floating logs, dragging a heavy chain after me with a ring spike at the end of it, which, with a small sledge hammer, I would drive into a log and give the signal to haul it up. Now that looks easy on paper, but I can tell you it was a ticklish job walking on and over the logs; they would roll when I stepped on them. I went under the first time I did it; but I pulled myself out and went on with my work in my wet clothes. Fortunately, I had very little clothing on. After attaching a log, I would run up and rush away another load of sawdust. It was run and rush all day long.

We were well fed for breakfast. We would have beans, potatoes, fried sow belly, barrelled pork, a dish of prunes, bread and coffee; same menu for dinner and supper with, occasionally, boiled dried apples in place of prunes. It was our habit to call each meal "beans." It was substantial. We got along well on this diet.

In the evenings we would go for a swim in the entrance to the locks; it was about seventeen feet deep. We had a strong diving plank running out about three feet above the water. It was very springy—so much so that I dove and went down so straight I struck bottom, and brought up a handful of dirt to show the others I had been all the way down.

The hired girl was a chunky, fresh young woman. All the fellows were older than I and she was too. They were all struck on her, but not me, no sir! She always saw to it that I got my share at the table.

I recollect she wanted to go up Fairy Lake to visit the Casselman girls. The men wanted to take her, but Fetterley was on to them, so he said I must, in a canoe. We left soon after supper. It was quite daylight. We expected to, and did, get back just after dark. When we were about halfway there, the water was quite rough. She became alarmed and asked me to run ashore till the waves calmed down. There were two small islands ahead of us and the main shore was half a mile away. No people living anywhere on the lake. I said, "We'll go on to the shelter of the islands." She begged me to run ashore. I wouldn't, but continued right on, soon reaching Casselman's. I waited by the canoe for about an hour while she visited at the house.

When we started back, it was getting quite dark. I could see ahead as I knelt in the stern. She sat in the bottom of the canoe, up front and facing me. She was getting quite fresh. As we entered the river, I could see a snag sticking up ahead of us, so I bumped into it. It jarred all the fresh-ness out of her. When we reached the landing, she ran to Mr. Fetterley to tell him she never wanted me to take her out again. I never did. I don't think she ever went again. When I told him of the trip, he just smiled.

I was there about a month. He had no more logs to saw, so I settled with him. I refused to work on a farm for his brother who said he would give me a cow if I would engage with him for the summer. It was a big cow and would have given us a lot of beef, but I didn't like him or his ways.

So I went to Huntsville early the next morning where I ran into Doc Howland, who said, "You're just the man I'm looking for." He and a friend had an invite to spend the day with Captain Pokorny at Gouldie's camp. Doc had a good horse and buggy. They were going to drive up but, not knowing the road, asked me to go along with them. I had nothing to do, so I joined them. It was a rough, bumpy road of about fifteen miles around by Grassmere, Bill Green's, and on to the Corners. There we picked up a Mr. Lawrence. The man with Doc was a minister, a young man. Lawrence had a good education, so when we joined up with Captain we were quite a learned party.

After getting acquainted, the minister and Lawrence went for a swim, both wrestling and playing like two little boys. We watched them for awhile until the doctor and Captain got into quite an animated talk on ferns, fauna, herbs, and mushrooms that grow in the woods; also, on what is good and useful to mankind. It was a very interesting day for me. We had lunch and left late in the afternoon. They let me and Mr. Lawrence off at the Corners. I proceeded on foot to the Portage, arriving, as usual, soon after dark.

Soon after this, Pop met with an accident. He and Arthur left me at the house to do up odds and ends while they went over to my clearing. We mostly cut through the woods to go there; it was much nearer than going around by the road. Then, too, we missed the Thompsons, whom we didn't care to have anything to do with as they were in the habit of stealing things from us. Pop and Arthur were going through the brush, each carrying an axe with the sharp edge up. In Pop's case, a twig or something caught the axe in such a way that it turned the edge down, meeting Pop's knee with such force that it cut a deep gash which bled very freely. Not having anything to bind it with, Arthur took off his vest and wrapped it tight around the knee. Then he helped Pop back to the house.

When I looked it over, I felt sure it had split the kneecap. The cut had spread open and looked very serious. As doctor, I took charge of it, first bathing it in cold spring water; then I took our Egyptian salve, making some good strips of adhesive plaster, binding and drawing the cut together in a good, neat way. I advised him to lie down for a couple of days. Then I removed the plasters by bathing them in hot water; and I tested the knee to see if the cap was injured. The joint seemed to be good. I rewound the wound in the original way. In a few days it was looking fine.

This was a good time to scatter grass seed; and we had a piece of land that was very stony and fit only for grass. Pop would not listen to our doing it. He must do it himself. As I said, the land was very stony. It was also rough and covered with stumps and, being wet, it was slippery. He slipped, striking his knee on a stump. It opened the old wound which had begun to heal so nicely. In spite of all I could do, it became inflamed and swollen. I decided we must have a doctor's advice, as I feared gangrene had set in. Really, his leg was so swollen it seemed to be as large around as my body. So I said to Arthur, "You had better go with me. Two can paddle to Huntsville quicker than one."

We carried our best canoe over to Pen Lake. We made good time out into Fairy Lake when we noticed a sailboat coming towards us. We both knew it was Doc Howland's boat; we hailed it. It was Doc Howland and a friend out for a sail, so we pulled up alongside. When I explained the case, he wrote a prescription as we drifted around in the middle of the lake, telling me to take it to his wife who, he said, would fill it.

We were soon at the office and away again, reaching home in half the time it usually took us. With the liquid from a pint bottle, I bathed the leg thoroughly and as often as it dried in. It worked like magic. The swelling was all gone in forty-eight hours, and the wound got well in a short time. The liquid was pure alcohol with magnesia.

During the winter of 1877–8, Pop made two gill nets, fifty by four feet, with one-and-one-half-inch mesh for big fish. He also made a net thirty feet by three, with one-half-inch mesh, thinking he could catch the largest of the minnows that run up the creek every spring.

One morning after the ice had thawed around the shore, especially at the mouth of the creek, I went down to see if the minnows had come and found the bottom of the creek black with them. I also saw two nice speckled trout in the shade of a log that spanned the creek about three feet above the water. I had walked out on the log before I saw them; I had not disturbed them. I motioned to Pop and Arthur, who followed me, to be quiet. They came near enough to see the trout. Pop said, "Stay where you are. I'll get the little net. Arthur and I will set it across the mouth of the creek. When ready, I'll motion you to splash the water. That'll drive them down and into the net." All worked fine, and we soon had two nice trout.

They were the first of the season. It was the last week of April and none of the lakes were open. Pop said, "We'll clean them, pack them in ice, and I'll take them down to Huntsville tomorrow. One for Dr. Howland and one for Postmaster Kinton." He would have walked at least twelve miles through snow and slush to do this. I judged he had two objects in mind. One was that the doctor ran the *Forester*, a Huntsville weekly, and he would no doubt publish it in the next issue. Then, too, Pop could get a nip of brandy; he had not had one for a long time.

He was doomed to be disappointed, however. That evening two men drove up from Huntsville, thinking our lake would be open and they could have some good fishing. We put them up, along with their horse and rig. One man was Mr. Hueston, a government surveyor on vacation with a friend. We had the trout packed in ice overnight, so they were nice and fresh. I was up early in the morning and put on a pot of potatoes, another of turnips, and also baked a big heap of corn pancakes. Then I fried the two trout, cooking them slowly in venison fat, which answered for lard or butter, over the hot coals from the log fire. They came out nice and brown and juicy. I also made a big pot of coffee. I can see it all now in my own mind as clear as if it were only yesterday.

All our dishes were tinware. The table sure looked good to me as we all sat down. I gave a large portion of the trout to each of the visitors. The trout weighed about two and a half pounds each before cooking, so with mashed potatoes, mashed turnips, and cornmeal pancakes they had all they wanted to eat; and also lots of coffee—everything steaming hot. I could keep everything hot on coals from the fire, and there was also the heat from the fire over the top of the dishes. It goes without saying we all enjoyed it. To prove they did, they remained with us all day fishing around the mouth of the creek but with no success. They drove away late in the afternoon, and I never met them again.

But in August of the same year Pop met Hueston in Huntsville. He had a contract to survey a large territory out in the Winnipeg region, at that time a wild western country and very cold in winter. He had come all the way from Toronto to get me to go with him as his special cook, saying he wanted me to cook for him only. He had enjoyed that breakfast and trout so much he wanted me. But Pop refused to let me go, so I did not see him. I should have liked to have gone.

We heard from him later. From his story, it was well I didn't go. It proved to be a severe winter in Winnipeg. They, about a dozen men, had nearly completed the contract (in fact, one day and they would have been through and could have returned home), so Hueston took all the men, leaving the cook to take care of the camp while he and his men finished the job. They returned to camp at dark to find the cook tied hand and foot and all their provisions gone. It seems some Indians had followed them, waiting for such an opening. That left them in bad shape; they were eighty miles from anywhere. They started at once, living on the way by digging in the snow at their old camps for any scraps they had thrown away on their way out. They all came out alive and well. Pop said, "Aren't you glad you didn't go with them?" Maybe so.

The lake opened up the twenty-fifth of April. In a few days we were catching lots of fish on our lay-out lines. Not satisfied with that, I would get up at the peep of day, jump into my canoe with a fifty-foot mason cord line and a spoon-style bait troll, and make a circle of the bay, about four miles around. In about two hours I'd return with four to eight lake trout ranging from three to seven pounds. As we could get some ice, we could keep them and take them to Huntsville, selling them at five cents a pound. Then, too, our rhubarb and watercress were large enough, so up to July we sold a lot of that. The rhubarb was so large it sold readily, three stems for ten cents. It was almost as thick as my wrist and quite long. A good deal of it we sold in trade to the stores. The Canns were always glad to take a lot of everything. Trade was just as good as cash to us.

Pop had also made a dip net four feet in diameter coming down to a point. He made it with the idea we could use it when fish were plentiful by dipping them up, especially at a deep pool at the base of a double cascade about a mile up the Oxtongue River, now known as Marsh's Falls.

As soon as the fish were running, we took the big skiff, rowing it around and up the river to the falls, about seven miles one way. There was no wind, so we couldn't use the sail. We arrived at the falls in the twilight. It was at that time a beautiful place with lots of water tumbling over into a deep, swirling pool at the bottom. We made several dips. I managed the boat, Arthur helped with the net and Pop made the dips, getting quite peeved at times because in the turbulent water I could not hold the boat just where he wanted it. The water was deeper than he had thought. By the time he gave up trying, all we dipped up were water-soaked roots of trees.

It was now very dark. Arthur and I wanted to camp overnight. We knew it would be difficult navigating the skiff down the river in the dark; the light on the water from overhead was all we could steer by. The light from the sky coming down between the trees made many of the turns and small bays appear like the river's course. But Pop was determined to leave. We did very well for a while until we ran into one of the bays and seemed unable to get out of it. Seeing a birch tree extending over the water, and thinking we could get some bark and make torches, we pulled in to it. As Pop grasped the tree, there was the most unearthly screech overhead. Pop said, "Let's go. It must be a lynx."

We got away from there on the double-quick, soon reaching the proper course of the river and out into the bay, getting home at dawn of day. We never tried fishing there again, although Arthur and I have been up there in the night a number of times. The noise which alarmed us came from a screech owl.

Waterfall in Muskoka

17

Dogs and Settlers Come and Go

AS IF WE NEEDED MORE WORK, we found we had to build a fence on account of Ruthven's cattle straying down through the woods to our clearing. They would trample down anything we had growing. There was a young bull among them which one day came down the clearing and ran for Pop, who was working near the old cabin with Arthur. They saw him coming at full gallop; Pop and Arthur could not get away. Pop, who had a big pick in his hands, clipped the pick off the handle and grasped it like a baseball bat. It was heavy and made of ironwood, good and strong. He waited until Mr. Bull was near him and swung it with all his strength, hitting the bull over the nose, near his eyes. The bull dropped to his knees with blood flowing from his nose; but he got to his feet and ran away, never showing himself again.

With lots of basswood trees, we started to split rails. We cut them into sixteen-foot lengths and split them with iron wedges Pop had gotten made for him in Huntsville. He also had two heavy iron rings made for a maul. We drove the rings into a piece of ironwood twelve inches long and six in diameter, making a ten-pound sledge. Either of us could swing it for hours at a time. Arthur and I, now being big and strong, could lift and lug all day long, never getting tired.

We built a snake fence on one side of the Baxter Road all along where we had cleared and planted. On the opposite side we built a long, straight fence. To get logs to the place, they being very heavy and at some distance, we got the use of McKeown's three-year-old oxen. Afterwards I worked for him to pay for their use. Then we built a brush fence next to the woods all around. We built it by felling trees one atop the other, piling loose brush on top of them. This made a bad place for cattle to get through, but they would; they liked the corn better than the leaves to browse on, especially during the summer and fall. So they occasionally broke through.

One rainy morning I was up in the woods with my gun looking for partridge. On my return, as I got near the clearing, I saw the cows in the corn. As soon as they saw me they ran and sprang over the fence. While their heels were up in the air and three or four in line, I fired at their heels. I don't know when they stopped running, but some weeks afterwards we heard Ruthven had said what he would do if he could find who filled his cattle's legs with fine shot. It kept them away for a long time. There was never trouble about the shooting.

When we cleared off the woods we left the nice sugar maples standing. We thought we could keep them from being killed when we ran the fire through. But, with all our precautions, the fire ate its way to the roots and killed them all. We had to cut them down and use them for the fence on the roadside. Arthur was standing on one, cutting it in two in the usual way, when something caused his axe to miss the log and drive into his left foot at the base of his big toe. It was a bad cut. It looked as though it had gone into the joint. I doctored it up in the usual way after finding he could wiggle his toe. I dropped into the cut some hot, boiled pine gum. We had found this was very good; it kept out any danger of proud flesh, and it helped the healing process. At any rate, he was all right in a few days.

We sure had a great time drawing those heavy maple logs and lots of others from the woods. The oxen would work fine for me at McKeown's, but we had to coax and beat them a lot at our place. Still, we made good use of them not only on the fence, but in drawing logs around to places where we could easily roll them up into heaps for burning.

One day in the spring Arthur and I went to Huntsville. We were late starting back. We hurried but, having quite a load, the canoe was deep in the water, making it slow travelling. As we entered the creek, the storm, rain, and big waves caught us. We got through the creek by dark and didn't stop but headed for the North Portage.

We could see the way by the flashes of lightning. The cracks of thunder were terrific and the rain came down in torrents. The waves became so high they would lift us up and seemed to throw us into the waves ahead, into the trough of waves and up again. We couldn't see this, but we could feel it all. As the wind and waves were in our favour, we didn't have to paddle. I was steering; all I had to do was keep the canoe so the waves would carry us along. I think that was the worst storm of many that we had ever been in. We pulled through to the Portage, soaking wet and half a canoe of water. Another case of all's well that ends well.

Being in such bad shape, we pulled ashore, packed our stuff on land, and turned the canoe over it to come back for in the morning. In the morning, our dog Shot was nowhere to be found. We found him on the other side of the Portage. He had gone there in the night and had made his bed under the canoe to watch it. Sometimes he didn't and we would find things missing.

Once we cached a lot of things; among them was a gosh hook, a tool with one edge like a hatchet and the other like a short sickle. It was a useful tool for cutting underbrush. It was also an heirloom, as Pop had brought it from England among a lot more tools. We later found it hanging in Thompson's house and never trusted him after that.

We never did visit the Thompsons. We happened on it because we had a meeting of settlers from all over the township, a great many of whom were Thompson's friends, who agitated the question of erecting a school building. We were all there, and there was some loud talking for and against it. There was a young man, one of Thompson's friends, who was better educated than any of the others. But he met with some snags from Sam Green who had a fair education and also from Pop. These two thought it was too soon to have a school. However, it was carried.

Later a nice little log school was built on one of Pop's lots. This lot contained only sixteen acres. But it so happened that it took in the corner of the bay and was at the end of one of Pop's big lots. Part of the clearing Pop bought from Pokorny was also on it, but it shut Thompson off from a view of the lake, a thorn in Thompson's side. More of this and the school later on.

During the summer we kept busy hilling up potatoes and corn and also weeding. I also worked for McKeown and Buchanan, doing the same thing and living with one or the other for two weeks at a time. I remember they both had cows, so we had plenty of milk to drink. At Buchanan's, Mrs. Buchanan would serve us last thing at night with a big bowl of cornmeal mush sweetened with maple sugar and lots of milk. We thought it was great.

One night Bill Buchanan, the eldest, and I went to a little lake on their place with a jack-light over the end of the canoe to see if we could get a deer. We paddled around for a long time looking for a deer's eyes to shine in the light. Bill had told me not to leave my hands in the water because the lake was full of blood leeches. I could see them as they came into the light from the fire in the jack-light; the water seemed to be full of them. By and by Bill got tired watching for deer, so we changed places, he taking the paddle and I the gun. Creeping close to shore as we sailed silently along, I spied what I took for the eyes of a deer. Taking careful aim, I fired at the eyes. There was a great scrambling in the woods, then something ran away. We pushed in to shore but could not find anything. Bill said he thought there were two deer, and the noise of running away was one of them. He felt sure we could find the body of the other. We didn't, so we returned home tired and sleepy.

In hot weather, it's as unusual to get a shot at a deer as it is to get any big fish. The only fish we could get were small yellow perch. We would drift in our canoe along and out from the shore a short distance where we'd drop our lines over the side, using a small hook and worm bait. The water being clear, we could see bottom easily at twenty feet. We could also see the perch as they came to nibble at our bait and we would hook them. In this way we had many a fry—small but good. We had a number of visitors from Huntsville and neighbouring settlers who liked this kind of fishing. Then, too, we had lots of nice red raspberries and huckleberries. Many a big dish of oatmeal pudding we had with the berries boiled in it.

We also had boats and canoes that people liked to use for a trip around the bay. Also, our shore was fine for bathing. One day we had some boys from down the lake come to visit us. Among them was a big fellow I nicknamed The Overgrown Infant. He was as good-natured as he was big. We did have some good times together swimming, boating, and canoeing. Many a time after Arthur and I had worked in the fields, we would strip off, paddle way out into the bay where it was very deep, dive over and swim and float about a mile out to the narrows, then swim back, picking up our canoe as we returned.

In June, Pop returned from Huntsville with a little hound puppy. He was a funny-looking pup; he seemed to have double ribs, which made him look like he was always filled up. He had very big feet and extra-long ears. Pop named him Dexter after a famous racehorse of that time. He was very intelligent and would go into the fields with us. He knew how to get under a stump where it was shady, and he also knew when it was noon. He would come out wagging his tail, as much as to say, "It's time to eat." In the evening he would do the same.

We also had an old female hound we called Vick who was nowhere near as sensible. Then we had Shot, a red spaniel no good as a bird dog. Later on, Pop brought home a big dog that was part St. Bernard and part mastiff. Very quick and wise, he had short ears and a bobbed tail. A man had given him to Pop to keep while he was away, with the understanding he was ours if he never called for the dog. We called him Toby, and we took to one another at once. We could talk to him like talking to a human being. He seemed to understand everything.

Thinking we had too many dogs, Pop decided to take Shot away and lose him while on a trip to Bracebridge. I took them to Huntsville so they could take the boat down to Port Sydney and walk the twenty miles to Bracebridge. I saw them to the boat and returned home. The next morning, to our surprise, Shot walked in on us. We didn't know what to make of it. The boat would not have stopped on its way to Port Sydney except to slow up at the locks. We didn't know until Pop returned and told us Shot had jumped over the side of the boat as they reached the locks. How did Shot find his way home? He had never been there before, and it was about eight miles in a straight line through the woods from the Portage. We could not see how he did it. We decided he had some intelligence, so kept him with us. Later on in the fall we sent him to chase Thompson's pigs out of our turnip patch. One of them turned on him, snapping out of his side a piece as large as a silver dollar. I thought we had better shoot him, but Pop said, "No. He'll cure it himself by licking it." Which he did. It soon healed so well that with his long hair the scar could not be seen.

About this time, we had a coloured man and his son settle on land in the bay at the back of the little Jack Island opposite the narrows. The man had grey hair, so we thought he was old. Seemingly, he was a nice sort of coloured man, and we called him Black Pete. Billy, his son, a half-breed, was about twenty years of age and a bad egg—he was in trouble most of the time.

A Mr. McClellan came to hire us to bring a lot of baggage from Huntsville and to take it to a place at the head of Ten Mile Creek Bay, about fifteen miles down and around the lake, beyond where Bigwin Inn now stands. We brought his goods from Huntsville in the punt with McClellan steering, and Arthur in the canoe carrying all it would hold. We left the Portage for Huntsville at daylight, returning at five in the afternoon. We carried all the goods across to our side of the Portage and loaded them into the big skiff or sailboat.

We advised McClellan to stay overnight with us, but he was over-anxious and refused. He said he could locate his place in the dark. We knew only roughly where it was. There was no one living at that extreme end of the bay and nothing for miles but the long line of dense woods. We doubted if he could find the place, but he was determined to go.

We reached the shore and travelled up and down it until he decided he couldn't locate his place. We couldn't see the clearing or the cabin that he said was on his location.

"What will we do?" he asked.

We suggested going ashore, building a fire, and camping out for the rest of the night. He didn't like that, so I said, "The nearest settler is about three miles from here, out on the big lake and across from the mouth of this bay."

As I turned, I saw the twinkle of a light which remained steady long enough for him to see it too. He said, "Let's go to it."

I was afraid the people would be in bed by the time we reached there, but he wanted to go, so Arthur and I, each with an oar, pulled that big skiff with its heavy load. McClellan steered for the light, which remained in sight all the time. We reached it after a long, hard pull and discovered it was from a cabin near the shore, where we found a young couple, Mr.

and Mrs. Brown, new settlers there. They were fine to us, giving us lunch and a shake-down. The lunch was good, consisting of the pigs' feet they were cooking for their breakfast next morning. We had cold potatoes, bread and butter with a fresh pot of coffee. The shake-down was a blanket on a board floor in a room at one side. We slept well.

After breakfast we found McClellan's place, unloaded, and left him there all alone. Soon afterwards we took his wife and two small boys from Huntsville to join him at their new home. They had been there only a few weeks when in the night a big bear came to see them. McClellan shot it with one bullet from his rifle. He estimated that it weighed 400 pounds, so they had some meat to start the fall with. They became intimate with Mr. and Mrs. Brown. After one year, disgusted with the severe winter, they all joined hands, deserted their clearings, and went to California. We never knew to what part.

In late summer the government declared that, as a preliminary to opening the land for location, all pine in the township of Franklin was to be sold at auction to the highest bidder. This brought in lumbermen to see what pine there was. Two fine fellows engaged me to show them the pine sections. I took them for miles in all directions, partly on foot and partly by canoe. We made our place the headquarters. They remained a week and saw all they wanted to, and then I took them to Huntsville in our big birch canoe. They were big heavy men. The canoe settled so deep in the water that the side slits or seams were submerged and started to leak. The canoe had never had such a heavy load before, so I had not previously had this trouble.

By the time we reached the island in Fairy Lake we had to go ashore to empty out the water. We were wet up to our knees. It was doubtful in their minds if we could reach Huntsville in the canoe. They were good sports and took my word for it that we could. The canoe was down in the water to two inches from the gunwales. Had there been any wave, I wouldn't have taken the chance. Well, we made it—wet but safe. I parted from them when they paid me, with a grip of the hand from both, never to see them again.

They didn't buy, so we didn't have any lumber camps. There was not enough pine in the township to interest them or any others, so the pine was left for the settlers' use.

Fairy Lake, July 21, 1875

That year a nice steamboat had been put on Lake of Bays. At first it ran from Baysville up to the Portage, back around through the narrows, down North Bay to what is now Dwight, then up the Oxtongue River to the falls. A man named Marsh, father of "The Ovegrown Infant" I've mentioned, had secured the land taking in the falls, where he began to erect a water-power sawmill which was of great interest to the settlers for miles around.

After they had the buzz saw in place, a party of three young men from Grassmere walked up to see the falls and the mill. One of the young men leaned over to see the saw. As he did so, a revolver fell out of his inside pocket, and as it struck the machinery it exploded. The bullet struck him over the heart. The shock paralyzed him for a few minutes. He recovered and walked to his home near Grassmere. One of the others who had gone on ahead secured a horse and drove to Huntsville. He returned with Doc Howland who, on examination, declared that the bullet had entered on a slant, striking the breast bone, curved and followed the skin around to his back. Doc removed the bullet and fixed him up so he was soon around and as well as ever. It was a narrow escape.

Soon after this incident, the steamboat stopped running into the Portage, passing by outside the narrows. One day late in October, Pop asked me to go out and meet it as it passed down the lake and give the captain an important letter to mail to a Member of Parliament. I hailed the boat. As it stopped, I pulled alongside at the gangway, handed the captain the letter, asked him to mail it, and thanked him for stopping. He gave the signal to go ahead before I could get away from the suction of the boat. With strong wind and wave against me, I could not pull away. They were towing a large skiff; this struck the side of my canoe, turning it over. As it came over, I grasped the gunwale and threw myself astride the upturned canoe. Seeing what they had done, they stopped. A young man jumped in the skiff and came to me. I got into the skiff and we pulled the canoe up onto it and emptied the water out of it. Fortunately, the paddle had remained under the canoe. I jumped into the canoe, thanked the young man, and paddled for the nearest shore, about a quarter mile away.

I went ashore, and in the freezing temperature of a north wind I pulled off my clothes, wrung the water out of them, dragged them on again, and paddled for home, a distance of at least two miles, facing that cold wind. Therefore, by the time I reached the Portage my clothes were frozen. I was none the worse for it.

A few days afterwards I went out to the place where I was turned over and dropped a hundred-foot line down with a heavy weight. It did not touch bottom. No wonder a drowned person never came to the surface. The depth of that lake was unknown.

18

I Shoot One Bear and Slaughter Two Pigs

ABOUT THE LAST WEEK IN OCTOBER, a Sunday, Pop said, "Let's go see if the corn is ready to cut." The corn field was up at the extreme end of our clearing. In getting to the corn, we passed through a big potato field and up a grade through the corn to a level of about two acres. We noticed lots of hills of corn had been torn out by the roots and carried away. I asked Pop what had done it. "Bears," he said. "They come in from the woods, pull the corn out by the roots, carry it off into the woods and eat the corn from the stalks."

Sure enough, we saw a path the bears had made in coming and going across the level patch of corn and then down in the woods. To our left was quite a deep hollow or small ravine which we had planted with corn; here we found a much larger path and much more corn gone. Pop said, "We'll have to lay for them tomorrow night. Arthur goes to Huntsville tomorrow and won't be back until after dark. The bears come for their feed about sunset."

So the next afternoon, Pop drew the charges out of the twenty-two-inch double-barrelled bird gun and put a heavy charge of powder in each barrel. Our guns were the old-style muzzle-loading shotguns. After the powder, we fitted two lead sinkers from the nets and plugged the holes with wood. We put a nice greasy cloth around them and forced them into the right-hand barrel; then fourteen double-barrel buckshot in the left-hand barrel, all on top of the extra charge of powder. We didn't think the gun might burst.

Floodwood in the Big East River, August 2, 1875

He primed the nipples with powder to make sure they would go off, put the caps on, lowered the hammers very carefully on the caps, and handed it to me, saying, "There. You'll have two shots for your bear. I'll take the single barrel." The barrel of that gun was about three feet long—a good old gun. He did the same with it as he had with the other, but used only fourteen double-barrel buckshot. He primed it the same way, saying, "Let's go."

The sun was setting in a clear sky. We went up through the potato field and up onto the flat to the path the bears had made. There was the stump of a small tree standing at the end of the path. Pop says, "Take your stand here. I'll go over into the gully."

I wanted him to let me go into the gully, feeling sure the bear would more than likely come there rather than where he wanted me to stay.

"No," he said, "I want to get a bear."

There was no use arguing; he went. I put my back against the stump. All was quiet. The sun was setting at my back and over the house. It was strange that I should notice this; usually, I would never have thought about it.

I had taken all this in while watching for a bear to come along the path. I turned my head to see if I could see Pop. As I did so, I heard a slight rustling at my right. I moved my head just enough to see a big black bear at my side. I didn't flinch, although I could have put my hand on his head as he looked up at me. I looked at him and he at me. How long we looked at each other I don't know. But he got tired first and started along the path in a straight line from the brush and entered the woods. He stopped about twenty-five feet from me, turned and faced me. I raised my gun. As I did so, I thought, "I must be sure."

I had both triggers up, aimed for his eyes, and pulled the right-hand barrel with the two lumps of lead. His head went down then up again. I had not lowered the gun, so taking careful aim again, I let him have the buckshot. He straightened out, never even kicking.

As I saw him lay over, I threw my hat in the air with a loud "Hurrah!" I turned to see Pop coming, rushing through the corn, trailing his long gun with his hair and long whiskers flying in the wind.

"Where is he?" he asked as he reached me. I pointed to the bear lying in the woods. He jumped over the brush fence and I after him with the big knife, one I always carried with me, drawn. I feared the bear might come to, but he didn't. Pop ran up to him, grasped him by the paw, saying, "Oh, oh, old fellow. We got you this time."

As it was getting dark, we dragged him to the brush fence and got his paws on my shoulders, giving me a good grip. Pop pushed him over on my back and shoulders. He was all I could carry; it bent me almost double. I got him to the house where we had a little porch over the front door. We hung him up by the hind paws, well spread out so, as Pop said, Arthur would walk into it when he came home. It was very dark when Arthur came. He was surprised and disappointed at not being in at the kill. This was the only bear I even got a shot at during my five years in the Muskoka bush.

A short time afterwards, for some reason I was alone (except for Toby, who was allowed to run loose; the other dogs were chained). Dexter remained in the house. I was carrying turnips down from a field next to the potato patch and not far from the corn field. I would go up with Toby at my heels, dig and trim a big bag of turnips as large as my head (they were rutabagas) and carry them down to the house. It was about a quarter mile from the field to the house, over a lot of rough, stony land. I remember it so well because a big one fell out of the bag. Since I couldn't stoop to pick it up, I plunged my long-bladed knife into the turnip and carried it to the house. I put my load down and returned for another bag. When near the field and not far from the corn, I saw a huge bear's head alongside a stump. I could see its big ears wiggling as it bit the kernels from an ear of corn. Toby had not followed me on this trip, so I ran back to the house for my gun.

As I was drawing the charge and reloading, Thompsons blew their call for dinner. I looked up to see the bear on top of the brush fence. He seemed to be much larger than the one I had shot. I finished reloading the gun and went up there and over into the woods but could not find him. After a lengthy search down in the swamp, I gave it up. I should have liked to have gotten him. We set a trap for him, but all we got were four of his big toes. He had torn loose in his struggles, leaving the toes in the trap. We didn't see him or any bear after that.

At the time I shot the bear, we had several deer hanging in the attic where they would keep for winter use. As the weather was cold, freezing at night, we had lots of venison. But I believe we liked the bear meat the best; it was quite fat from having fed on our corn. It was also juicy and tender. I would boil it in large chunks as large as a man's fist. When it was nicely cooked, we would sock our forks in the big pieces and just bite it off in big mouthfuls. It was very good with corncakes, potatoes, turnips, and coffee. I used the fat for frying fish, venison steaks, and pancakes; and I used a lot of it for shortening in bread. It made the bread tender and easy to eat, and it gave it a nice sweet taste. It was fine for currant bread, the only cake we ever had. Others thought so too. We were living high at this time; all of us built up more that fall and winter than ever before. We were also getting lots of the fish that were running up on the shallows.

The first of our net fishing came while in the midst of harvesting. One nice evening when we first tried the nets, we took the two nets Pop had made over to Pen Lake. It was a question among us as to where we would set them. Pop favoured the little sand beach to the east of North Portage, Arthur and I the stony shore to the west. We settled it by placing one net in each place.

The nets were fifty feet long by four feet deep. We got a good set for each and left them for the night. Next morning bright and early we were over there to see the result, going to the one at the beach first, since Pop was sure we would get a lot of fish. He was disappointed; there wasn't a sign of fish in it. So we moved over to the other net.

Pop stood in the bow of the boat to take in the net, Arthur helping him, and I paddled the boat from the stern. It sure looked hopeless. When we reached the net on the rocky shore, Pop started to take it in and said, "There's one. And there's another." And so it continued to the end of the net. We took in twenty-two nice salmon trout—there seemed to be one every two feet. They would weigh about three pounds each.

This was encouraging, so we went in for net fishing. Pop had made four more nets on rainy days and at night during the summer, all the same size. We set them at various places on the rocky shores and on a shoal about two hundred feet out from North Portage. This place was the best, so we placed three and sometimes four nets around it. We would place the nets out early or just before dark, after working all day harvesting our crops.

The crops were fine. My, it was nice to see the potatoes roll out of the hills, often as many as nine, some as large as my foot. The rutabagas, as I have said, were as big as my head; we had one exceptionally large one which measured eighteen inches across and eight inches deep. Our corn was White Flint, early and fine to eat as green corn and to have ground into nice meal. It was a heavy crop. Our beans and peas were also good; they were cranberry beans and marrow fat peas. We had also grown a lot of hay, oats, and wheat. The hay and oats we had no use for except to feed the horses of visitors who would drive up from Huntsville at times. The wheat we would thrash out clean and boil it whole to eat in the winter. We all liked a big dish of it in place of meat at breakfast.

We worked early and late. One night after we had set our nets and had returned to the house for supper, we decided to go back to the nets. As we reached the north side, we could see someone in a canoe out at the shoal by our nets. It was still light enough so we could see as we rowed quietly out. We found Black Billy spearing fish that were caught in our net. We got close to him, he unaware. When he saw us he dropped his spear into his canoe and started for shore. If a black man ever turned white, he did; he was so badly surprised! He no doubt thought we would shoot him or tumble him over. We chased him close to shore when Pop said, "Let him go." To Billy he said, "We let you go this time. But don't let us catch you again." I think he was glad to get away. We never saw him at the nets again.

We caught so many fish, we sold some to the settlers and in Huntsville, mostly in trade. We also salted them down into anything made of wood. I know we had two big wooden washtubs and a fifty-five-gallon salt-pork barrel all filled with brine. Then, too, we had a large quantity salted and smoked.

At the end of the season, Sam Green told us that whitefish ran up on the shoals. He said they were nice and would weigh about one pound each. They always came on the shoals the last of the season or right after the salmon stopped. I persuaded Pop to let me take the fifty-foot, one-and-a-half-inch mesh net to see what I could get. This was after he had refused to try it. As I was leaving early in the morning with net and canoe over my head to carry them across the Portage, he said, "In the morning, you'll find the net frozen in."

It was cold and clear when I reached the shoals on the opposite side of Pen Lake, out about a half mile from the Reverend Hill's farm. Putting out from a point of Fraser's land, I found the wind blowing inshore with small waves—just right for me to start at the other end of the shoal. I had laid my net in the canoe, so all I had to do was drift along the shoal sideways, pay out the net with my right hand, keep my canoe in position with paddle in my left hand, and drift along. After I had the net out, I paddled back alongside of it to find I had a good set. It was four feet, the floats lay on top of the water, with the sinkers on the bottom. I concluded it was a nice set so left it until morning.

In the morning I found my net wasn't frozen in but was full of fish end to end, top to bottom. I drew it in from the land end, pulling the canoe along sideways. The canoe drifted with the strain of pulling the net in. I had a full canoe.

I was soon back to the little beach near North Portage where I landed, straightened my net out on the beach, and removed the fish. I had seventy nice whitefish. As Sam Green had said, they weighed about one pound each. Besides whitefish, I had about twice as many suckers and catfish. Pop and Arthur came over to see how I was getting along; they were surprised. We carried all the fish over to the house.

We ate a lot of whitefish. The balance we cached in the snow at the back of the house, alongside the hill facing north, where they would remain frozen all winter. But before we had occasion to use them, the foxes got at them, eating them before we were aware of it. The suckers and catfish we kept for the dogs.

We sure had a successful year in our hunting and fishing. Arthur started the first of the seven deer I mentioned by catching a short-prong buck in the bay in front of the house. He had no gun with him so he chased it around and caught it by the tail, killing it by stabbing it above its kidneys. From the holes in the hide, he must have stabbed it six times. This spoiled the hide for sale. It was also the worst kill of the seven; the others we shot from time to time as we used the hound to drive the deer into the lake. We did get two as they swam out into the lake to cross without being driven. Sometimes it was Pop who would get one, then Arthur or myself. As the saying goes, it was more by good luck than good management.

We were also lucky in selling potatoes and turnips, especially turnips, to the settlers. We figured we had raised 150 bushels. We sold a big portion of them and the same amount, about a hundred bushels, of potatoes. Marsh, at the falls, ordered twenty bushels of turnips. He had a number of men working for him. Arthur and I delivered them in three big loads in the skiff.

The first load was so heavy it weighted the gunwales down near the water, not leaving four inches to spare. We rowed the boat all the way. Since it was late in the afternoon, there was no wind, so we couldn't use the sail. We rowed through the narrows, around into North Bay, and up the river to the falls. Our progress was slow, so we didn't reach the falls until almost dark. The men were all at supper. Arthur and I unloaded the boat, carrying the turnips up a steep bank to a shed. When we got through, Marsh settled for the turnips and we were invited to supper.

As we went in to eat, we decided to stay overnight; but when it came time to turn in, we found there was no room for us. However, since a fog had sprung up, we decided to lay around somewhere. It was dark and we feared we might go astray in the bays of the river.

We were all right until quite late in the night, when we had to leave the bunk house for an open shed. They would not let us build a fire on the cleared space and, since it was too dark and foggy to go any distance in the woods where we could have built a fire to keep warm, we stood and walked around; then we lay down in the shed with a wide board over each of us as a covering against the cold and fog.

This did not keep us warm, so we got up and walked some more. Were we glad to see the first peep of day? Well, I guess! We were numb with the fog and cold and were glad to get inside. As soon as the cook opened up, we got him to make some coffee first. After we drank about a quart each, we made for home as soon as we could see through the fog. We did not get caught that way again; we started out early in the morning on the other two trips. However, we didn't catch cold or suffer from it.

To eat up the turnips and all the poor or waste of our crops, we secured two pigs. And thereby hangs a tale—of a pig, not a pig's tail! Pop swapped for the larger one. I received a little black runt from the Buchanans in part payment for my work with them. I started to drive him ahead of me; he was a wild little cuss and would dodge this way and that. However, I managed to hold him ahead of me for about two miles on a narrow bush road; but after reaching Brunel Road, which was much wider, he got away from me.

I chased him back for half a mile and caught him by the leg. I threw him over my shoulder and carried him, squealing, most of about three miles to the Portage where he was quite content to stay in a pen with the other one. We fed them well on corn nibbins, mostly; they both waxed fat, so by March both were big, fat, and ready to be killed.

We took advantage of the spell of mild weather to kill them. It was left to me to stick them; I had helped in the killing of pigs. We took the little one first. I stuck him with my knife, a six-inch blade, in the way I had seen it done: by turning him on his back, grasping his snout, and running my knife down his neck to reach a vital spot which lies just under the breast bone. In this way, they die and bleed at the same time.

I was very successful with that one; he died very quickly. But my knife evidently was not long enough for the big one; after sticking it, I let it go. It bled profusely, as it should have, but it continued to live and run around grunting and full of life until Pop got his gun and shot it.

Then began the butchering. The first act was the scalding which has to be done in order to scrape the hair off the pig's hide. To do this, we turned our big room into a slaughterhouse.

We first hung our big sap kettle full of water over the fire to boil, When it boiled, we dipped it out with a big pan, pouring it on the body of the big pig as it lay on the floor to scald it and loosen the hair. The little one we dipped into the boiler, half its body at a time, first its head part, then the back.

We scraped and butchered them on the floor, as it was good hard pine, tongue and groove. We finally hung them up, first cutting them through lengthwise so we could carry and hang them up in the attic where they would freeze. Cleaned, they weighed about 350 pounds.

The meat was very fine and good, having been cornfed; it was firm sweet meat. The fresh pork bacon didn't shrink in frying, coming out as large as before being fried. The pork came in good as a change from fish. We had eaten up all the bear and deer meat by this time, and we had sold so much of it that, in one way or other, the balance was not sufficient to see us through the winter; so the pork tided us over. Well, we had lots of fresh pork; but what a shambles that room was in! When we got through, we soon cleaned it up.

19

On Our Own for the Winter

ON A SATURDAY soon after we'd delivered the twenty bushels of turnips to Marsh's Falls, I took a load of fish to Huntsville in the old punt. I went to get the mail, too, and all I took with me was one hard-boiled egg for lunch. I arrived in Huntsville, sold the fish quickly, received a letter and two packages in the mail, and returned to the Portage by sunset. I went into the house and dropped the papers into the paper rack.

Pop and Arthur sat by the fireside, and as I turned from the rack, Pop said, "And didn't you get a letter?"

"Yes," I said. But I couldn't find it in my bundles or pockets; therefore, I decided I had lost it. Pop was very angry. I was too, to think I had been so careless.

"I'll go back and see if I can find it," I said. I knew just about where I had been after I received it.

I did not stop for any lunch. I had eaten my one egg in Huntsville at noon. I recrossed the Portage, reaching the foot of the creek in the dark. Since I knew I could not see anything if I went to Huntsville, I pulled into shore at William Casselman's place and tied my boat secure to a tree. I left it and walked across a field to Casselman's big barn which I found full of nice, sweet hay, found the ladder leading to the haymow, climbed up, and burrowed down in hay deep enough so I could cover myself overhead in a sitting position. I went to sleep almost immediately and did not awaken until sunup.

Hunt's shanty, Huntsville, July 21, 1875

I could see the sun shining bright through the hay and the particles of frost frozen from my breath. I jumped out, fearing I might be seen by someone; but I need not have been afraid as it was Sunday morning. I did not see anyone, so I jumped into my boat, arriving in Huntsville early.

As it was Sunday, there were very few people around. I walked everywhere I had been the day before but could not find the missing letter. I returned to my boat and sat down to think, jumped up again as a bright idea struck me, got out the oars and never stopped rowing until I reached the Portage, a row of ten miles.

Then I hurried across the one-and-a-quarter miles to the house and to the paper rack—to find I had put the letter in with the papers the day before without noticing. This was the bright idea that came to me when I sat down to concentrate and think in Huntsville.

I had been away thirty-six hours with only one hard-boiled egg for lunch, but finding the letter made us all feel better. But not the contents. It was from Mother in Philadelphia. She said Lidie, the youngest, then about nine, was seriously ill with typhoid fever. This broke us all up, as she was the favourite with all the family. So there was nothing to do but Pop must go to her.

We did a lot of scurrying around to raise money to pay Pop's way to Philadelphia. The first thing we did was take a load of fish and venison to Huntsville. We took our largest canoe with the fish, venison, and the three of us. It made a heavy load. We took with us for eats a big loaf of my currant bread done up in a large blue checkered handkerchief.

When we reached the creek, we found it was too shallow in places to float us, so we decided to portage over to Fairy Lake. Arthur and I carried the canoe, one at each end, it resting on our shoulders with everything in it except our lunch and paddles, which we left for Pop to carry.

We arrived in Huntsville, disposed of the venison and fish to good advantage, and bought some necessary clothing for Pop. We decided to eat our lunch on a point of land just outside the river, but when we came to look for our lunch it was nowhere to be found. Pop had neglected to pick it up when we stopped at the creek. I had taken it out of the canoe and placed it on top of a stump while we arranged our load; this was at Hood's Landing, in front of and not far from Hoods' house and clearing. So we decided to push on in hope it would be there or that at least the Hoods might have found it and kept it for us. We might have had lunch in Huntsville, but Mr. Cann had sold the hotel and five acres of land to a Mr. Scott and, as we needed the money, we couldn't afford to pay for three of us at Scott's.

Well, we went up through the creek and arrived at Hoods'. As our load was much lighter, we could float over the shallows by scraping the bottom of the canoe occasionally. Mr. Hood and all the family came down to the landing; it was not quite dark. We asked them if they had seen our lunch, and he said, "I guess someone took it. But never mind. Come have supper with us. It's all ready to sit down to." We accepted. They had it all ready, with our currant cake all sliced up. We had a good laugh over it and a good feed, too.

They liked my currant cake so much that we let them eat all of it; it was a treat to them, especially to the five children. Mrs. Hood wanted to know how I got it so sweet and tender, so easy to eat. I told her how it was made with the bear fat for shortening, which gave it the sweet taste. She could hardly believe it. They all enjoyed it very much.

Often after that, we would stay for a meal. If it was dark when any of us reached there, they would have us stay overnight with them. We found them nice, friendly people. The eldest boy, Bill, and John, two years younger, both younger than Arthur and me, had been up to our place several times and stayed overnight with us. The family consisted of Mr. and Mrs. Hood, Bill the eldest, Lizzie about fifteen, John, Martha, and Bennie, a little fellow of four, bright like all the family. I got to know them all very well.

We scoured around among the settlers, selling them fish and venison for cash. I remember the McKeowns, Buchanans, and Dickies had some small amounts of American money which they let us have. In this way, and with what we had received for fish and venison we sold in Huntsville, we made up enough to pay his way by stage to Bracebridge, then by boat to Gravenhurst, the beginning of the railway from there to Philadelphia.

Arthur and I took Pop to Huntsville and saw him off on the stage. We returned to the Portage to fight it out alone for weeks to come.

We were glad to have a letter from Pop about two weeks later, stating he got through all right to find Lidie had passed the crisis and would get well; that was good news. He said he would return in the spring.

So Arthur and I settled down for the winter. First we cut lots of firewood and gathered the last of the potatoes, turnips, corn, and so on, and laid in some flour, salt, coffee, and tea. We also took a lot of corn over to Grassmere as soon as it was dry enough to have ground at the mill. We worked in the woods, cutting out the brush in preparation for cutting down the trees later.

Arthur made the trip to Huntsville when we received the first letter from Pop. Then later on, I went down to Huntsville to get some supplies and the mail. As there was no mail in when I got there, I waited for the five o'clock stage. This made it late for me, so it was dark crossing the Portage. I left the canoe on the north side because I had several packages. Among them was a pound of currant crackers (noughatines) which I had bought as a treat for Arthur and me; we both liked them and had not had any for years.

Well, I got home all right, but the crackers were gone. I had lost them on the way across the Portage. We lamented the loss, thinking some animal would eat them. The next morning I started out on a hunt for the crackers. I found them alongside a log I had climbed over in the dark. I had come the long way around by Baxter Road to the clearing. We sometimes did this when it was dark as it was hard to see the turn for the short way in. This made it so I had to cross a stony field with logs lying around, making it a rough trip down to the house. We enjoyed the crackers all the more after thinking they'd been lost.

I was sorry to hear on my return that Toby's owner had come and proved his ownership to Arthur or, as Arthur said, "I would have believed he was the owner by the way Toby took to him." We were sorry to lose Toby, he was so wise, big, and strong.

The lakes remained open and almost free of snow. We got through the late fall and winter up to Christmas with an occasional visit from Dave Dickie and a return visit. We had read all the old papers; we had read them over more than once. Dave loaned us two novels, one on the fall of Pompeii and one on the natives of Australia. They were so interesting that once we remained up until three in the morning, forgetting all about time. This, however, kept the house warm as we had to keep a bright fire going, the only light we had to read by.

Once in awhile we would see the Pokornys go by. They never stopped. Then, too, we would see one or another of the Thompsons on the road or out on the lake, but never to talk to. Black Pete and Bill kept away. McKeowns, our next nearest neighbour, had no occasion to come our way, so it was an exception to see anyone. Also, outside of seeing Mrs. Dickie, we never saw a woman except on our trips to Huntsville. I think we made only three trips while Pop was away.

At times we would take the gun and travel for miles through the woods, returning with some partridge, or a rabbit or squirrel. We always had the common red squirrel but, strange to say, that year we had some fine, big grey, black, and even white ones. They were very wild; we would see them occasionally but never shot one.

The strangest thing to us was to have little birds come to our back door for scraps even in the coldest weather, some very pretty coloured ones, green and yellow, and some with pink top-knots like linnets, and a lot of crossbills. They were very tame. We liked to see them and listen to their twittering, especially early in the morning.

The weather remained good and the lake was open except for about a hundred feet from shore in front of the house. The ice was about two inches thick, very smooth and with no snow on it. This was the condition on Christmas Day 1878.

As we sat in the house with the door wide open, we heard the baying of a dog in the woods to the east on the opposite side of the clearing, coming towards us. We got the guns as quick as we could, and found a deer had run out on the ice, falling down. The dog was ahead of us, so when we reached the deer all we could do was watch it die. The dog had caught it by the throat and severed its jugular vein. It was a sorry sight to see it die. It opened its eyes and looked at us in an appealing way as if asking us to help it. I never saw a more human appeal than it gave me as it breathed its last.

The owner of the dog came soon after. He proved to be George Meredith who, with his two sons, had settled on two lots on the road between the Portage and the Corners. Pop had tried to hold these lots, thinking my brother Will would come on from Philadelphia with his wife and baby Belle. He was wise enough not to come. I was glad to hear

Meredith had taken them, although we had done some underbrushing on them in order to hold them. Meredith was an all right sort of man, keeping to himself and never interfering with others; he was big and strong. We divided the deer in the usual way, which gave us half the meat. This fresh meat came in good.

The weather turned cold Christmas night, freezing the lake over. Then snow came and covered everything. It sure was a fine sight to see the clearing, trees, and lake covered with its white mantle. We could see far across the bay and over on the peninsula, from the narrows down to a bay at the neck of the peninsula, and across to Rat Bay, which led to a bay off North Bay, a shortcut to what is now Dwight. On this peninsula there was a high bluff that faced our house, adding to the beauty of the scene. It all made a fine sight to look over, especially on a clear moonlight night.

Bill Thompson's old father and mother had settled with two adopted children on land close to the neck and bay, immediately south of their son's lots. The children, a boy and a girl, were younger than Arthur and me. We later visited the family. They had built a nice log house. The old lady would keep a big loaf of bread and a bowl of dried apples, stewed, on the table so the children could eat them when they felt like it. As Arthur and I were welcome to eat with them, we didn't refuse any opportunity to call on them.

While Pop was away, we both worked in the daytime, and read or sat looking in the fire at night, keeping warm as the weather grew colder.

We were alone for several weeks when, one day early in February, we saw a team of horses come out of the narrows onto the ice. The lakes had been frozen over for some time, so the sleighing was good. This proved to be an old man with his horses pulling a big homemade sled. We watched him as he came towards us. He was moving all his worldly goods from the Bobcaygeon area up to the Magnetawan River, a long way to the north of us.

The man proved to be a sociable fellow about seventy years of age, well preserved and as hard as nails. We were glad to have him stay with us. We put the team in the old cabin; as it was winter, there were no fleas to bother them. One was a tall, brown horse and we had a time getting him through the low doorway; the other was a white mule, not so tall as

173

the horse, and he passed through without any trouble. We put the home-made sled under a shed we had built of slabs left from building the house; it was where we had housed our two pigs. He had some oats and we had lots of hay and straw, so we made the horses comfortable.

We took his luggage into the house. He had some bread and bacon, and some coffee that he insisted we use with our potatoes, fish, venison, and other things. He remained with us three days and nights, and we were sorry to see him go. He was afraid of a thaw coming on, usual in the month of February. He bade us goodbye with many thanks. We never heard whether he got through or not. I presume he did, as the thaw held off long enough.

20

Fighting Over Land

SOON AFTER POP LEFT US, I took Shot, our bird dog, for a walk through the woods to my place; since the weather was quite mild, I hoped to get a partridge. About halfway there I heard a noise as of a lot of men chopping. The noise seemed to come from the lot between Thompson's and the bay, the sixteen-acre lot that deprived him of a view of the lake. I immediately started towards the sound and found Thompson and a dozen of his friends cutting down the trees on the lot.

I went up to Thompson, telling him to stop because he was on my father's land.

"No," he said. "I'm located on this lot."

"How can you be?" I said. "In the first place, it's not open for location. Also, we have some land cleared on this lot. My father bought Pokorny out in 1875."

He said, "I have a letter from the government to prove I am located on it." I asked to see the letter, and he said, "I won't show you the letter, but here is the envelope it came in."

"That doesn't prove anything. As my father's agent, I order you off the lot."

He said he wouldn't go, so I called to the men to listen. "Men, as my father's agent, I wish you to bear witness to the fact that I order Bill Thompson off this lot. I also tell you that he will not be paid for any work done on it by any of you or Thompson, as my father has the first claim on this lot. I also deny that Thompson is located on it. As all of you must know, Franklin Township is not open for location. So I warn you and Thompson to get off this lot."

They continued to work. I returned to the house and wrote Pop the particulars. The next day I walked to Huntsville to mail it. The weather was mild. The lakes had so much water on top of the ice that I couldn't walk on them. I crossed the Portage and turned into the woods on the north side. There was no road through the woods but plenty of snow and slush. It was a rough tramp of eight miles through to the Chaffey Road, then four miles to Huntsville; it was up hill and down, with swamps to cross through all the way from the Portage. Across the creek, there was a rough, low bridge made by settlers, then a rough woods road around Hugh Taylor's farm and down near Fairy Lake, then through the woods to the Chaffey Road. Sometimes I was up to my knees in snow, then again in slush. I wore moccasins made of real buckskin, with my trousers tucked inside and tied around my ankles.

I reached Huntsville, mailed my letter, ate my lunch of bread and cold venison steak, and started back. The moisture had soaked into the buckskin, so my moccasins were wet. Seeing I would be in the dark long before I reached the Portage, and not wishing to go through the woods in the dark with the snow and slush, I decided to take the road running alongside Fairy Lake and around Pen Lake, through Grassmere and by Bill Green's and the Hill's place, then on through the woods to the Corners where I turned into the Baxter Road, going by Meredith's place, my own clearing, Thompson's, and on to the Portage. It was dark long before I reached the Corners. It was fourteen miles coming this way from Huntsville, so by the time I reached home I had walked twenty-six miles; but I didn't think anything of it. It was several days before my moccasins were fit to wear; they had to be rubbed as they slowly dried to keep them from stiffening.

Pop didn't answer my letter. But we knew he would come as soon as he could, so we were on the watch for him. About two weeks afterwards, at night, Arthur and I were sitting, one on each side of the fire. It was very quiet. As we sat looking into the fire, I heard a faint sound as of someone calling. I looked at Arthur; he had heard it too. I said, "Pop!" We both ran outside and heard it again. It came from way off on the other side of the Portage. We both started on a run, never stopping for cap or coat.

We found him sitting on a log at the corner where Brunel Road came to Portage Road, about a mile from the house. He was all in. We got him to his feet and, with his arms over our shoulders, we practically carried him to the house. After drinking a lot of hot tea and getting warmed through, he told us he had walked from Toronto, walking all night and reaching Bracebridge the second night. He put up one night at a hotel in Bracebridge where he was trusted for a supper, bed, and breakfast, leaving there early in the morning. When he reached the Portage Road he found he could go no further; so he gave our usual call which, fortunately, we heard. However, he was all right the next morning.

He told us he had received my letter and couldn't rest, but he had no money to pay his way. Owen, who didn't want him to come back at all, refused to lend him the money; but after some persuasion (also, I judge, seeing Pop was bent on coming) Owen gave him enough to reach Buffalo. He also gave Pop a job lot of stockings from Dolan's, as he was going out of the hosiery business, thinking he might sell them for enough to carry him through. He was able to sell them for enough to reach Toronto; from there he started out walking. It was said to be 220 miles to the Portage. He was more than fifty-six years of age, so it was a pretty stiff walk in the depths of winter with hard, frozen snow and ice covering the ground.

He had seen the Crown lands agent in Toronto, who told him the lands were not open for location, so Thompson could not be located on any lands. Pop was up and around the next morning ready for a scrap with Thompson. We all went over and found Thompson at work with his two boys and a couple of men clearing up the trees they had cut down.

Pop opened up on him at once by saying, "So you are located on this lot, are you? You know you cannot be. I've just come from the Crown lands office in Toronto where they told me the land was not open for locating. So I verify my son's instructions to you to get off his lot. As you know, I bought Pokorny's clearing and have worked the land since 1875. Furthermore, I have bought these sixteen acres from the government, giving me the sole rights, as owner, to it. So I order you off, and I will not pay you for any work you do on it."

Thompson said, "Do as you please."

We returned to the house. Pop said, "I have not bought the lot, but I was told in Toronto that that was the only way to secure it." Since Pop had two lots that he intended to locate on, and as this lot was at the end of one and facing the lake, he had the first claim on it. Thompson had no claim because it was at the side of his lots. Therefore it was up to Pop to secure the lot by paying fifty cents an acre to the Crown lands agent in Bracebridge, a Mr. Lount whom Pop had met several times, getting good information from him about the law on free grant land.

Pop said to me, "The only way we can get money is for you to go on to Bracebridge and take the bear skin with you. Sell it for the best you can get. With the money we have, you can make up eight dollars, the full price for the sixteen acres. You'd better start for Bracebridge in the morning. You'll be able to get a better price for it there than you could in Huntsville." He thought I could get at least seven dollars for it. With the two-fifty we had, I could pay for the lot, leaving a balance.

I left early in the morning, going by way of the lakes to Huntsville; it was good walking on the ice and a hard-beaten road from Huntsville to Bracebridge as there were lots of teams and the daily stage running over it. I walked all the way and reached Bracebridge just after dark; I stayed with the Hendrys overnight.

Early next morning I was out with the bear skin rolled up under my arm. The first dealer I applied to turned it down on account of the bullet and shot holes in the side of the head. They were detrimental to the sale of it.

The next dealers, two brothers, quizzed it over thoroughly, asking me how much I wanted for it. "Seven dollars," I said. They finally offered four twenty-five. I picked it up, asking them if they would take it as a gift. I said, "You know it's worth ten." I walked out with it under my arm and had not gone fifty feet when a man in a sleigh hailed me to ask me what I had. I told him. He would also have me tell him the story of how I got it. Then he offered me five dollars. "No," I said. "I want at least seven." After a lot of dickering, I got five dollars and seventy-five cents from him. With what I had, that would leave me a grand total of twenty-five cents after I paid for the land.

I went on to the Crown lands office and paid for the lot, getting a receipt for it. Mr. Lount was a pleasant man. He said, "Tell your father to go ahead and serve an injunction on Thompson. It will not cost you anything if you tell the judge I advised it. Have Thompson brought up in court in Huntsville for a hearing. Also tell your father to show this receipt for the payment for the land. Thompson will have to show a cause for why he should not be stopped from further work on the lot until it is open for location. Then, by your paying for it now, your father will have first claim to it. Also tell your father to enter his claim for location at once. It will be open for location very soon."

I arrived home that night. Pop went to Huntsville the next day and had papers served on Thompson to appear in court, giving him five days to prepare his defence, and to stop operations on the lot until the case was settled.

Thompson employed a smart lawyer to defend him. He also had several witnesses to show his right to the lot. Howland and Hill, justices of the peace, heard the matter. Pop presented his case himself.

Thompson and his witnesses were sworn in after Pop entered the cause for the injunction. After they gave their evidence or version, Pop was sworn and gave a long story. Then I was called. Thompson's lawyer, in a sharp tone of voice, said sneeringly, "And what do you know about this?"

I said I was on the stand only to corroborate my father's story. And I added, "You have one witness who has sworn falsely when he says he did not know of any reason for my father's claim to the lot. He knew my father had bought a clearing on it from Pokorny, as my father and brother were underbrushing on that lot when your witness, Alex Buchanan, came by. I suppose he was prompted by Thompson to find out all he could. We explained to him all about the lot. Now he denies knowing anything about it."

The lawyer jumped up at this, saying, "Do you think the moon is made of green cheese?"

"If it is," I said, "that's where you ought to be. However, I think you are smart enough to know from the evidence that my father owns the lot." I was called down by the JPs, so I could say no more.

The case was finally dismissed, Hill and Howland deciding the government would have to determine who had the greater claim to the lot after the land was open for location. They would not serve an injunction

Peninsula Lake, July 25, 1875

either. It was an expensive affair for Thompson. He had to pay the lawyer and mileage for his witnesses. However, he continued to work on the lot, getting it in shape to clear about five acres.

While this was going on, it was decided that we ought to have a post office on the Portage. Pop had a petition drawn up to request the government to appoint an office to be called Osborne Portage. Arthur and I started out one morning late in February to have the petition signed by all the settlers we could locate. After Pop and I signed it, we had Pokorny sign; he was the nearest settler to the Portage; then Dave Dickie.

From there we crossed the lake outside the narrows to a point of land at the outer end of North Bay where we found four of Thompson's friends at work. We got their names then struck through the woods to Sam Green's on the other side of the big peninsula. From there, we went on to a gang of Thompson's friends who were clearing land alongside Three Mile Creek Bay. I put it to them to sign. One big husky in the gang of Thompson's friends gave me some pretty strong language. I said, "You may talk as loud as you like, but a post office is not for you alone. It's for the benefit of all the settlers in the Township of Franklin, so let your friends sign even if you object to it."

At that he gave way, saying, "Let's put him on this stump so he can tell us all about it." Before I could protest, I was lifted bodily and placed standing on top of a big stump where I made my first speech and read the petition to them. They were all so pleased that they all signed without exception. They were a hardy lot of men; but like all of Thompson's friends, they held a grudge against us. I can see the picture of that scene today, away off in the woods, everything covered with snow and no access to it except by water in summer and ice in winter and through miles of trackless woods.

We parted from them, aiming to trek through the woods to the Bobcaygeon Road—we judged about six miles. We had gone about halfway, not far from where McClellan had settled at the head of Ten Mile Creek Bay, and back from the bay about a mile in the dense woods; here we came to a new clearing and a log cabin.

Seeing smoke from the chimney, we went to it and knocked on the door. We heard someone say, "Come in." At the same time, a venerable old man opened the door and invited us in, looking at us in surprise. There was only the old man and his wife, two very pleasant English people. They must have been seventy years of age. They were just about to sit down to dinner, so would have us join them. We had a very pleasant visit. They had a number of things for dinner that we had not had in a long time: pot roast of beef, butter, canned milk, and pie.

Their son had studied to become a doctor. He had gone to Baysville for supplies and left the old couple all alone and far from any human being. It was plain to see that they were well educated and came from the English aristocracy—why they came, we never knew. Their name was Hart. I never saw the son. A number of years afterwards, I learned he married Martha Hood; they made their home in Huntsville, where he had a good practice. At his death he left his widow in good circumstances.

The old folks bade us goodbye, hoping we would call again; but we never did. We left two partridges, which we had shot along the way, as a thank-you for lunch and their signatures.

From there we set our course to strike the Bobcaygeon Road, which was still a couple of miles away. The road was merely an opening through woods that had been burnt over years before. It was growing up in young pine trees about ten feet high, and the branches grew close to the ground.

As we walked through snow about a foot deep, clear and smooth, we saw fresh partridge tracks crossing the opening. I had a gun and, telling Arthur to stay where he was, I crawled through among the trees and soon saw two partridges close together on the snow. I aimed to kill both with one shot; one lay still, the other flew up, sailing over my head without a flutter of its wings. I felt sure I had hit it. I called to Arthur to watch where it landed, as it had gone his way and over his head. It sailed off into the woods, across the road, and down among the trees. We found it dead in the snow.

The sun was throwing long shadows, so we hurried along. I judge we had gone about three miles when we came to a cedar swamp where the snow was trampled hard with partridge tracks. In fact, the birds were all around us among the trees at the side of the road. We had gotten away from the burnt-over section and into hardwood trees. I had the gun, and it was no trouble to shoot two at a time. Arthur, who was some distance away, called to me; when I reached him he said, "Look up!" The trees were full of partridges feeding on the buds in the sunset shining on the tops of the trees and the birds. He said in a wondering tone, "It looks like a dream, doesn't it?" Well, it sure did.

We couldn't shoot them because I had used all our gun caps. But I had some matches. So I aimed the gun at the birds that were on the ground and more on a level with us, telling Arthur to touch off the gun with a light from a match as I aimed it. We got five in this way and were sorry to leave the others; but our matches were gone. The sun was going down and we were at least ten miles from home.

Soon after leaving the partridges, we saw just off the road to our right a little slashing and a cabin with smoke coming from the chimney. We went up to it to find a man, woman, and a little baby in arms. They were just ready to eat. He was a tall man, and afterwards we got to know him as Long Joe. They were glad to see us. He said, "All we have to eat is boiled wheat, but you're welcome to share it with us." That was all they had. Could we help them eat it? No. We gave them six partridges and thanked them, saying we had eaten. A couple of years afterwards they were found by some hunter; the man was dead from starvation, and the woman and baby barely alive. The mother and baby survived and were sent to relatives near Toronto.

From there we soon reached the Gouldie brothers' hut and camp at North Bay, where Dwight is now. We found a young man and woman sitting close together on a log. He was quite young, and she was the wife of a Mr. Frazier who occupied the hut when the Gouldies were away. They sat in front of a log fire in the hut and we didn't like the looks of them; so we did not stay. It was too soon for the Gouldies to be there; they came only in the spring and fall to trap, fish, and hunt. From there we had seven miles to walk on the lake ice to reach home.

Our petition was finally filed and forwarded to Toronto. It was turned down. The authorities considered it too soon to grant a post office. They would take up the question again when there were more settlers. We had done all we could; Arthur and I must have made around forty miles that day through woods, across bays on the ice, and on ground covered with snow a foot deep.

It was good walking on the ice as it was like snow-ice from the sun melting the snow and penetrating down into the ice, which sort of honey-combed it; then it froze at night.

During all this time, Pop had made two more nets. We also scraped the corn from the cobs at night and on stormy days; by the end of February we had eight bags of nice clean corn. We had built a big strong hand-sled and with Pop's help dragged it across the Portage to Pen Lake where Pop left us to drag it on the ice, which was just right for good walking or skat-ing. The sled slipped right along; Arthur was on skates at the back, I on foot at the front. We pulled that load on the ice at least six miles to Bill Green's place. It was a half-mile from there to the grist mill at Grassmere.

The road was too rough to pull the load over it, so we carried the bags of corn on our backs or across our shoulders to the mill. We had to wait some time for our turn. There were several men waiting, and I heard one say, "Yes, they are big huskies but they're not strong. They're fat and lazy."

They meant Arthur and me. I could not stand for it, so I said, "That barrel of flour is yours, isn't it?" It was standing on the floor.

"Yes," he said.

"These eight bags of corn are mine," I said. "I will bet them against the barrel of flour that either one of us can lift it on our shoulder. You men can say which one of us shall do it."

"You cannot do it, so decide for yourself," he said.

I asked the boss if he agreed to it and he said, "Yes. If you do it, the flour is yours. If not, the corn is mine."

I was not at all afraid of losing. So I turned to Arthur and said, "How about it?"

He gave a sailor's hitch to his trousers. He was as mad as I was at what the men had said but, as was his custom, he let me do the talking. He tipped the barrel so he could lay endwise on it, reached over and grabbed the barrel at the opposite end, and with a grunt swung the barrel up onto his neck and shoulder, saying, "Where will you have it?"

"Outside," I said. "It's ours."

I helped him get it to the sled which we had brought up empty to the mill. We soon had seven nice full bags of fine, almost white, cornmeal.

The shrinkage in grinding and the toll reduced it one bag. Then, too, the seven were not as full as with whole corn, which weighed before grinding about 115 pounds each. We didn't think anything of carrying them one bag each over our shoulders the half-mile to the mill from the lake and back again filled with meal.

We had got out so we could see for about six miles down the lake straight ahead and at least two miles across when we saw a black fox crossing the ice from east to west at the widest stretch. Arthur had the skates and was pushing the sled; I was pulling. He couldn't see the fox, so I stopped and pointed it out to him, saying, "Can you head it off before it gets across?"

Since Arthur was on his skates, he could go like a streak. He took the gun and was soon flying over the ice. The fox saw him coming and the race began. The fox kept right on for the shore, Arthur was cutting to head him off, and I came after, pulling the loaded sled. It was a fine sight: no one to be seen, the jet-black fox streaking for the shore, Arthur after him swinging his arms with the gun in one hand, and I pulling the load. It sure would have made a great picture, with the sun just on the line of the horizon, the ice as white as snow, the black fringe of trees all around the lake, and the three black objects gliding over the ice. The fox won the race. We watched it cross Hill's clearing and enter the woods beyond. He was a beauty, and we were sorry we could not get him.

We hadn't had anything to eat all day, so when we reached North Portage we were all in and had to rest. After a rest, we found the snow was too soft to think of pulling such a load, so we each took a bag of meal as far as a spring of fine water that was open all winter. After a good drink we felt better; we shouldered the bags and didn't stop again until we reached the house.

After eating, Pop joined us. We brought the sled and all in one trip. The snow was freezing, so we could pull it through. It was dark long before we got back. Arthur and I said that it was the hardest day's work, and the most exciting day of many, that we had ever put in. I was afraid that Arthur might have strained himself in lifting the barrel, but he was none the worse after a night's rest. Pop said the bet was all right as it turned out, but it had been a big chance to take.

In the middle of March we had an exciting experience in connection with our dog Dexter. During the winter evenings he would sit on his tail in the back room we used for our dry wood and storage. He would watch for mice. I said he would never amount to much as a deerhound; Pop said that a dog that would hunt little animals would also hunt big ones. And so it proved.

One day after we had eaten our noon lunch and were all sitting near the fire, the dogs too, with the door wide open and the sun shining bright, Dexter suddenly jumped up and ran out the door to the top of a heap of firewood. He sniffed the air, sprang off, and ran through two feet of snow to the ice on the bay, where we could see a nice big buck crossing the ice. It was a fine sight: the ice was white with a good surface for running; and nothing to be seen on the white surface but the deer.

I was first to realize what Dexter was after, so I grabbed the long gun and gave chase. The deer had seen Dexter and was running at high speed over the half-mile ahead of him, aiming for the nearest point of land which we called Wooley Point. The deer crossed this point, ran out on the ice again and went around Little Bay, crossing another point and into another little bay. He repeated this at three points, then ran into a bay in the corner of Big Bay which led to the neck of land to Rat Bay.

When I reached this last point, I could see the deer about to enter a cedar swamp at the end of the bay, with Dexter close to him. Dexter had not opened his mouth up to now. He could not have been more than ten feet behind the deer when he sent out a loud baying that reverberated over the lake and around the hills in all directions. It sure sounded like good music.

I ran into the woods to find Dexter wagging his tail and with a grin to his mouth as if he thought he had done a big thing. He had caught the deer by its hind leg, then by its side, next by the fore-shoulder, then finally by the throat, severing the jugular vein. It was breathing its last when I reached it.

It was a full-grown deer with perfect antlers, but rather thin at the end of a hard winter. The fresh meat came in good. We all thought it fine of Dexter, who was only eight months old. He jumped a hundred per cent in our estimation; and we never had any reason to reduce our estimation: he proved to be a born deerhound.

A day or so after this, we were up in the woods felling trees where Arthur and I had underbrushed. It was a cold, windy, snowy day. We were cutting trees a short distance from each other when something hit me on top of the head. I had only a thin muskrat-skin cap on and, as everything was going black, I had enough presence of mind to throw my arms around the tree. By the time Pop and Art reached me, my head had cleared. It was a dead, dry, hard piece like a little tree that had come straight down endwise, kerplunk on top of my head. It was about ten feet long and three inches thick at the butt, tapering to nothing. It didn't even break the skin, although there was a sore lump on my head for days afterwards. All in a day's work.

We continued felling the trees until it was time for syrup making. We followed the same routine as I described before. I sure enjoyed the nights watching the fire as it boiled the sap down to syrup. We sold some of it to settlers and some in Huntsville.

And so we continued until the sun melted the snow; the brush dried up as fast as the snow disappeared, and the lakes opened up.

Huntsville, August 6, 1875

2 1

There Is No Law Here

POP MADE A DEAL WITH KINTON, store-keeper in Huntsville, to take our barrel of salted trout on sale if we could deliver it. To get the barrel across the Portage, we placed it on two long poles, Arthur at one and I at the other, with Pop at one side to keep the barrel steady. We carried it across to Pen Lake, depositing it between the seats in the back part of the flat-bottomed punt. I rowed it down to Huntsville alone. The water in the creek was deep enough, so I had no trouble.

At Huntsville, I ran it alongside the steep grade leading up to the store and post office. I couldn't see anyone to help me, so I tied the boat at each end securely to stumps, put one foot on each seat, grasped the edges of the barrel with my fingertips, and lifted it out of the boat to the bank. As I got out of the boat, I looked to see Doc Howland and another man standing on the high platform of the store watching me.

I rolled it up the bank to the stoop, asking Kinton where he would have it. "Get it up here," he said.

Doc said, "Get your platform scales. I want to see what it weighs."

While they got out the scales, I worked the barrel up several steps to the platform and put it on the scales, all without any help. It weighed 216 pounds.

Doc, taking my upper arm, said, "You must be strong."

I said, "If that weighs 216, then I must have lifted as much as 400 pounds in lifting logs over stumps in clearing our land." I honestly believe Arthur and I have lifted that much.

Corduroy road near Huntsville, August 7, 1875

I don't know whether Kinton ever sold the fish or not; I do know that we got a lot of things from him on account which we never had to pay for.

Soon after the lakes opened, I went out trolling and caught one nice six-pound salmon trout. As I came near the landing, I could see Pop and Arthur talking to a stranger. I pushed ashore, turned my canoe over, and started for the house with the trout in my hand. The stranger called to me to ask what I had. When I answered, "A trout," he said, "Don't you know it's against the law to take trout at this time?"

"Law," I said. "There is no law here."

"Yes, there is," he said. Then he showed me his game warden's badge. I asked him if I should throw it back in.

"No. But don't take any more."

I said I thought the law was against taking trout in the fall when they were spawning. "No, it is now," he said. I think he was wrong. However, after some further talk we invited him to stay overnight. It was now past sundown, so he accepted. I cleaned that fish for supper and he ate his share of it, law or no law, and enjoyed it.

In the morning, I cut off two big slices of venison. As I was broiling it over the fire, he asked me what I had. I said, "Some steak." I wanted him to think it was beef. He didn't say a word until he had gotten away with a big share of it; then he said, "That was a fine venison steak, as nice as any I ever had." As he was leaving, he said, "Be careful. Don't let me have to arrest you." He never bothered us, and we went on fishing and killing deer whenever we could or felt like it.

We ran the fire over where we had cut the trees down and were clearing it up when we saw smoke rising from the little lot. It made Pop mad. Thompson was going to clear the land where they had cut the trees down in spite of all the objections. We reached the lot to find Thompson and his two boys watching the fire, which had not reached to where we stood. We went over to them.

Thompson had got up on a high log and the boys were on the side opposite us. He would not answer Pop when he called to him, so Pop moved closer. When Pop got within reach of him, Thompson swung around, making to kick him in the face. Pop grabbed his foot, pulling him off the log, and they both rolled over in the brush. Thompson got Pop underneath, and Pop grasped Thompson's long black hair. As he pulled Thompson's face down, he would raise his forehead up and bring Thompson's face down on it with a bang. The blood began to fly from Thompson's nose.

I could see it all plainly and knew Pop had the best of it. But Arthur couldn't see from where he stood, so he thought Pop was getting the worse of it. He jumped in, hitting Thompson with a slap aside the head and pushing him off. They both got up. I was watching the boys, big as Arthur and me, to see they didn't take part in it. They only looked on with tears rolling down their faces, they were so scared. The men had a lot to say to each other in a loud tone of voice and in loud words. As we were leaving, Thompson said, "If you ever interfere with me again, I will be prepared for you."

We returned to the house. The next day the constable drove up from Huntsville to serve a summons on Pop and Arthur for assault and battery. They were to appear the next day in the courthouse in Huntsville; Thompson had brought the charges against them. We all had to go, I as a witness for both of them and against the two Thompson boys as witnesses for their father.

Doc Howland and Reverend Hill were the JPs. They held court in a one-room rough frame building with no room for witnesses, so we were all turned out to await our turn while they interviewed Pop and Thompson. Then they called in the eldest Thompson boy, then Arthur, then the younger boy, leaving me to last—at Pop's request, as I found out afterwards.

When I was called in, Doc asked me to tell all I knew about it. Pop interrupted, saying I would corroborate the evidence of the other witnesses; but Doc said, "I want to hear of it in his own way." I repeated my story as I have told it. The justices asked, "Is that all you know? Did you hear anyone speak of shooting?"

I instantly said, "I heard Thompson say, 'I will be prepared for you if you come on this lot again,' or words to that effect."

That settled it. The conclusion was that Thompson committed the assault when he tried to kick Pop, so Arthur and Pop were declared not guilty. It cost Thompson a lot to bring the charges into court. We could have made him pay us, but Pop said, "No, it has cost him enough. Let him go." Thompson continued to clear the land from the lake up and beyond the road, feeling sure he would get the lot.

At a meeting of settlers at Thompson's house, it was decided to erect a schoolhouse; therefore, a nice one-room log house was erected by the settlers joining together. The school was built just north of the Baxter Road, across from Thompson's house. Pop gave his consent to the location.

A Miss Fraser was engaged as teacher. She lived with her parents across Pen Lake and opposite North Portage. The settlers who sent children to school agreed to pay a little for each one for maintenance. The teacher would be paid by the township and the Province of Ontario.

At this time, we had an evangelist come through visiting any of the settlers who would put him up free of charge for a day or more. I think he gave the name of Stuart. He put up with us for several days while going around visiting the other settlers and talking religion. He had the Moody and Sankey books and literature, and he could talk religion all right. He would hold meetings at different homes, and once in the new school building. He seemed to affect Pop so much that Pop said he believed he talked from his heart. After he thought he had been in our neighbourhood long enough, he asked me to take him in our canoe around to Colebridge and the home of Zack Cole, an old settler—a long trip.

It was Sunday. As we got to the landing, we could see a nice little birch canoe turned up on its side close to where we landed. As the Reverend Stuart landed from my canoe, he made a remark about it that I thought, if Pop heard it, would make Pop change his thoughts as to the religion being lived up to; it filled me with contempt. I met him several times under conditions that were not in his favour; in fact, it gave me a sort of prejudice against all preachers of the Gospel. He was a man some years older than my father; I judged him to be seventy at least, a vigorous old man. Many years afterwards I met his son, who had a church at Dwight. I also met a grandson in Philadelphia who had charge of a fine Baptist church there.

About May 1st we were notified the land was open for location; all squatters had to enter their claims at once. All settlers with families could locate 200 acres each. All were to make out an affidavit as to their intentions, and location of lots preferred. To get title to the lots, they had to clear fifteen acres of land, erect a habitable house, and live in it at least six months each year for five years; then a clear title would be granted to those who complied with the law. The government reserved the right to all minerals discovered on the land, less a percentage to the owner. Pop was located on two lots of 100 acres each. He was also granted, at fifty cents an acre, a small lot of six acres at the end of one of the lots.

The sixteen-acre lot was the one in question as to whether Pop or Thompson was entitled to it. They did not refund the eight dollars I had paid for it, but held the money until it could be proven who was entitled to the land.

It was five years before the matter was settled. The title was due on it, and an official was sent from Toronto who settled it by compromise: the title went to Pop, who agreed to pay Thompson in lumber for his work on it, and it allowed Thompson a short road to the lake through the lot.

Being eighteen years of age, I was duly located on two lots comprising 193 acres. I did not build a house; it was considered that living with my father on adjoining lots was sufficient.

After we were located, everything went along quite peaceably among all concerned. We planted as much or more than we did the year before, working the land every day with an occasional trip to Huntsville or Baysville or Bracebridge. We took trips around the lake visiting and being visited by Dave Dickie, Old Sam Green, and the Gouldies when they came in the spring and fall, and also doing some fishing, always poor in the hot weather.

Early in the fall, at sunset, we had the constable drive up. We saw him at the house as we came down from the field. When Pop saw him, he said, "And what now?" He had no doubt that Thompson had sued him again.

The constable wanted to engage one of us to take him around the lake. He had a summons to serve that night on Black Billy, who was then living at the foot of the lake near Baysville, one to serve on Zack Cole at Colebridge, and one on McClellan at the head of Ten Mile Creek Bay. I was deputized to take him.

We talked this over as we ate our evening meal with the constable, and I decided I should take the old log canoe, which had been returned to us. Pop had rigged it with outriggers for oars and iron brackets. It was easy to row but, being narrow with a round bottom, it was easy to upset. The constable said he was used to a canoe. We put in plenty of hay so he could lay in the stern, a pillow for his head, and a seat to sit on for a change. He was fixed very comfortable; he lay in the stern as I rowed from the forward seat.

It was dark as we left the Portage for Baysville straight down the lake for thirteen miles. We routed Billy out of bed and served the summons (all summonses were for debts contracted in Huntsville). From there we struck off for the opposite shore to the right side of the main part of the lake and the fourteen miles to Colebridge. There we routed Cole out, and were off for McClellan, eight miles out of Cole's Bay, through the narrows into Ten Mile Creek Bay to the head of it. We served the summons on McClellan and started for home, another eleven miles, and arrived just as daylight was appearing.

It had been a wonderful trip. I did all the rowing as Jack the constable lay or sat in the stern. He was a jovial chap about forty years of age, I judge. He repeated all the jokes he had ever heard and told all the stories he could think of. Some of them would do for the greatest liar in the world. He also sang all the songs he could think of; he had a good bass voice.

After we left McClellan's he went to sleep—his work was done. I continued to pull at the oars mechanically. Was I tired! Well, just imagine: I had worked all day with the hoe, then rowed the big canoe so many miles. As I say, I rowed mechanically to the clickety-clack of the oars, no doubt asleep at times. There was no wind or waves, just a still, quiet night with a starry sky overhead with nothing to break the stillness except the jumping of a fish or the call of a loon in the distance. It was a trip never to be forgotten.

In settling with him, he allowed me mileage at five cents per mile. I never received a cent of it. I was to be paid at the courthouse in Huntsville. I judge Pop got it all right; at least the constable told me it was paid to Pop in full for my services.

About this time we had a visit from several members of the Hanes family of Huntsville. It was a large family of well-built boys and girls. Hanes came up to our place with his two sons and the old granddad, the postmaster, to have a fishing and hunting time of it. The two boys were big, husky fellows, the youngest my age, twenty, and the other about two years older. The granddad was somewhere past seventy and all were a jolly lot. They put up with us and had a good time.

With the nets, we managed to get some fish and, also, a few nice trout by trolling. We put the hounds out to try for a deer, but we had no success; the deer would run to some other lake and the hounds would follow. Once Dexter and Vick were away all one night; they had a long run of it. Pop said the deer must have gone to Mary's Lake, a good twelve miles from where they started, as the crow flies, and not far from our side of the Portage. Well, all the men would go off through the woods hunting and return with a partridge, squirrel, rabbit, and once a porcupine.

We would all get together for supper, sitting at the one table. The only thing remarkable about it in my mind was to see the old granddad drink his coffee. They had brought loaf sugar with them, and the old man would take two or more blocks of sugar into his mouth, holding them so he could drink the coffee through them, melting the sugar as he drank. He claimed that that was the only way to use sugar with coffee; I tried it and found it good. They remained with us four days and nights and declared as they left that they had enjoyed every minute.

A few days later two Ojibway boys came and, after asking permission, camped down at the shore. They were the same ages as Arthur and me, fine and clean in their ways and dispositions. They had one canoe, some traps, a good rifle each, and one good revolver. They also had a tent and a live beaver which they had trapped by the toes; they kept it alive and it was quite tame. They were equipped with cooking utensils—in fact, everything for camping out. They had worked their way from Lake Michigan at the request of their father and mother, who had charge of a lighthouse on that lake. The father and mother were raised around Lake of Bays but had to leave when all Indians were ordered onto a reserve. They had never returned, so they had let the boys come to see their old hunting grounds and to find two kettles they had cached away before leaving.

The boys told us all this from time to time. They found the place described to them by their father, but the kettles were gone. I asked them what the kettles were like. They described them as being like gypsy kettles or broilers, one iron and the other brass. I told them I had seen two such kettles at Pokorny's, but warned them to be careful if they went for them. Pokorny would be very nice to them so as to get them to camp with him. "If you do, he will work on you until he gets everything you have, so look out. He is a slick white man." All this came out during the two weeks they camped on the Portage. They were fine Indian boys, as fine as any white boys I had ever met.

Arthur and I had a good time fishing, swimming, and canoeing with them. One day we took a trip to Baysville, Arthur and the youngest in our canoe and the oldest and I in theirs. We always let the Indians steer and paddle—they were more adapted to it. Along the way on this trip we stopped at a beach halfway down the lake for a swim in the altogether, laying on the beach in the sun. We did not have to wear any trunks as there was nobody anywhere near us. We picked and ate a lot of late huckleberries, too. Then we paddled on down the lake for miles in the altogether. When out on the lake, we were like real Indian boys in their natural garb. We had a fine trip, spending the whole day—twenty miles. Another day the eldest and I went down to Huntsville. Did we make that canoe fly! I just guess we did—we made the ten miles in a little over an hour. It was a nice day, no wind, and clear, cool, and smooth water.

We were very sorry when they left us to camp on Pokorny's place, where they remained until it became too cold for camping. Pokorny had done just what I had told the boys he would do. He had worked on the boys by telling them they would have the two kettles, that Mrs. Pokorny would do their washing and mending and cook for them. He would see that they had a good time, too. He also said he would take them over the ground where their people had lived; in fact, he used every means in his power to get them away from us. They told us all this as they were leaving for home.

They had described to us the location of the Indian village where their people had lived. It was at the northwest corner of North Bay and west of where Dwight is now. It extended up the grade and on to where we had found the black cherry trees. Their father had told them of having black cherry trees in the village, so we were sure of the location.

When they passed our place on their way back to Lake Michigan, all they had left of their nice outfit was one canoe, two paddles, one gun, and one blanket. We could see this as they prepared their load to cross the Portage and while telling us of their experience with the Pokornys, who had kept them from coming in contact with us. I was sorry for them and wondered how they would work their way home to Lake Michigan. They got through all right; I found out by a strange coincidence later on.

22

Burnt Clothes, New Duds, and Ready to Leave

IN THE EARLY FALL of 1879 we had a letter from Mother. In it she said
Owen had started in the hosiery business on September 1. This started
me thinking: if I were there, I could work for him as a knitter, as I had
been before leaving Philadelphia. In answering that letter, I said I wished
him all the success it was possible for him to have. I did not say anything
to lead him to think that I wished I was there with him; but it was in my
mind all the time thereafter to get back to old Philadelphia.

I didn't let it get the best of me, as it was time to prepare for the long
winter; first, by cutting a lot of firewood and getting it under shelter, then
harvesting our crops, which were good but not as good as the previous
year. The bears had not bothered us or our corn, so we didn't get one.
Nor were we as fortunate as we had been in getting deer; we only got two,
both good big ones.

We were also preparing for the fishing season. We decided to build
a camp on Pen Lake so we could stay near our nets overnight. We built
an angle cabin of logs with walls six feet high and a bark roof to keep the
rain off. We built it just beyond the little sand beach north of the Portage
and near the point of land at the entrance to Wolf Bay. The opening of the
camp was facing the lake, with a stone wall to act as a windbreak and to
build a fire against for cooking and keeping warm at night. At one corner
of the opening was a large cedar tree, the roots of which grew in such a
way as to make a nice seat covered with moss; it was almost inside the
camp and close to the side of the fire and to our balsam-brush bed. Our

Log shanty with flat roof, Huntsville, July 1875

dog Shot took charge of it after we got to using the camp. It made a nice bed for him. We took possession of the camp by the last week of October. It was fine for us, large enough so we three could sleep in it. The fire and blankets kept us comfortable even on cold, snowy nights.

We had eight nets, each fifty feet long and four feet deep. We set four of them around the shoal which was about a hundred feet of deep water from the camp. The rocky shoal was about two hundred feet long, with water covering it except for a few rocks that stood above the water at all times. It was out in front of North Portage, about a quarter mile, with its broadside on the beach. The beach was wide and long enough for us to hang our nets up on stakes to dry after we removed the fish. It was also handy for mending them.

We caught a lot of trout, so one or another of us took trips to Huntsville to sell them. I frequently went alone. On several trips I stayed overnight with the Hoods, especially if it was dark when I got up through the creek. The Hoods always treated me fine. I have gone to their house when all were in bed, and as soon as they knew it was me, Mr. Hood would say, "All right, Tom. Come on up and roll in with the boys." They had three beds laid end to end alongside one wall of an upstairs room: one in the first corner for Mr. and Mrs. Hood and four-year-old Bennie, the next one for Bill and John, and the next for Lizzie and Martha. I never made a mistake in the pitch darkness, as the boys would wake and speak to me. They were a jolly family with no pretenses. I was always one of them. I would have breakfast with them and then go on to camp. The boys came to see us at camp.

On one occasion Pop and Arthur took a load of fish down to Huntsville in the old punt. We never left camp until we had the nets in and the fish out. That made it a late start and a late return. On this occasion they did not return until after dark.

I had the nets all set and was back in camp with the spaniel keeping warm on the cedar roots. It was moonlight and very, very clear. By and by I could hear them coming, first by the click of the oars, then by the voices, so I knew they had someone with them. When they got near enough, Pop gave the usual call; I knew by the sound of his voice he had been drinking, so I didn't answer until they were nearer. It so startled

Pop, who was standing up, that he stepped on what he thought was a flat rock just under the water; but it proved to be only a shadow he had seen. He went under for a good wetting. He thought he could wade ashore, but they pulled him in and came to the camp. There were two men with him.

I had made hot coffee, fish, bread, and potatoes aplenty for all; they ate hearty. Then one of them pulled out a quart bottle. After it had passed to the three of us the second time and was being handed to Pop for the third time, I seized the bottle, saying, "He has had enough, and unless you promise to put it up for the night, I'll smash it." They consented because they knew I meant it. Arthur and I never drank any liquor of any kind. As for Pop, I never saw him more maudlin than drunk; but I knew if he drank more, he would become unbearably disagreeable. I kept him from this condition a number of times.

Very soon all three men were asleep in the camp, so Arthur and I made a brush bed close to the wall where we could get some heat from the fire. The men left us the next morning.

About the first of November, Pop and Arthur left me to go to Huntsville, to the locks, and on to Port Sydney with all the fish we had. They would be gone until the next night, so I repaired the nets, leaving them hanging on the poles to dry. Then I took Shot, the spaniel, and went over to the house to feed the dogs, three hounds, the youngest a good-sized pup we called Banjo.

I found them all right and glad to see me. I gave them a good feed of fish and cornmeal mush, turned them loose for an hour, meanwhile cleaning and fixing things in the house and around, and returned with Shot to the camp. I had lunch and a canoe trip into Wolf Bay but did not meet anyone. Soon after, Miss Fraser, the schoolmarm, with her brother and sister passed in their canoe on their way across the lake to their home on the opposite side. The boy said, "Hello," but the others did not speak.

Then I positioned four of the nets in my canoe so I could let them out with one hand while paddling with the other. I placed these four at intervals around the shoal; of the other four, I placed two along the shore west of the Portage, one at the shoal in front of Hill's place across the lake, and the other not far from the shoal near Fraser's. By the time I returned to camp it was dark, so I lit the fire and made supper for myself and Shot.

After eating, and being tired, I lay down to sleep. Shot was in his place on the cedar root and was soon asleep. After a long time, I couldn't get to sleep, so I got up and went down to the canoe. Shot followed me. The late moon was overhead in a clear sky and everything was so quiet and nice. With Shot, I got into the canoe and paddled quietly around to all the nets just for the trip and to see if the nets were all right. We returned to camp, and I lay down with all my clothes on, our habit while at camp. I could not get to sleep.

I thought I could get to sleep if I took off my clothes. So I took off all but my shirt. I only had to take off pants, knit jacket, shoes, and socks; I placed them in a heap at the foot of the bed, in a corner opposite to Shot; and, I thought, far enough from the fire to be out of danger from a spark. Feeling sure they were safe, I rolled up in a blanket, lay down, and must have fallen asleep at once.

How long I slept I don't know, but I awakened suddenly to find that dawn was showing. Shot was wide awake and I think he woke me by barking. I looked to see if my clothes were all right, only to find a heap of red-hot fire where I had piled them. With a handful of brush from the bed, I swept the red coals into the main fire. My knife was red hot, so I got it into water at once so I could use it for a long time after.

My shoes and felt hat, which were a little to one side, escaped with a piece burnt out of the hat brim and the toes of both shoes badly burned; but I could wear them after trimming them down. My hat was the same, and my socks were burnt up along with the knit jacket and pants. So I had only my shirt which, fortunately, I had kept on.

I lay down again to think, "What now?" My first thought was that I must get across the Portage to the house before the schoolmarm and her brother and sister came across for school. So I wrapped the blanket around me Indian fashion, bare feet and bare legs, and hiked it through the woods to the road and across the Portage on the double-quick; not only because I wanted to get some clothes, but it was cold and frosty with ice in some places.

I judge I made that mile and a quarter in the shortest time I ever had. Shot followed me all the way. I built up a fire while hunting up a pair of pants, or parts of a pair which were more "holey" than righteous. I succeeded in patching them enough to hide my nakedness, but such patches!

Well, I fed the dogs and returned to camp. Then I fed myself, took the canoe to bring in the nets, and decided I had the largest catch of the season. By the way, we had formed a pool at the edge of the lake so we could keep the fish alive and fresh until the next day, when we would take a lot of them to market in Huntsville. I filled the pool with nice live trout, not one less than three pounds. The dead ones I put into a wet, mossy place in the woods where it was cool and shady. I had about eighty in all.

I then hung up the nets to dry on posts along the beach. When they were dry, I started to look them over for any torn places when I noticed the schoolmarm with her brother and sister pass by on their way to the Portage, landing not far from me. As they turned in landing, they saw a deer swimming out of Wolf Bay. They called, "Arthur, Arthur," thinking I was Arthur, whom they knew. I had never met them. I turned to answer them and they, all three speaking at once, said, "There's a deer in the lake," as they gestured towards the point. The point of land hid it from me, so I ran to my canoe, pushed out, and saw a fine big buck swimming towards the shoal.

I always kept the old shotgun in the canoe when at camp, and the paddle also, so I was not long in giving chase. As he saw me, the deer turned and headed for the main shore, nearer and to the left of the shoal. I got in ahead of him and turned him towards the shoal. When I thought he was near enough, I shot him.

The shot struck him just back of the right ear. The blood flowed, his head went down, then up, and he was swimming away as if nothing had hit him. The gun was loaded with fine birdshot and a light charge of powder, so it did not have force enough to kill him. I gave chase again, caught up to him, turned him towards the shoal, and when near enough, grabbed him by the tail, pressing him down and away so he could not strike at me or reach the canoe. My paddle was heavy hard maple; I raised it and brought it down edgewise between his antlers, striking him one blow on the top of the head which killed him at once.

I strapped him to the canoe, working him into the shallow water; then I jumped out, took the strap off, and pulled the canoe up as far as

I could and slung his body sideways to the shoal. I worked my canoe around so I could tip the one side of it under his body, then went around him and grasped his legs to roll him into the canoe, getting a lot of water in, too. I didn't mind that as long as I could get the loaded canoe floated. I paddled to shore near the camp, pulled him out, and dragged him up to a tree that had a big limb just in the right position. Over the limb I threw a basswood rope and secured it to his hind feet; but I couldn't pull him off the ground, as he was too big and heavy. I finally got his body off the ground, but I couldn't get his head or neck up, so I was compelled to butcher him in that position.

After I had him skinned and cleaned, I cut his head off and pulled him up high enough so the dogs or animals couldn't reach him. The skin I threw up over the limb of the tree. I gave the spaniel a good feed. I made a bundle of parts and head and took them over to the house, fed the hounds, and hung the head up on the second floor where it would keep. It was a nice set of antlers, perfect in every way and large for that kind of deer.

Then I returned to camp to finish mending the nets. The spaniel was asleep. After I cooked and ate lunch, I felt I had earned a good rest, too. I lay down and slept until sundown. I got up, broiled a piece of fish, and with bread and coffee, made a good meal.

Pop and Arthur had not come, so I set the nets the same as the night before and went back to sleep. It was getting real cold and dark, so I prepared everything for a quick meal for Pop and Arthur; I was sure they would come soon. While waiting, I summed up the fish and deer: eighty nice trout and about two hundred pounds of venison. Not a bad day's work. I felt proud of it, being all alone.

As I expected, Pop and Arthur soon came home as hungry as beavers. We soon sat down to eat, and Pop said, "What luck?"

"Bad and good," I said.

"Well, give us the bad first."

When I got through telling about my clothes being burned, he said, "Well, that's the first time I ever heard of a man having all the clothes burnt off his back and him not being burnt at all." It was kind of a joke to him.

Then I told them of the fish and the deer, and they had to go look at the carcass of the deer hanging from the limb. Pop declared it would go at least 240 pounds, live weight. "It's the biggest we ever caught," he said. After sizing up the fish, we returned to our places by the fire to talk it over.

Pop finally said, "You had better take the deer and all the fish you have and all we get in the morning, also the deer hide, and go down to Huntsville and dispose of all you can. Then go on to Port Sydney and sell the rest for what you can get. Then foot it to Bracebridge, where you will be able to dispose of the hide. Get anything you can for it. With your cash receipts, fit yourself and Arthur out for pants, boots and socks, and a shirt each. Stay with the Hendrys overnight and return the next day." This would mean by water at least thirty miles, then twenty by land from Port Sydney to Bracebridge one way.

Then we lay down to sleep to be up and around before sunup, get in the nets, remove the fish, and have breakfast. While Pop and Arthur strung up the nets, I cut the deer into quarters, packing it in the front end of the canoe; with the fish piled up in the middle, I had just enough room to kneel in the stern to paddle and steer. I got away about eight o'clock and before the wind came up. I made Huntsville after stopping at the Hoods' to give them two nice big trout, which they thankfully received.

I got the new hotel man in Huntsville to come down to my canoe and pick out what he would like to have. He took half the deer and a lot of fish. I sold the other forequarter to Doc Howland with some fish as part payment for his services from time to time. The hotel man paid me in cash. This left me a quarter of venison and about half the trout. A man came down to see what I had; he liked the venison but didn't want too much. I cut off about ten pounds from the top of the leg for him. I sold and gave some trout in trade or to be traded out later at the stores. Then I sold a few trout to Hanes at the post office. That left me one leg of venison and twenty-four trout.

When I left Huntsville, I stopped and sold all but six of the trout at the locks. It was getting late for me to complete my trip to Bracebridge, so I did not lose any time pushing off down the river for Mary's Lake. As I neared the outlet, I could see the waves rolling up and into the river.

I pulled ashore and took off almost all my clothes, fastened everything I could to the canoe, and jumped in, determined to do or die, as the saying goes.

The waves were coming from a sweep of four miles directly from Port Sydney. I headed into them. They were so wide apart at first that my canoe would plow into the one ahead, so I shipped a lot of water before I got out far enough to turn quarter the wave. Then I ran for a long way, always getting further out. I could see two islands way off ahead, to my left and far out of my way. But if I could get in the lee of them, I could make up for lost time. The next swing of the canoe brought me so that I came up along the far side with very little wave.

I soon landed on the first island. I pulled ashore, unloaded, dumped the water out, and put on my clothes; I could see the waves were much smaller beyond the islands. I made fairly good time from there to Morgan's, landing down the river in Port Sydney. I pulled in to find the venison leg had blistered some from the water. I doctored it so that it looked pretty good, then brought Morgan down to see what I had. He took all the fish but demurred at taking the leg of venison on account of it having been wet. I finally let him have it at a reduced price; I had no time to waste. He paid me in cash.

Then I asked permission to leave my canoe in a closed shed on the wharf. I told him I was going on to Bracebridge. He said, "You are making a long trip of it. Hadn't you better stay overnight and go on to Bracebridge in the morning, do your business and come back here for the following night?" I could have got a room with him for twenty-five cents a night, but I refused. I hadn't the money to spend for lodging. So I rolled up the deer hide in a rope to form a pack strap and started on my way.

I reached Bracebridge in time to look up the Hendrys for a night's lodging. The next morning, I left as soon as I could get away from them. Before leaving, I had insisted on his coming up for a few days with us at the end of the following week. We would be through net fishing by then, and Arthur and I would take him up to Oxtongue Lake for a deer.

I soon disposed of the hide, in trade at a store; I bought all I wanted and, in fact, spent nearly all the money I had. I made a bundle with a rope, forming a head loop so I could carry them on my back without using my hands. I reached Port Sydney without mishap, got my canoe, and was away for the Portage.

I got through the creek just about dark, so I did not stop at the Hoods' but went right on to the camp where they were waiting for me with a good supper. I had not eaten since leaving the Hendrys at breakfast, so I was good and hungry. I had covered neary forty miles by water and over thirty by land, not including walking around at the different places. Pop was well pleased with all I had done and thought my purchases were good for the prices I paid. He also thought I had made quick time. It wasn't so bad to make it in less than two days because I didn't leave until late the first day; then, I spent a lot of time in Bracebridge. I was none the worse for it.

As to my purchases: I first bought two pairs of heavy felt pants, black-and-white check, one-inch-square checks, all wool, forty-inch waist and thirty-two-inch leg, short so they stuck into boots or moccasins; three pairs of heavy wool socks size twelve; two pairs of knee-high heavy boots, all leather with thick and wide soles, size ten and a half; two common shirts; a two-piece suit of wool underwear for Pop (he was the only one of us who wore underwear), and a felt hat for Pop so he would make a better appearance when he went to town. We all wore homemade muskrat caps in winter, went bare-headed and mostly bare-footed in summer. I'm sorry I've forgotten the price I paid, but it was enough. I also bought two pairs of solid buckskin moccasins, sewing cotton, needles and incidentals, and two scarves coloured and striped lengthwise to tie around the waist, leaving the ends hang down to a depth of two feet, with fringe on the ends; this was a universal French style. They gave a sporty appearance and a feeling of warmth too. Arthur and I wore something of the kind all the time. When we got these new duds on, we felt quite dressed up.

For a few days after this we had cold, rainy weather—windy with some snow; it was very miserable. One day we went down to visit the Hoods. On returning, the wind and waves were so strong, Pop said, "Better pull for shore and wait for the wind to settle." We landed in the bay west of North Portage, built a fire and prepared to stay awhile.

Arthur left us for a tramp through the woods. He was gone so long, we began to wonder what had become of him when, lo and behold, he appeared with a big head of cabbage. He had come across a clearing with a nice patch of cabbage which should have been collected and helped himself to a big, solid head. We sure enjoyed that head of cabbage; it was as sweet as a nut. We cut it up into big slices with our hunting knives, taking big bites of it. We were hungry, so we soon ate it all.

As soon as the wind went down, we got to camp and put out the nets for the last time. The weather was too bad; the fish had almost stopped running, too. We had a big lot of fish salted down for winter use. We were unable to get the nets up until late the next day on account of wind and wave. As we got them to camp, we made big bundles of them; each of us carried a bundle weighing about a hundred pounds.

It was very dark when we crossed the Portage; I, as usual, led the way. We turned into the shortcut for the house. It was a dark place with a black muck bed to our left. We had cut an opening through here for a shorter road across the Portage but, as there were no teams to pass over it, it had grown up; there was nothing but a footpath which we had made by our frequent trips across the Portage.

We could not see the path. I led the way by feeling with my feet to keep them on the path. Pop was close at my back and Arthur close to Pop's back.

"Pop, I'm going to get out of this," I said.

"Where are you going?" he asked.

"To Philadelphia," I said. This was a surprise to him. I hadn't hinted that I thought of leaving. "And I would advise you to get away, too. You told Mother you would sell your rights at the first chance you had. I know you've had three chances to sell, but like unto the old lady and her cow, she would like the money but would like to keep the cow, too. Now, I would say put a match to the house and let someone else get an independency out of the land. I can't see anything for the future for me, and nothing but a hard, solitary life for you and Arthur. So let's all go back to Philadelphia. We children can get work, so we can take care of you in comfort."

This got on his nerves, so he angrily called me down for a young fool, going on and on, winding up by saying, "You can go to your Mother if you wish, but I will stay here to live and die on the place, and be buried in a hole at the back of the house before I'll go back to be dependent on my children."

"I guess Arthur will stay with you. He's cut out for this kind of life in the woods," I said. "I'll stay on until we give John Hendry a good time. He'll be here tomorrow to stay for a few days. Arthur and I will give him such an experience, he will never forget. Then I'll go and get a job to earn enough to pay my way to Philadelphia."

That settled it for that time. This all passed in the pitch of darkness; we could not see each other as we talked. Nothing more was said about it until after Hendry had come and gone.

23

They Decided to Die Together

ARTHUR AND I met John Hendry in Huntsville the next day; we reached the Portage some time after dark. We had everything ready so we could leave the next morning for Oxtongue Lake, a nice lake several miles east of the Portage, away up the east branch of the Muskoka River. We did not wake up until daylight so were late getting away.

Arthur was in one canoe with the two hounds, Dexter and Vick, and a lot of utensils for cooking, an axe, and the double-barrelled shotgun loaded for deer; he had quite a load for one canoe. I was in the other canoe with John Hendry, the long single-barrel gun, one fishing net, axe, and numerous articles such as blankets, a lot of bread, potatoes, and cooked beans—in fact, enough eatables to last us and the hounds for three days. Everything being ready, we shoved off, leaving Pop standing on the shore with Banjo and Shot at his side. He had no desire to go with us.

We paddled side by side. We soon passed through the narrows into the open lake, swung to the left and around into North Bay, then headed for the mouth of the river. The river was very deep and about a hundred feet wide, with no current of any kind. We reached a fine double falls, two beautiful cascades in quick succession. It was a natural falls surrounded by virgin forest, mostly pines. Marsh was changing the looks of everything with the sawmill he had built to the left of the falls; it was changing the natural appearance. It is now known as Marsh's Falls. Here we had to make our first carry to reach the smooth waters above. Hendry, not used

Muskoka River at Huntsville, August 5, 1875

to such work, was of very little use to us; but Arthur and I, being like unto little giants, did not need his help.

After this carry, we paddled for a number of miles up this quiet river to a long, rough rapids. We had a carry of half a mile to get above this stretch of rushing waters. After clearing the rapids, we paddled on up the river to another stretch of rapids and, to get beyond this, we had a carry of three miles. I helped Arthur take off the canoe over his head and a big bundle done up in a pack strap.

A pack strap is like a harness for a man. The straps pass around the pack with two loops for the arms to pass through with a broad strap to circle the forehead. The pack rests on the man's back, held there by the straps around the arms and head in a very comfortable position. So, with the canoe upside down and balanced over the head and the paddles lengthwise resting on his shoulders, a man can carry a heavy load for miles, just bent forward and balancing the canoe with his hands gripping the forward thwart, or seat.

Arthur started with the hounds and Hendry followed with a small pack he insisted on carrying. I followed last with my canoe and pack. Each canoe would weigh sixty pounds and our packs at least a hundred pounds, so Arthur and I had big loads. They had a good start on me, but I caught up with them about the end of the first mile; Hendry was all in. There was only a narrow footpath to follow up the hill and down, and it was rough walking. As Hendry was a small, light-built man, I wasn't surprised at him giving out. So I told Arthur to take it easy; I would go on through and return to help him get Hendry over. I made the full trip of three miles without a rest and returned to find they had only reached halfway. Arthur couldn't leave Hendry, so he waited for me to return.

Poor Hendry! I could sympathize with him; I knew what it had been with us in our first experience carrying a small pack through the woods. I have not said anything about the annoyance from flies while travelling through the woods. In the spring, black flies almost eat you up. Late in the fall, mosquitos and dog flies are terrible, even on the water. When it is calm and warm, I have counted as many as a dozen big ones digging through my heavy pants as I sat fishing or rowing a boat. So Hendry, being fresh meat, was bothered by the skeeters. Arthur and I had gotten so tough and used to them we didn't mind.

We finally got him across to the smooth river where it passed under a log bridge of the Bobcaygeon Road, about a half-mile below Oxtongue Lake. On the opposite side of the river from us was a deserted log cabin where a man and his wife and child had settled a number of years before our time. Zack Cole told us of it.

Zack and his two sons were on snowshoes looking for deer and trailing a big toboggan loaded with blankets and axes so they could, if necessary, camp overnight. They came across this cabin and wondered who could have built it. There were no signs of life. They forced the door open to find the body of a man, and a woman and child unconscious and near death. They built a fire, got some hot water, and succeeded in bringing the woman and child back to life. The boys put them on the toboggan and took them to their home many miles away.

The woman and child recovered their health. She said her husband was taken sick and then the deep snow came. She did not know where to go for help so, when they had eaten up everything, they decided to die together. She thought he must have died soon after she became unconscious. Cole buried the man near the cabin, and no one had occupied it since.

By the time we reached the lake it was raining. We pushed on to the opposite side, a short distance up the lake, opposite the mouth of the river; here we found a good place to camp. It stopped raining but, as it looked like more to come, we cut a lot of wood and built a fire. We had no tent, so we cut forked sticks to hold canvas on edge, and we cut a lot of balsam brush for beds. Then we cut some long, forked poles and drove them into the ground near the fire; we could turn a canoe upside down over them, and we could stand there out of the rain and, at the same time, get some warmth from the fire. We made all the preparations for the night that we could.

Then Arthur took the hounds to the end of the lake and turned them loose into the woods. Hendry and I moved along the lake about a mile. The hounds soon started a deer. First it ran away from the lake, then it turned; that brought the deer to the water about a mile away from us.

This lake was only about half a mile wide. We paddled as swiftly as we could, but the deer beat us to the shore by about a hundred feet. I took a shot at it; it hesitated and ran off into the woods. The dogs swam across the lake and took up the trail, driving the deer to the upper end of the lake where there was a party camped. We soon heard two shots of a rifle, so we presumed they got our deer. But the baying of the hounds started again, so we weren't sure and didn't go to see the campers. The hounds came back not far from us but, instead of entering the lake, the deer continued on and, as we could hear from the dogs baying, crossed the river. Where it went we never knew.

We returned to camp. It was now getting quite dark and commencing to rain. However, Arthur and I took the net and tied one end to a tree leaning over the water, letting the net out as we crossed the mouth of the river. We dropped the sinker with a big cedar float attached to one end of the net. We knew it must be very deep by the way that sinker and float disappeared; we wondered if we would ever see our net again. We paddled back to the tree to see how the rope held. By the slant of the rope, the net seemed as if it must be on end. We left it for the night.

We placed our canoe up on the poles over or close to the fire. We could stand or sit under it sheltered from the rain and keep warm by turning first one side, then the other, to the fire. Since it was raining hard, we ate supper standing up under the canoe. Fortunately there was no wind, so the rain came straight down. We rigged the other canoe on edge over some balsam brush so Hendry could roll up in a blanket and lay down. He was all in. He didn't complain, but I bet before morning he wished he was back home. As it rained steadily all night, Arthur and I stood up, sheltered by the overhead canoe and keeping warm by repeatedly turning around to the fire. Hendry went to sleep rolled up in the blanket and got some heat from the fire.

By late in the night the dogs had not returned. We decided they would find a hollow log or some place of shelter from the rain to spend the night. But along about midnight, we heard a faint whine from somewhere near where we had put the dogs out, away around the shore from the camp. We decided it was Dexter, so we lifted the overhead canoe down and carried it to the lake. I got in, took my bearings from Dexter's whining, and presently saw his white body in the bushes close to the water. I pushed the end of the canoe to him and he jumped in, crawling to me as I knelt in the canoe. He pushed his nose between my knees, whining and shivering from the wet and cold, but wagging his tail in thanks for my coming to him.

I got back to the fire as quick as I could. Arthur had taken him in his arms and was holding his paws over the fire. He called to us to look at Dexter's paws with the firelight shining through the web between his toes. We sure felt for him and praised him for coming back. He had followed his own trail back to the lake through miles and miles of dark, soggy leaves and wet brush. He was only a year and a half old. Vick came back the next day at noon. It was a question between us of which dog was the wiser: the one who returned promptly, or the one who found a place to keep dry and did not return until daylight showed the way. We did not reach a decision.

The first thing in the morning we raised the net. The lake proved so deep it was like lifting it straight up. Almost at the outer end of the net, we found one nice brook trout. He was a beauty, black as could be, shading down to a light tan with red spots circled with a light bluish ring all along its black sides. The spots looked like little eyes, the red forming the pupils. It would weigh about three pounds. The meat was dark cream and very fine and juicy after being broiled in pieces over the hot coals. I think we ate all of it for breakfast. We did not set the net again, so this was the only fish we caught. And the last trout I caught before leaving the country.

We remained three nights without getting anything. Since the rainy weather continued, we decided to return.

Arthur said, "Let's ride the rapids down the river."

"That will be risky with our heavy, loaded canoes," I said.

He didn't think so. He said the Gouldie brothers had told him it was no trick at all. They said there wasn't any danger as the rough water was only in short runs with eddies between each rapids. By doing this, we could save hours of hard work, missing all the carries except at Marsh's Falls. I asked Hendry if he would take a chance with me in my canoe. "I'm with you, if you think it can be done," he said. That settled it.

Early in the morning we started. Arthur and the hounds, a lot of camp sundries, gun, axe, some pots and pans in his canoe—altogether a heavy load since we and everything were wet from the continuous rains. He led the way. I was in the other canoe with Hendry, the net, blankets, gun, axe, and other things.

We travelled side by side down the river and under the bridge and below. When near the rapids, I called to Arthur to stop at the bottom of each rapids and wait for us. I did this because I didn't know the rapids. Then, too, the river turned its course, making some short bends so we would be out of sight of each other at times; if anything happened to him we could pick him up. And by waiting at the foot of each rapids, he could pick us up if anything happened. He was to follow the same rule all the way down. I used this precaution since I wasn't sure of Hendry.

We were soon flying along in the swirling rapids. I guided the canoe through the rapids to the swirling eddies below when Hendry put his paddle in to help. He did not show any excitement in coming through, but as soon as he dipped his paddle he caught a crab, as the saying goes. In this case, a whirling eddy caught it and, before I could tell him to let go of the paddle, the edge of the canoe was down to the water. It righted as soon as he let go, so we didn't get any water in. The paddle disappeared instantly, sucked down by the whirl. Arthur, who was waiting for us, could see what happened, and said, "A close shave, that."

We waited some time for the paddle to appear, but it never came to the surface. It might have been the same with us if we had turned over.

It was enough for Hendry. He settled down in the bottom of the canoe and did not say a word as we shot through the other rapids and on down to Marsh's Falls. We didn't think it was much of a trick to run the rapids; but how we did fly down them, reaching the falls in half the time it would have taken us if we had carried around them. It gave an extra punch to the trip.

We were glad when we arrived at the Portage and glad to dry out. We had been soaking wet all three days and nights at the lake and on the trip back. We dried out very soon and drank lots of hot coffee with plenty to eat at supper. Soon after, we retired for the night. None was any the worse for it next morning. All Pop said was, "You were foolish to stay up there in the rain. There was no chance of you getting a deer or fish either in such weather." When we told him we had run the rapids, he said, "A wonder you didn't try to ride over the falls!" He seemed to think it was a foolish trick with such heavy loads.

As it did not rain all day, and as a finish, I took Hendry and a net over to White Fish Point on Pen Lake so he could see the operation of setting a net. Not that I expected to get any whitefish; it was too early for them to be running up on the shoal, but it was worth trying. He was very much interested to see me set the net all alone from a canoe. He was delighted the next morning in taking it up with a dozen nice whitefish and lots of suckers and bullheads.

The next morning I took him down to Huntsville and saw him off on the stage for Bracebridge. He was delighted to take the whitefish and two nice fresh trout with him. He never thought we would not meet again for a good many years.

24

Coming Back, Never No More

ON MY WAY BACK from seeing Hendry off, I called to see the Hood family. I made a deal with Mr. Hood to work and live with them until the eighteenth of December, just about six weeks, at ten dollars per month or two-fifty per week cash. This would give me fifteen dollars.

Pop gave me the old skiff to sell or trade if I could. I traded it to a young settler east of Hill's place with the understanding he would have to get it across the Portage. I took in exchange an open-face silver watch, a small but good coat only two sizes two small for me but I could get into it; and with the deal, I took a nice pullover wool shirt, dark blue, that I could wear. The watch would gain only two hours and a half in twenty-four, but I sold it for two-fifty. I also got a lot of potatoes and other produce. I sold the potatoes and all the produce in Huntsville.

Pop and I thought I did well; it was an old boat when Pop got it and we had the use of it for three summers. It was big and awkward, but it would carry a big load. It would sail all right; but when it came to rowing it, that was another story.

Hood had two cows, a yoke of oxen, two nice big horses, some pigs and chickens. It was my work to look after all the stock, cut firewood, and cut down trees to clear more land. He was not a hard man to work for. He and the boys would work with me, especially when up in the woods. We most always drove down to Huntsville on Saturdays, taking the whole family in a big bobsled with a box body. We would fill it with hay, and all five children and Mrs. Hood would huddle together in the hay while Mr.

Hood and I would take turns driving. I was like one of the family and enjoyed these trips as much as they did. I was two years older than Bill Hood, the eldest; Lizzie was two years younger; then John, Martha, and Bennie, about two to three years between each one.

Sometimes it was very cold. On one return trip, a hundred-pound bag of salt burst open. We stopped at once, but the salt piled up in the snow. I scooped it up in my hands and found that salt and snow is very cold. I thought my hands would never get over it; they were deathly cold, just like ice. After that, Mr. Hood had to do all the driving—I could not hold the reins. But, like a good many other things, I survived it.

You can imagine me with the five children huddled in the straw in the bottom of the sleigh. There were three boys and two girls and me and we kept close together. I got a piece of wool blanket and kept rubbing my hands. Then the two largest boys, who had woollen mitts on, would each take one of my hands and rub them in their warm ones; so by the time we reached home, they had thawed out.

It was a tough job getting up at daylight and going out to bring in enough wood to last all day. I also had to go out in the fields with a box hand-sled and cut open a pit of carrots for the horses, or a pit of turnips for the pigs, a pit each of beets and potatoes for the house—with the thermometer down to thirty and forty below zero. On reopening one of these pits or after having removed a lot from it, it would look in the dark like stalactites—the frost would form all kinds of shapes. I really enjoyed the life at the Hoods, except that they did all they could to get me to take up with Lizzie, a scrawny girl of fifteen. But I had Philadelphia in mind, and kept her at a distance.

As I said, I engaged with Hood to remain until the eighteenth of December. Within a day or so of that time, Mr. Hood arranged to have a threshing bee for the nineteenth. He did not want me to leave. I was very useful to him, saving him a lot of work that otherwise he would have to do. I liked him very much. Then, too, he was not a well man. He didn't complain, but at times he would say, "My stomach feels bad." I didn't realize how bad he was or what the trouble was. But he lived only two years after I left him.

He was afraid he would not have enough men come to the threshing, so he persuaded me to stay for the nineteenth. I hated to do it: I wanted to visit Arthur and Pop for a day before leaving them on the twentieth. I had figured to reach Philadelphia for Christmas. However, as Hood had been so good to me and paid me in cash up to and including the eighteenth, I felt I must show my appreciation. I said I would stay over and see how he was fixed for help.

We were up early and getting ready for the threshing. It would be an all-day job. The men began to come. We got the machine going, with Bill, John, and me up in the barn pitching the sheaves of grain down to the men. We were kept busy up to noon when there came a let-up in the work. I looked out to see a lot of men standing around, as there usually was at a bee of any kind—many come for the big feed. When I saw this, I called down to Mr. Hood and asked if I could go. "Yes," he said, "and thank you for staying over."

I shook hands with the boys, bidding them goodbye; jumped down and went over to Mr. Hood to shake hands goodbye.

"What are you going to do when you reach Philadelphia?" he asked.

"I'll go to work for my brother for a year," I said. "Then I'll become his superintendent."

Now I had no reason for saying this, but how true it became! I did go to work for my brother and one year after he asked me to take charge as foreman, a presentiment of coming events like unto my leaving Philadelphia when a party asked me when I would return. Offhand I said, "Oh, in about five years." And here I was preparing to leave for Philadelphia five years after. All this gave me the impression that coming events do make themselves known to people at times.

Well, I left Hood and the boys and went on down to the house to find them very busy getting dinner ready. Sitting beside the stove was a young fellow I didn't like. He was a no-account, just a hanger-on at such doings. I shook hands with Martha, Lizzie, Mrs. Hood, and in bidding them goodbye, Mrs. Hood asked if I would ever come back. I said, "Oh, in about three years." This presentiment did not come true.

As she said goodbye, I looked at her. "There's a boy you can have for Lizzie," and I pointed to the bum sitting by the stove. "Never," she said. "I would have liked you."

"Never," I said.

With their best wishes and request to stay for dinner, which I refused with thanks, I took the path which led up to their clearing to the woods and through the woods when I heard little Bennie calling. I looked back to see him running after me. I stopped. When he reached me, he said, "Ain't you coming back no more, Tom?"

I picked him up as I said, "No, never no more, Bennie boy. Be good and grow up big so you can help daddy." He said he would.

I carried him to the edge of the woods and put him down. He ran back home. Strange, but of all I heard afterwards, he turned out the best man of the boys. John died two or three years afterwards. Bill lived to get married and raise a family, but he became addicted to strong drink. He was considered a smart man in a deal but not over particular in his dealings.

The last I heard of Lizzie, she took up nursing and went to Minnesota, never marrying. Martha married a Dr. Hart who had a good practice in Huntsville. When he died he left Martha a nice home that she turned into a tourist home. She was living in it when I last heard of her. That is the story of the Hood family as I heard it from others. I never met them after I left to return to Philadelphia.

After I left Bennie, I had about a mile of wood road and three miles of trackless woods to travel through. There was lots of snow to tramp through with only a sight of Pen Lake, which was frozen over. I had only the light of the sky overhead as my guide to the Portage road. It was dark when I reached the house.

Pop and Arthur were at home. As I entered, Pop said, "Well, I guess you've changed your mind and are going to stay here." Why he should have thought that I don't know, unless it was my being a day late in returning. I didn't ask his reason for saying it, but said, "No, sir. I leave here the first thing in the morning."

"How are you going?" he asked. "You haven't much time now to reach Philadelphia for Christmas."

"I'll foot it to the end of the railway at Gravenhurst," I said.

He did not say any more. We ate supper in silence, then talked over how I would travel. Pop told me to take a ticket to Hamilton, then go around to the different scalpers or ticket agents, saying I could get a cut on a ticket to Buffalo. He still stuck to his idea of staying on the Portage.

Arthur promised to remain with him but take advantage of any opportunity to persuade him to give it up. Then we retired for my last night on the Portage. I slept well, as I was very tired; it had been a hard walk up from Hoods'.

The next morning we were up early. After breakfast I bade Pop good-bye. He had very little to say. I didn't have any packing to do as all my possessions were on my back. I still wore the old felt hat with the piece burned out of the brim, my little sack coat two sizes too small for me, but I thought I looked good; a blue pullover shirt, my heavy felt pants, a pair of wool socks, high leather boots with my pants tucked down in them, and no underwear. I did have a woollen muffler, wide and long, that I could put over my head to cover my ears and part of my face, and wrap twice around my neck. I also had my narrow, fancy scarf which I wore around my waist, tied in a bow knot at my side, the end hanging down. This was a French Canadian idea and a good one; it kept the clothing close to the body and very comfortable.

So, with twenty-one dollars and twenty-five cents, I started for Philadelphia.

Fairy Lake, July 29, 1875

25

Would I Ever Reach Philadelphia?

ARTHUR CAME WITH ME for about four miles. He was going to visit with Tom Steele. When we reached the turn of the road into Tom's, I bade Arthur goodbye.

There was about a foot of snow on the road, so I had to break my way through it to Port Sydney. I went by road because the lakes were not frozen over. After leaving Port Sydney, I had a hard-beaten frozen road all the way to a little village called Falkenburg; it had one hotel. When I left the Portage, the weather was quite mild; by the time I reached Falkenburg, a walk of twenty-five miles, it was down to zero.

It was dark and I was tired, so I went into the hotel and enquired for a room. The good-natured proprietor told me they were all taken. He expected a gang of lumbermen in during the night and they had secured all his rooms. After I explained where I had come from, he said, "I can make up a bed for you in the attic. It will be cold, but I can give you lots of blankets." I was glad to take it rather than walk six miles farther to Bracebridge. So, after I had eaten with him and family, I retired.

I felt pretty cold as I entered the attic. I bundled up in the blankets and soon felt warm. I slept till after daylight, awakening to find my breath had frozen on the blankets, and fine snow had sifted through the shingles, covering the bed white. As I looked up, I could see daylight between the shingles. Just imagine, if you can, sleeping in such a place.

I wasn't long in getting down to the bar-room, where they had a big sheet-iron stove, red hot, with a crowd of men surrounding it. They made

Peninsula Lake near North Portage, July 26, 1875

room for me, so I was soon warm and comfortable. They were all fixing up to leave, pulling on socks and moccasins. It is an actual fact that I saw one man about my age pull five heavy woollen socks on each foot and buckskin moccasins on top of them, lacing on the uppers outside heavy woollen pants. I had one pair of socks inside leather boots (boots are much colder for the feet than moccasins). They were a jolly crowd. They asked where I had come from and where I was going. They said, "You're not dressed well enough for this weather." I did not make any answer to that as breakfast was called.

I ate a good breakfast with the gang. They were on their way up north to Lake Nipissing for the rest of the winter and spring. When I came to settle for my accommodations, the landlord said, "Boy, I think you ought to stay over. It is a terribly cold morning." No doubt he realized how thinly clad I was.

"No," I said. "It's only six miles to Bracebridge. I can make it."

"Maybe so. But I have known men to freeze to death on a morning like this in going less than six miles."

I was anxious to be on my way. I bundled up, pulling my muffler twice over my head and around my neck, covering my ears; I put one thickness over my mouth to breathe the sharp air through. I tightened my belt sash around my waist and struck out for Bracebridge.

It sure was cold! Long before I reached Bracebridge, it seemed the cold air, as I met it, came in front and out the back of me. To say the least, I was cold. By the time I reached Bracebridge, I was so stiff I could hardly walk.

I entered the first hotel that had a red-hot stove. I shuffled up close to it, took off my muffler, and loosened my belt sash to let the warm air penetrate through me. I soon began to feel the warmth of the fire. My tingling ears caused me to raise my hands to them and find the lobes of both ears frozen so stiff it seemed as if I could snap them off. I went out, picked up some snow, and rubbed my ears with it gently as I walked on to the next hotel. By the time I reached it, my ears had softened. I entered the bar-room, where I soon warmed up. I remained there until I was thoroughly warmed and rested. I didn't suffer any bad effects from my ears; I really felt fine as I started off for Gravenhurst, more than ten miles over a hard, icy, well-beaten road.

After walking several miles, I reached a long, straight piece of road where I would see a black speck on an up-grade some miles ahead of me. I soon discovered it was a man going ahead of me, so I sped up to reach him. He discovered I was coming, so he waited or walked slower to give me a chance to overtake him. We were the only signs of life to be seen, so we were glad to meet and walk along together.

He was a strong, well-built Irishman and claimed to be seventy-four years of age. He had walked as far as I had, coming to Bracebridge from the opposite direction and reaching it the night before I did. He had put up overnight but got away before I reached there, and he was much fresher for the walk than I. He could sure step out for an old man.

We walked for some miles. Lake Muskoka was along one side and between the lake and the road was all pine woods. The roadbed was beaten hard by the stages and sleighs passing over it during the week. The snow and ice was hard and crumbly and as high as the top of a rail fence; but we did not see any fence or team or human being. He had the advantage of me as he had moccasins. They are much easier for walking on ice or snow than hard leather boots; he could get a grip whereas I would slip at most every step.

We trampled along side by side. Sometimes we talked; oftener we did not say a word, as we required all our breath to fight against the cold, sharp air and the exertion of walking. We had travelled several miles in this way when we saw a frame house back in the pines a short distance from the road. The only sign of life was smoke issuing from the chimney. My friend said, "Let's find out who has the nerve to live there, miles away from a human being, at this time of year."

At our knock on the door, a deep, gruff voice said, "Come in." As we entered, we saw a big, tall, well-built man standing against the opposite wall, his left elbow resting on a shelf or mantle attached to the wall. There was very little furniture, and that homemade. There was a fine big range or cook stove, and on a wooden bench alongside of it an object covered with a shawl looking as though it were a person bent over the stove.

After a few words of greeting, the man invited us to have a drink from a big bottle he took from a cupboard. I refused. My friend joined him in a couple of rounds, and I sat on a stool while they drank and talked. I judged he was a Scotchman, about fifty years of age.

I could not take my eyes off the bundle leaning over the stove. Presently I heard sobbing and saw the bundle shaking. I could not stand for that—I knew it must be a woman. So I said to my friend, "Come on. We must be on our way." As they were shaking hands goodbye, I stepped over to the bundle and pulled the shawl to one side, and a woman's face turned itself up to me.

The features were of what had been a comely woman, but it was a most wretched and pitiful look she gave me, with tears running down her face and her hair bedraggled. I threw the shawl back, covering her face, and turned to the man. He was facing me with a very angry look. I faced him and said, "Are you a man? If so, get this woman out of here."

"That is none of you damned business," he said.

"No," I said. "But if you have a soul in you, get her away. Or the blame will rest with you for her life or sanity."

"Go on about your business," he replied. "I will take care of mine."

"It's up to you," I said. So we left them to their misery.

We had miles to go to reach Gravenhurst, many miles of virgin pine forest. As we approached the lights of Gravenhurst, it being some time after dark, the white snow covering the ground and a clear, bright, starry sky overhead made it so we had no trouble to see our way.

When close to the village, we both saw a fine big whip lying in the road; we both ran for it. I picked it up. The old man wanted it, for it was a beauty, a Simon Legree type, black leather cowhide all studded with bright brass rivets. I carried it into the first hotel we came to. There was nobody in the bar-room, but as we entered the proprietor came around from the back of the bar. We made ourselves known, and I asked for a room for the night and a call so I could get the first train out in the morning. "It leaves at seven in the morning," he said. As we were leaving the bar-room, I said, "Will it be safe for me to leave this whip in the corner here?" He assured me it would.

I was down to the station by 6:45. It was all in darkness and a heavy wet snow was falling. After looking around, I espied a streak of light as if it were coming from under a door. I stepped up to the door and knocked. The door opened a few inches and a voice bawled at me, "What do you want?"

"The train that leaves here at seven," I said.

"The train's been gone this half hour," he said, and slammed the door shut. It seems they were afraid of being blocked by the snow and, as there were no passengers expected, it left an hour ahead of time. The next train would leave at five in the afternoon.

I returned to the hotel, not in the best of humour, and said to the boss, "You're a dandy man to be running a hotel for the travelling public and not knowing the time the trains leave." When I explained, he said he was sorry.

"Maybe you did it for what little extra you might get out of me, but you won't do it," I said. "Which is the road to Severn Bridge? I am going to walk it. The next train will never get out of here if this snow keeps up."

"In front of the house, and it's eleven miles to Severn," said a man in the hotel. "You had better not go out in this wet snow." The snow was falling; each flake like a wet snowball, they were so big.

"I'm on my way," I said.

As I was leaving, I caught sight of the whip, which I had forgotten. I called to the boss to give the whip to my friend of the night before, as I stepped out the door never to see the whip or the people again.

The snow soon stopped falling. I reached Severn Bridge about noon to find I had to wait until the five o'clock train would come. So I gained nothing by my walk except the difference in train fare. This more than paid for a dinner at the hotel in Severn Bridge. And so that concluded my trek of more than fifty miles from the Portage. I made it in two days, which was not bad, considering the hard walking.

The five o'clock train finally arrived and on time. I reached Allandale at nine to find the train laid over until seven the next morning. I secured a room with another man in the Orangemen's Club and Hotel; I agreed to share the room as it was a reduction in expenses; and, besides, there was no single room vacant. This man was much older than I and proved to be a good sport. He showed me through the lodge rooms and explained the pictures to me and gave me the history of the Order. At this time, the rival Orangemen and Fenians were both very strong in parts of Canada. I had a very interesting night.

I boarded the train which would get me to Hamilton by noon; from there I would book through to Buffalo, New York. Just opposite my seat in the train were two young ladies about eighteen or twenty years of age. They were nicely dressed and up-to-date for those times. Their hair was done up in a pyramid on top of their heads to a point, and lots of it. I could see it plainly as they didn't wear hats. The hair was a natural black and very bright, like unto a horse's mane; their complexion was a sort of copper colour. At first I thought they might be Assyrians, and their features were too regular for Italians from any part of Italy. After puzzling my brain to decide on their nationality, I gave up.

I became interested in the countryside we were travelling through and, for a while, they passed from my thoughts. I was roused from my reverie by hearing the girls say, "Why, Papa, we wondered where you were."

A big broad-shouldered man was bending over them as he said, "Oh, I was in the smoker." As he said this, he turned as if looking for a seat. I moved over, inviting him to sit with me. My, was he broad!

He squeezed me over close to the window. As he thanked me, I said, "That's all right, chief." He looked at me very hard. "You never saw me before, or I you," I continued, "but I recognize you as a full-blooded Indian."

"Yes, I am an Indian chief, and they"— he pointed to the young ladies—"are my daughters. My wife a full-blood, too. Her father was a chief and died soon after we were forced onto the reserve."

The girls were looking at us as we talked. They no doubt could hear some of our talk, as they smiled intelligently at me on some of my remarks to him. This opened up a conversation in which I told him about the two boys who had camped at our place in the fall, and what a good time we had together.

"Yes, they are my nephews," he said. "My brother, who would not stay on the reserve, was given charge of a lighthouse on Lake Michigan." As he said this, I was sure of him. But what a strange thing that I should hear of the boys in this way. I had often wondered if they had gotten back to their home safely and alive.

We had about three hours to talk before they got off the train. He told me all about his people going on the reserve, about his life around

Lake of Bays (or Trading Lake, as he knew it). He was very much interested to hear of the changes in his old hunting grounds.

He asked me to go with them to their home to see their nice community. He said, "You'll find it is up-to-date with any white man's city. We have a fine post office, banks, theatres, hotels, and schools—every convenience of a city." I should have liked to have gone with them, but I had to refuse as I wanted to reach Philadelphia for Christmas. As they were leaving, he shook hands with me and said, "If you ever can come to our city, ask for me. I will see you have a good time. Goodbye."

I reached Hamilton at noon. I had to lay over until two o'clock. My ticket only called for Hamilton, so I scoured around to the railway agents or scalpers to get a reduced fare to Buffalo. I saved a little by taking a ticket to a place called Meyersville, where I would have to lay over an hour and a half or until the train for Buffalo came along.

While waiting, I went into a barber shop for my second shave. I needed it. It was about a year since Arthur and I had a shave by borrowing a razor from an outfit of a man who was travelling through and had stopped with us on the Portage for a day and night. That was our first shave; I leave it to you to imagine how we looked after we got through hacking the hair off. Now I was covered with soft, light blond hair and my moustache was more than a quarter-inch long. The barber wanted me to leave it on, saying he could colour it for me; but I refused. I told him I was on my way to meet my Mother whom I hadn't seen for over three years, and I wanted to look a little like I did when I saw her last. So it came off with all the rest, and I had a haircut, too.

The train came at four o'clock. The conductor told me he was due in Buffalo at ten. My train for Philadelphia left one minute after our arrival, so I had to get a ticket and catch my train for Philadelphia in one minute. He said I would reach Philadelphia at ten-thirty the next morning. He said, "When we get into Buffalo, there will be a man waiting with a lantern. So you just watch me." I did, and as we were slowing up for Buffalo, he motioned to me.

I went out on the platform of the car with him, and he called to the man with the lantern, "This man wants a ticket for Philadelphia."

"You have only one minute," he said. "Jump off as soon as you can, but be careful. The ground is covered with ice and is wet." It was raining too. As I got off, the man said, "We have got to run for it. Come on."

I followed him through slush and mud until we entered a small room. There was no one to be seen. He banged his fist on a counter and called, "Come on there. Wake up. This man wants a ticket for Philadelphia."

A man came in, and my man said, "Hurry. Get him a ticket."

The man did so, saying as he laid the ticket on the counter, "Ten dollars, please."

I gave him a Canadian ten, and he said, "Five percent on that."

"I guess not," I said. "Money is at par."

"Fifty cents more or no ticket," he said.

I plunked a fifty down on the counter, saying, "You beat me. This is what I depended on for a lunch on the way to Philadelphia."

My escort said, "There goes your train!"

I grabbed the ticket, saying, "And so am I going, too."

I caught the tail-end rail and sprang aboard. I think the station was located near where the old station is now, on Mechanic or Exchange Street. It's now the Union Station. I know it was a miserable place.

I had run away from the lantern light through rain, slush, and mud and it was dark as the ace of spades; but I made it, which was all that mattered. I was so relieved to think I was on the last train to Philadelphia, but to my sorrow, when we reached Waverly, the conductor very pleasantly told me, "This train goes to New York City. You will have to lay over until nine in the morning." It was then three—another six hours to lose. Would I ever reach Philadelphia?

I went into the station, lay down on a bench, and dropped off to sleep. As soon as people moved around, I woke up to daylight. I went into the city and saw some nice-looking felt hats called the General Grant. I thought I could spare the price of one-fifty and get rid of my burnt-brim hat. I got a good fit and thought it looked good on me; so I felt quite dressed up. I got a light breakfast and the train came along. The conductor said he was due to reach Philadelphia at ten-thirty that night.

It was a long day for me; but, like all days, it passed. It was dark hours before we got in, so I couldn't see any old landmarks until we entered North Penn Station; it was then the station for all the trains, the station we left from more than five years previous. The station was a solid mass of people. Since it was Christmas Eve, they had come to meet the last train.

As I got on the steps, I looked over the heads of the vast crowd, wondering if there was anyone who would know me. I felt sure there was no one who would know me in my rig of black-and-white checkered pants tucked down inside my boots and my backwoods rigging. I remembered the station, so instead of going through the crowd to the front exit, I swung to the right and to the back of the station where the train came in.

The station was at Third and Berks streets. I walked up the tracks to Norris, down Norris to Second, over Second to Diamond, down Diamond to Front. Coral Street joined both Diamond and Front. I knew the streets as well as if I had never been away. I walked up Coral to Susquehanna Avenue corner. I knew Mother lived on Coral, but I didn't know just what house in the row of houses above Susquehanna; so I stopped on the corner.

Everything was very familiar to me. I stopped under the faint light from a coal-oil lamp post; as I stood there, some boys came along serenading, just as I had done years before. I asked them if they knew Sam Osborne. They gave me a stare as they said "Naw," and ran away. As I turned and looked up Susquehanna, I saw a man coming down towards me. Although the light was poor, I recognized him at once as my brother Owen. I figured he was on his way to Mother's to see if I had shown up. He was on the side of Coral Street opposite to where I figured Mother lived, so I waited. But instead of coming straight across, he jaywalked; and when in the middle of Coral Street he turned, looked at me, and went on.

I gave him time to show me which house in the row Mother lived in. I followed slowly after him for half a square, when he turned and went in. I gave him time to get settled, then I went up the steps and pulled the bell. The door soon opened and Mother stood before me. My first thoughts were about how much better she looked than when I saw her last. Just three years and three months had passed.

I saw she had no idea who I was, so I said, "Does Sam Osborne live here?"

"Yes, sir," she said.

"Is he in?" I asked.

"Yes, sir," she said.

"I want to see him," I said. As I said this, I stepped up to the door sill as if to enter the house, and she threw her arms across the doorway. When I laughed, she said, "I know you now, my boy!"

Afterwards, she said she was puzzled as to who I might be. When I asked for Sam, she thought I was after him for something he had been doing, as he was always getting into trouble. But when I laughed, she recognized me at once.

Owen, Emma, Sam, and Lidie were soon in the hallway to greet me. It was a great meeting. I inquired for the others as soon as I got my breaths—which was almost squeezed out of me. Mother said, "They have all gone to the station to meet the last train. We felt sure you would get here for Christmas."

They had been looking for me the past six weeks, as Pop had written to say I had made up my mind to return to Philadelphia but could not say just when. So they decided I would surely be on the last train and had gone to meet it and me. As Mother said, if they saw me they would not know me; and no wonder, dressed as I was. Also, when Annie and Marie saw me last I was a poor, thin boy, not weighing over sixty-five pounds. I returned weighing 185 pounds and almost six feet in height, rugged and strong. Owen, who I had thought was tall when I last saw him, seemed now to be a small man in comparison, not near as tall as I.

Well, I had to hide when we heard the others coming. I heard them say, "No, we didn't see anyone we thought might be he." I was shut in an adjoining room, and Owen opened the door, saying, "Did you think he would look like this?" What a surprise! They could hardly believe their eyes. There was Annie with her friend Will Chapman, and Marie with no friend.

After this meeting, there was brother Will to come. He came in soon after, and when he saw me he just grabbed me and said, "Well, well. The biggest one of the family and the tallest, too." I was the largest there except Lige. He was so big at that time that I could hide behind him; he was as good-natured as he was big.

This about ends my five years and three weeks in Canada. As I have said, when I left Philadelphia I did not weigh over sixty-five pounds. Just previous to my return, I weighed 185¾ pounds. I stood with my boots on five-feet eleven and a quarter; I wore size ten-and-a-half boots, and my chest measured forty-five inches, standing easy. So much for the healthy country—despite all the hardships I endured. Really, I have not told half of the hardships and the laborious work we three—Pop, Arthur, and I— endured during that five years.

I went to work for Owen the day after Christmas following my return, a piece-work job. I was very anxious to earn all I could, so I put in every minute on the job—sometimes twelve hours a day. The work, being shut in, and the late hours I was not accustomed to, resulted in my losing fifty pounds in six months; I never regained the loss.

Six months after I left Canada, Pop notified me that if I didn't return I had better have my location transferred to Arthur, who was then past eighteen. As well, if I didn't return in time, a friend of Thompson's would jump my claim. As I did not intend to ever return, I transferred it to Arthur; eventually he received title to it. At the time I transferred it to him, there were fifteen acres cleared. Arthur never built on it; he lived with Pop or in Pop's house.

Now, in 1934 and at the age of seventy-five years, or sixty years from the time I left Philadelphia for Canada, I have written, in my own way, this truthful story of my actual experiences, and without exaggeration. A lot more could have been told …

AFTERWORD

Fates of the Osbornes

J. Patrick Boyer

THOMAS OSBORNE, SEEING "no prospect for the future" in primitive Muskoka except "a hard life for the years to come," urged his father, William, and brother Arthur to join him so they could "all go back to Philadelphia." Previously he'd ensured his mother and sisters left Muskoka before winter set in. When he himself quit the district, with the frigid air and heavy snows of late 1879 descending for yet another Canadian winter, Thomas vowed to a young friend inquiring if he'd see him again that he would not come back, "never no more."

A half decade before, Thomas had only just started working in a Philadelphia textile factory when his father abruptly took all the family, except the two oldest boys, to Ontario. In the interim his brother Owen, who'd refused to go to Canada and had even held back sending their father money received from the sale of his own business interests, had parlayed his growing assets into a successful knitting mill. Thomas, now eager to resume familiar work upon returning to Pennsylvania, could not wait to join Owen. There was safety in steady routine. There was security in a steady paycheck and a nearby grocery store. He'd already had, in five years, enough adventure to last a lifetime. The youth who'd shot bear and paddled with Indians, who'd gazed in rapture at night skies filled with stars and winter trees filled with wild partridge, began making stockings in his brother's busy mill. The reluctant pioneer had come home to city living, his only dream now to become superintendent of the textile mill.

Thomas did well enough as he reverted to form, but only by fitting like a small cog into the vast wheels turning American industry and commerce. Back in a city with its social patterns and expected behaviours, a maturing Thomas almost predictably took the next step into respectable life as a stolid citizen. Whereas in Muskoka he'd skirted efforts by others to match him up with marrying-age women, and instead avidly pursued adventures with other young men, those inclinations simply underscored the limited choices available in Muskoka's backwoods and his overriding resolve to avoid local entanglement in order to get home to the big city. In 1882, when he had turned twenty-three, Thomas married attractive and thoughtful Carrie Barber of Philadelphia, after which the domesticated couple proceeded to populate their home with a succession of seven little Osbornes, five of whom would survive infancy.

Thomas rose steadily in the textile business, from skilled worker to plant superintendent, at the prospering Pennsylvania stocking mill. He owed his advance to a combination of personal ability and being a brother of the factory's owner, Owen Osborne. In time Thomas and Carrie relocated their family to New York State, where he progressed to an even more senior position, supervising a knitting factory in Oneida, living at 113 McGuire Street. For a quarter century he fulfilled himself in this work, more independent than working for his brother, still in a city setting, content in the demanding embrace of his own family, a valuable man undistinguished in the American labyrinth of industrial management, his sense of adventure as atrophied as the once hardened muscles of his pioneering youth.

It almost seemed there were two Thomas Osbornes. Had those wild homesteading adventures in Canada ever really even happened?

As months turned to years and years became decades, those blighting experiences and charmed joys of his youthful Muskoka years seemed like a remote dream, as alien to city businessman Thomas as, when in Muskoka, his abandoned city life had then appeared to be. Now, like a veteran safely returned from a foreign battlefield, secure with a clean place to live and grateful to have survived, Thomas had taken refuge in the routines of family and work, and in the order of a city setting. He was content to be alive, enjoying quiet patterns and creature comforts—a warm soft bed to sleep in when he grew tired, an apple in a kitchen bowl waiting for him to get hungry.

Over these decades, as well, Thomas Osborne's family responsibilities and the demands of running a busy mill crowded out time for reminiscing. Nor was any other veteran of those Muskoka struggles available to swap pioneer stories. And even if Thomas did have the luxury of open time and an inclination to talk about the past, nobody who was then around him would really understand, or much care.

Thomas shrank from being the bold youth who shot game, saved lives, and paddled miles by moonlight, assuming instead the unheroic proportions of a businessman focused on producing better hosiery in his comfortable haven. So it went, and the years of his life were eaten up. He was sixty-eight when Carrie died in 1927. In time the quiet widower moved to southern California, to be near one of their adult sons already living there.

Meanwhile, back on the Osborne's north-Muskoka homestead, life had become far more promising than Thomas had been capable of imagining.

When he quit the Portage in 1879, it was because he found himself "in rags, as it were, and no prospect for the future but a hard life for the years to come," proving how one's appraisal of a situation is coloured by one's state of mind. Though transformed by necessity into a hardy Muskoka woodsman for several years—outwitting death, overcoming the wiles of desperate men, becoming a skilled cook, artful fisherman, fine hunter, and expert canoeist—Thomas was as reluctant to remain in Canada as Owen Osborne was to join them at the Portage. At some level the two brothers seemed to agree, even if just through their tacit preference for the city. One engineered the return to civilization of his mother and two sisters from their ordeal east of Huntsville, while the other regularly stalled in sending their father his own much needed money from Philadelphia.

William and Arthur, however, enjoyed increasing success in Canada by carrying on with the inspired vision that had first led Osborne senior to one of Muskoka's most remote corners, to stake out a homestead on one of the district's least promising bits of farming land.

William always had a keen eye for opportunity. The man who'd seen brighter prospects in keeping a village inn at Montsorrel, only to then move the entire family across the Atlantic in search of a main chance in Philadelphia, then again relocating with most of them to southern Ontario in the hope of starting some new business in Dundas, and when that didn't pan out in Toronto, had next shifted his focus to available lands just then opening for settlement in Muskoka. William was savvy and innovative, as his son Thomas indicates through various passages in this book, and as son Owen recorded in his own 1927 book *The Story of the Stocking: Reminiscences of a Manufacturer*. Owen documents how his father improved efficiency in the mechanical operations of textile mills by a number of innovations.

Even though William Osborne had to guard against his tendency to indulge in alcohol, he was stone sober in evaluating Muskoka prospects. He did not rush to grab the next most convenient farm lot, as most settlers did in Muskoka's 1870s land boom, intoxicated as they were by the rush for the district's "free land." William spent over a dozen weeks studying areas not yet opened for settlement in north Muskoka, where he reasoned that his potential opportunity would be greatest if he got in ahead of others. After a quarter year studying maps and listening to villagers talk in Huntsville, and with the benefit of extensive and deliberate reconnoitering, William settled on land in isolated Franklin Township. It was at the farthest end of Peninsula Lake, one of the interconnected lakes in the extensive watershed system around the village of Huntsville.

Even then, William did not locate land that held particular promise for farming, but instead bought out a squatter's squalid shanty on land not yet surveyed and not even open, in 1875, for a free grant. Far past the end of even the crudest roads into the bush, Osborne's chosen real estate was so remote that he could only reach it on foot or by canoe or rowboat. Added to this list of negatives, the place was a jagged welter of rocky outcropping and steep slopes, enough to deter any prospective farmer. "Captain" Pokorny, from whom he'd bought it, had after all squatted here not to grow food, but to escape the law and survive by his devious wits and his suitcase of cash.

William Osborne wanted all the land here he could get. He bought squatter's rights from Pokorny, would stake his own claim, and would get his son Thomas to claim free grant land next to his lots as soon as he turned eighteen. He bought up whatever else he could from others. To William's chagrin, after Pokorny sold him his Franklin Township rock pile, he just moved around the bay and re-squatted on an adjacent piece of property to continue his hideaway existence, rather than move away as was the deal. Only after Pokorny died in the 1880s would William add the old Pole's second property to his own holdings, by purchase.

The one positive thing about this real estate was its strategic location. The Osborne land straddled a narrow divide between two watershed systems, as suggested by the name South Portage for their front yard, and North Portage which was their "back forty." To the southeast spread the large Lake of Bays, and to the northwest the series interconnected Peninsula, Fairy, and Vernon lakes, linked by a lock on the Muskoka River south into Mary Lake since 1875, and by a dredged channel between Fairy and Peninsula lakes since 1887. By occupying the space between these two great water systems, as William Osborne understood from the very beginning, he could prosper as gatekeeper.

Things were even turning out better than Thomas could imagine. When he was still at the Portage steamboats were only starting to make their appearance in north Muskoka, but William had looked to the future in deciding to settle this straddling patch of land. He realized it would be only a matter of time before economic development would touch these lakes of north Muskoka, the way it had been fostered around the district's central lakes Muskoka, Rosseau, and Joseph once they became linked by a canal and lock built on the Indian River at Port Carling in 1872. Another sign that had registered with William Osborne was how rustic McCabe's Landing had been transformed into booming Gravenhurst once the Northern Railway reached there in 1875, connecting to steamboat traffic on the central Muskoka lakes, spawning new trade, commerce, industry, and vacation resorts.

Looking for opportunity in the future, just as he had done in his past, William Osborne envisaged a similar hive of activity—at the only place a connection between north Muskoka's two watershed systems could be made. He and Arthur remained, after his wife, daughters, and then Thomas, had all departed. The pair would bide their time, and wait for prosperity to come to them. William gave up his marriage for this dream of freedom.

In the closest approach of these water bodies at the Portage, notes geographer and Muskoka historian Gary Long, "a mere five-eighths of a mile separates Portage Bay on Lake of Bays and Wolf Bay on Peninsula Lake—a tantalizing proximity tempered by the geographic reality that Lake of Bays stands 103 feet higher and a line of high hills runs along the narrow isthmus." Daunting cliffs and precipitous slopes, he explains, "meant that even the natives' portage trail didn't take the shortest line across." Connecting the lakes would be an engineering challenge, "but the Portage was the only place it could be done."

A proposed short canal across the Osborne lands between Peninsula Lake and Lake of Bays was never built. Such a canal seemed likely, once a channel had been dredged from Fairy Lake east into Peninsula Lake, to extend the reach of shipping from Huntsville. Yet the barrier of overcoming a rocky drop of more than a hundred feet proved an insurmountable hurdle because of the projected construction cost. For William and Arthur, however, the exact means of transit between steamboats on Lake of Bays and Peninsula Lake did not much matter. The inescapable reality was that all freight and passengers would have to cross their land.

Consistent with his original strategy, and as money became available through William's selective sales of non-essential lots for summer cottages, he bought out other properties on the northern side of his Portage lands to overcome the problem that his original grant did not reach all the way to Peninsula Lake. Thus, to the southwest he acquired some eighty-three more acres fronting on Lake of Bays and into Portage Bay. The piece he bought from Pokorny's estate in the 1880s included the western side of Osborne Lake. To monopolize this prize corridor required owning as much of it as he could, not only for controlling the road across his own land, but to prevent others building nearby competitor routes parallel to his.

Initially a road had been built across this awkward stretch of Osborne land, around the rocky ridges and over swampy mud areas. In 1887 it had been upgraded and gravelled. At the same time steamboats such as Captain Alfred Denton's *Northern* and *Florence* had appeared on Peninsula Lake, while Lake of Bays Captain George Marsh, who also built a sawmill that Thomas writes about, owned and operated two other steamers, *Mary Louise* and *Excelsior*. By 1891, with the development of resort hotels around the lakes and the opening of a leather tannery in Huntsville, to which barge loads of tan bark were tugged by steamers, the Osbornes would open their front door, step onto the porch, and watch bustling port activity with passengers and freight arriving and departing at South Portage, and shops open for business.

Once the Northern Railway from southern Ontario reached north Muskoka and beyond in 1886, the same transformation that swept Gravenhurst a decade earlier occurred in parallel for Huntsville. Not only did the village surge with sawmill activity and population growth, but heavy industry in the form of tanning leather sent prosperity and new forms of commerce rippling east into Franklin Township. The road over the Osborne land between Peninsula Lake and Lake of Bays became a lively thoroughfare. Freight wagons lumbered back and forth. Passenger transit was available, both in the form of a buggy and also a wagon bus with rows of seats. All vehicles were horse-drawn and operated by Arthur Osborne. The Osborne's "Transfer Line" had now come into its own.

One man's bottleneck, as William had foreseen, could be another man's ticket to prosperity. In 1897 the roadway that had been gravelled a decade before was now upgraded by paving. The building of more lodges, summer cottages, and many more steamboats all reflected the drive of entrepreneurs to expand their operations into the surrounding hinterland. Those activities included not only vacationers in transit and sportsmen hunting and fishing, but harvesting trees for lumber and hemlock bark for tanning too. Nobody in this expanding commercial empire of north Muskoka could bypass the Osborne-controlled transfer zone, it seemed.

But a threatening cloud loomed on the southern horizon. A group of central Muskoka businessmen and entrepreneurs was planning a new line, the Bracebridge and Trading Lake Railway. It would run east and west between Baysville and Bracebridge at the *south* end of Lake of Bays, scooping this potential hinterland away from Huntsville and into the economic orbit of Bracebridge, linking all Lake of Bays business to the

Northern Railway's north-south line at Bracebridge. The Bracebridge and Trading Lake Railway Company also intended to continue the tracks west from Bracebridge to Beaumaris, joining up by rail with the entire central Muskoka lakes navigation system. Whether the highly attractive vacation areas around Lake of Bays and its surrounding village communities of Baysville, Dorset, and Dwight could be drawn into Huntsville's sphere, or would instead fall away to Bracebridge and south-central Muskoka, would be determined by what happened on Osborne's land in the race to see which group of entrepreneurs got their railway built first.

The neck of land between North Portage and South Portage, considered impossible for a canal, was now urgently reconsidered for a train. When a contracted engineer from the Grand Trunk Railway arrived to look over the steep incline in 1889, he pronounced that running a railway over it was out of the question. A more enterprising local man, however, was more inventive in rising to the challenges of the Canadian Shield.

George Marsh first displayed his entrepreneurship building and operating a sawmill at Marsh's Falls when Thomas Osborne was still on the scene. Then, as noted, he started operating the steamer *Mary Louise*, which began his venture into transportation. By 1895 this line of business had grown to include five boats on the connected series of north Muskoka lakes, still separated only by the lands Thomas had, in his day, cleared and planted. After negotiating a lease with the Osbornes for a right-of-way across their lots, George Marsh laid out a railbed snaking up from South Portage, tight around the shore of tiny Osborne Lake, through a narrow rock pass over the hump, and down the lengthening steep slope to North Portage on Peninsula Lake.

Everything about Marsh's "Portage Railway" seemed miniature: its short mile-and-a-half track, the narrow gauge of its rails, its two tiny second-hand locomotives that previously had only been used for light work marshalling cars in level rail yards. When operating now on the steep grade, the small engines pulled the train at such slow speed that good-humoured passengers soon bequeathed it the mocking nickname "the Portage Flyer." Many of them liked to descend the open-sided cars and stroll alongside, helping lighten the load while picking wild strawberries. When they leisurely climbed back aboard, they could resume their same nearby seat. Something else small about the miniature train was its brief season of operation, since winter was out of the question. All in all, no other railway could boast, as the Portage Flyer did, to be "the world's shortest commercially operated railway."

Slow or fast, small or large, transportation across the Osborne corridor brought more buildings, services, wharves, freight-handling equipment, storage facilities, and population. New steamboats were being constructed onshore at South Portage, again in view from the Osborne's front porch.

Another sign of progress was the opening of a post office. William Osborne's earlier effort in the 1870s to become postmaster here, and to have the community known as "Osborne Portage," which Thomas describes when getting all settlers to sign the petition for postal service, was turned down by Ottawa officials as premature. But by 1904, thanks to the economic boom and population growth around their homestead, a post office opened at South Portage. In the same decade, major new resort hotels, including the prestigious WaWa and Britannia, were built on the shores of Lake of Bays. Passenger and freight traffic increased.

While the Portage Flyer cut heavily into the horse-drawn operations of the Osborne Line, the astute Osbornes had negotiated employment terms along with the lease for a right-of-way across their land. Arthur Osborne became mechanical superintendent of the Portage Railway. Meanwhile, the land-rich Osbornes also collected rents, lease payments, and proceeds of sale from anybody wishing to open a store, build a home, or start up a spin-off business.

The commercial opportunities continued to expand. When sawmill, steamboat, and railroad owner George Marsh died, right after taking his inaugural ride on the Portage Flyer, an even more ambitious entrepreneur bought up Marsh's many assets in 1905. Charles Orlando Shaw, owner of Huntsville's tannery, was developing the vacation potential of Lake of Bays through shipping and, in 1920, by opening his lavish Bigwin Inn resort on the lake's largest island, whose Native structures and graves had been explored by Thomas and are written about in this memoir.

All this, and more, was possible because travel had become easier. The Portage Flyer continued operating for decades, to the mid-twentieth century, and today serves Muskoka tourism in a different role as an attraction relocated to Huntsville's Pioneer Village heritage centre. The rival Trading Lake Railway between Baysville and Bracebridge was never completed, to the chagrin of its proponents (including my great-grandfather James Boyer, who was a director and the railway company's secretary), although shares were issued, government grants lobbied for, funds raised, the line surveyed, and some roadbed constructed.

The two Osborne men who remained in Muskoka after Thomas returned to Pennsylvania made a rewarding life for themselves amidst all these economic developments changing the district.

Like his brother, Arthur found a woman to fall in love with, Annie Lowe, but unlike Thomas, he managed to find her in Muskoka, on a farm just three miles north and east of the Portage. He was twenty-six and she twenty when they married in 1887. Annie left the homestead of her parents, Jacob and Mary, and moved in with her husband and his father, William. Arthur and Annie had four children in the coming years, although first-born Owen, named for Arthur's increasingly prosperous eldest brother, died in childhood.

William's own marriage, of course, had come to its effective end through the years of separation from Esther. He had vowed to die and be buried in Muskoka, while his wife and most everyone else in the Osborne family knew that she would have faced a diminished and difficult future in the Franklin Township log farmhouse. There were worse fates than living apart.

In the 1890s, when he reached his seventies, and as Arthur and Annie's growing family needed more space, William moved out of their shared homestead at South Portage and began enjoying his money and freedom. He spent the rest of his life at boarding houses in the vicinity of Huntsville, a free man who could come and go as he pleased. He who had walked from Toronto to the Portage, lacking money for a fare, now rolled south from Muskoka in the comfort of a parlour car, his eyes closing as he dozed off, scarcely seeing the jagged rocks and swamps along the sides of the railbed. William made frequent trips to the United States to visit his scattered children and grandchildren. Back in Muskoka, one of the places he stayed, at the turn of the century, was a newly built hotel overlooking North Portage.

One visit to the U.S. took William to Queens, New York, where he lived awhile in 1910 with daughter Anna and her husband, Elijah Woodelton, before returning the next year to a boarding house in Huntsville where he resided until dying, in 1913, at age ninety-two. Despite his wish to be buried in Muskoka, his body was shipped by train to Philadelphia, with Owen continuing to have his way in matters pertaining to his father. His casket was lowered into a family plot beside Esther's, where she'd been interred since her own death in 1895, at age seventy-one.

Arthur's fate continued to be tied up, in a large way, with the small railroad. The Portage Flyer kept chugging along in productive service, under his watchful attention, but in 1912, when he was fifty-one years old, a flatbed car he was riding became unhitched. On the steep incline it quickly gained unimpeded runaway speed. Understanding the threat of the looming crash, Arthur saved his life by leaping off. But Muskoka rock took its toll. Arthur's smashed leg healed slowly. He would walk with a limp the rest of his years.

By 1915, with a gimpy leg reducing his ability to maintain railroad equipment, thinking about his limited prospects in this small seasonal community, and having dutifully fulfilled the promise Thomas, on leaving Muskoka, had extracted from him to stay and watch over their father to the end, Arthur Osborne tendered his resignation from the railway. He and Annie moved to southern California, to be near one of their adult daughters already living there.

Yet in an ironic twist of fate, now that none of the Philadelphia Osbornes lived in Muskoka, Owen was at last drawn to the place. He who opposed the original Canadian gambit in the 1870s, would not move from Pennsylvania with the family, and even thwarted the Muskoka homesteaders by stalling to send William his own money, became a seasonal Muskokan.

The oldest son's interest started when his father conveyed, at one point, some of his extensive Portage Bay land to him. Then, after William's death in 1913 and Arthur's departure from Muskoka in 1915, Owen managed to get pretty much all the rest of the property, some 290 acres, including an island in Lake of Bays. On an eighty-three-acre peninsula of these Franklin Township lands he then built a fine summer residence. He delighted in bringing wealthy friends from Philadelphia, entertaining them with dramatic and astonishing tales of how his Osborne family settled and opened up the very area in which they now found themselves.

Thus the Osborne family embraced, in the very same generation, both types of "Muskokans" — the permanent and part-time residents, the former often of pioneer stock who struggle to make a go of it working in a difficult economy, the latter generally wealthy people from southern cities who enjoy the scenic splendors of Muskoka's summer season and hire locals to do the work. Whereas Thomas recounts full details of how he and Arthur cleared land, chopped firewood, and built a small birch-bark canoe themselves, for his part Owen paid, in a typical year, Maud Thompson $65.35 for care of the property, Gordon Thompson $15 to work on his boat and cut wood, Vance Allison $5 for locating a well on the property, Thomas Johnson $13.06 as caretaker of the grounds, and $40 to Gordon Thompson for "cutting remainder of wood and cleaning brush at Lake of Bays."

In California, other stars aligned. Widower Thomas Osborne, living with his son James Lawrence, generally called "J.L.," reconnected with his brother Arthur, who, after relocating to the golden state with his wife, Annie, started cattle ranching in Riverdale County, east of Los Angeles. Getting around on horseback overcame Arthur's problem of a lame leg.

As the two brothers again began spending time together, they entertained one another recalling their youthful adventures, swapping story after story, lamenting over one thing, laughing about another. Although their adventuresome life together, in what Thomas now referred to simply as "Northern Canada," had long since sunk into deep memory, it had continued to reside there, and was now resurfacing.

The more they reminisced, the more vividly episodes of their survival in the 1870s stood in heroic contrast to Thomas's relatively lack-luster decades since. As in their youth, the brothers again sparked off one another, two veterans who'd been through the same battles, on the same front, able to finish each other's sentences, capable once more of sharing a thought without exchanging a word.

All those years which had since passed since they'd been together in Muskoka now turned out to be an ally. Time, as editor of a compelling narrative, served them well. While older folk may forget who they saw a week ago or what they ate for supper the night before, most can recall with crystal clarity the smallest details across distant decades. That was the case with Thomas. With time on his hands and living with his son in the expansive California atmosphere, he could focus without interruption on the Canadian chapter in his life. In this rare combination of circumstances, by 1934 Thomas felt compelled to record the saga.

He was now seventy-five. Even if recalling events five-and-a-half decades after he'd lived them was no particular challenge, writing them was. He was suffering pain from neuritis in his arm. Still, this impediment could not stop a man who'd once struggled out of icy waters, put a blade into his foot, and overcome blackfly bites that made his neck, hands, and face resemble hamburger meat. Thomas first wrote out the story in pencil. Then he added to and corrected his draft memoir over a number of years. At last, believing he'd accurately captured the essentials of his pioneer story, he wrote the final manuscript in good, using pen and ink.

By 1942 his son J.L. Osborne, with whom Thomas continued to live in California, had become so fascinated by the tale his father had been writing that he wanted to see for himself the wild northern place where his father lived as a youth. He also wanted to discover the fate of the Osborne properties at the Portage. Maybe there was some asset to which he was, unknowingly, entitled. Travelling to Muskoka, J.L. visited Huntsville, scouted the Osborne homestead lands, and carried his father's manuscript with him everywhere, in part to help him identify places, in part to look up people mentioned in the story.

When J.L. Osborne showed the document to Harman E. Rice, editor of the *Huntsville Forester*, the astute newspaperman recognized its potential as a compelling feature article that, if serialized, would encourage readers to buy his publication week after week. Rice proceeded to publish the book-length Osborne memoirs, under the heading "Early Settlement on Peninsula Lake: The Story of a Pioneer," in installments for some twenty-four weeks between October 29, 1942, and April 22, 1943.

Thomas had done *the great deed*: he had created a published record that made sense of his life. Five years later, in 1948, this fearless man who had survived the worst nature could throw at him in Muskoka was struck down by a car in San Diego while attempting to cross 12th Street at its intersection with "E" Street. His leg was broken, but worse his skull was fractured, causing massive internal bleeding. After clinging to life for two more days, Thomas Osborne's once adventuresome life in the Canadian wilds ended in this final drama at a California hospital in San Diego County, on May 21, in the darkness of 3:00 a.m. His remains, cremated in San Diego, were buried in Philadelphia.

Arthur, now the only remaining member of the Muskoka Osborne triumvirate, continued living on his ranch, then moved into Riverside to live at 277 N on 6th Street. That was where, in 1959, he died at age ninety-eight.

Only five of Thomas Osborne's ninety years were spent in Muskoka. Yet, just as a strange combination of conditions contributed to the writing of his compelling memoir, after his death a second rare confluence of circumstances made that short span from 1874 to 1879 stand out, at least from where we see it today, as the most memorable chapter of his long life.

The first of these components was the enduring interest about the Osbornes in Muskoka. Because William and Arthur had created a strong Osborne presence in the crucial Portage area between Lake of Bays and Peninsula Lake, a local appetite existed for their saga as homesteaders in the district's early rugged days. That created a demand for Thomas's story.

A related component was that Thomas had supplied that demand by his compelling memoir about the Osborne's pioneer experience, which folded seamlessly into the beginning era of modern Muskoka.

A third component materialized two years after Thomas's death in 1948, when two of his in-laws, C.A. Bates and Jean Crosby of Bethesda, Maryland, typed his hand-written manuscript and had several copies bound for Osborne family members as a hardcover book with the title *Canada Pioneers* on its green canvas cover. This private limited edition included a preface with biographical information about Thomas we otherwise would not know today. *Canada Pioneers* also reproduced two photos of Thomas and Arthur Osborne that bookend their lives. The first, showing the brothers wearing good city clothes, was taken by a Toronto photographer in May 1875 on the instructions of their mother. Esther reasonably thought the picture might be the only lasting memento she'd have of her two sons, then about to head into Canada's untamed north in search of her quixotic husband. The second photograph was taken sixty-five years later in Los Angeles, when eighty-one-year-old Thomas and seventy-nine-year-old Arthur, again together and once more clad in suits, posed in August 1940.

The fourth component, one of those serendipitous events without which all would have been lost, occurred three-and-a-half decades after that private family edition of *Canada Pioneers* had been created. One of Thomas Osborne's grand-nieces, discovering the tome in the course of sorting through hoarded artifacts following the death of the last member in a branch of the family in 1985, perused the contents and spared it from the dumpster. She sent it, instead, to Huntsville's Pioneer Village, just in case it might be of local interest. The package was opened, but the book simply placed with other uncatalogued material.

There *Canada Pioneers* languished in storage for a half-decade more. One day Pioneer Village curator Barbara Paterson came across it. Recognizing the importance of Osborne's story, she sent the book to Boston Mills publisher John Denison, then gaining deserved renown for publishing a number of important titles about Muskoka. In 1995 the work duly appeared as a paperback, its true nature obscured by a whimsical title, *The Night the Mice Danced the Quadrille.*

Owen Osborne died on November 18, 1929, just as that autumn's fateful Great Crash of the stock market caused billions of dollars in share values to evaporate overnight, ushering in the Great Depression of the 1930s and causing textile mills and other factories to close. At his death Owen was worth well over $3 million in shares and bonds. If land values had been added, that figure would have approached $5 million.

Mary Shook Osborne, Owen's second wife, whom he married after his first wife, Catharine, died in 1910, inherited the Muskoka properties fronting on Lake of Bays. For years thereafter, she arrived in style from Rydal, Pennsylvannia, to spend her summers at the Portage, accompanied by her new husband, John Campion. Mary is still remembered today by old-timers for the expensive gifts she brought for distribution to local children. The older folk now were those children who received red-painted sleighs, books, clothing, and first-aid supplies.

Not only do such memories endure in this section of Muskoka, but place names also bear witness to the pioneering Osbornes. Although the early effort by William Osborne to become postmaster and to have the community known as "Osborne Portage" was turned down by Ottawa officials as premature in the 1870s, the Osborne name would become attached to the locality all the same.

The deep little lake on their property that nestles amidst the rocky ridges between Lake of Bays and Peninsula Lake, though never officially named, is locally called Osborne Lake. The height of land at the southern edge of this section is known as Osborne Mountain. The peninsula now occupied by homes and cottages where Owen's cottage stood is still identified as Osborne Point.

The isolated area where the Osborne's first homesteaded became a busy place. Records of the original Franklin Township land grants now in the Ontario Archives at Toronto, and subsequent transfers of title traceable in the Land Registry Office records at Bracebridge, reveal complex sets of transactions for the Osborne properties at the Portage. Apart from the legal records, the history of so much activity over the years on this small neck of land between the top of Lake of Bays and the eastern end of Peninsula Lake remains evident today in the puzzling configuration of properties, buildings, roadways, fences, and signage. After nature first made a rocky jumble of this unique place, humans managed to complicate it even more.

William stayed in the district the rest of his life. Arthur kept on as long as he was needed and physically able. Owen in time ventured north, a wealthy manufacturer who built, on land his father and brothers first claimed and cleared, a posh summer residence in place of their flea-infested log cabin, his motor launches replacing their heavy crude rowboat and homemade canoe.

Thomas would not return in person. But in reliving the Muskoka experience through his vivid memories after a half-century of estrangement from the district, he returned in the way of all writers, by creating this memoir of the most fascinating adventure of his life. Of thousands who faced pioneer testing, Thomas Osborne was among the few to memorialize his experiences, not writing mundane letters or cryptic journal entries, but in this book's dramatic real life saga. His true tale is as emotionally compelling as it is historically revealing.

What we can celebrate in *Reluctant Pioneer* is not only the resilient adaptability of humans, nor even the act of survival itself, but above all the spirit of optimistic realism which infuses both.

Muskoka Road south of Gravenhurst, September 14, 1873

ACKNOWLEDGEMENTS

THE LATE BARBARA PATERSON of Huntsville, inspirational curator of the town's Pioneer Village heritage centre, added some details of Osborne family history through her research. Barbara was instrumental, two decades ago, arranging with publisher John Denison of Boston Mills Press for a 1995 publication of Thomas Osborne's manuscript. For his part, John Denison is to be acknowledged by all who treasure Muskoka and Ontario history for the large number of splendid books he published over several decades to preserve provincial heritage.

Genealogist Sara Brower of Philadelphia searched census records, archives, probated wills, and rare books in the United States for information about the Osborne family, bringing to light many nuggets of information to enrich the Osborne saga. She also reviewed Owen Osborne's small book, *The Story of the Stocking: Reminiscences of a Manufacturer*, checked Osborne family records in England, and obtained the death certificate for Thomas from California.

Carol Williams of London, Ontario, provided the 1875 and 1940 photographs of brothers Thomas and Arthur Osborne, as youths and old men, from the original typescript copy of *Canada Pioneers*, a book now owned by Mark Miller of New Jersey. The volume had been given to Carol's grandmother, Fannie Thorne Miller Wipperman, a friend of the Osborne family.

Dominic Farrell of Toronto and Gary Long, now of Sault Ste. Marie, assisted in procuring the drawings by George Harlow White.

Gary Long, a Muskoka historian closely familiar with the geography of the Portage and its waterways, displayed avid interest and conducted research on the land holdings of the Osbornes in that vicinity.

Huntsville history volunteer Janet Fisher drew attention to the 1940s serialized publication of the Osborne narrative in the *Huntsville Forester*. Elspeth Hogg of Port Sydney, another ardent member of north Muskoka's volunteer historians, assisted making this new Dundurn edition possible, as did Huntsville councillor John Davis.

Roy MacGregor, who grew up in the same area well-known to Thomas Osborne, contributed an engaging and instructive foreword to this book. He was also persuasive that the title *The Night the Mice Danced the Quadrille*, given to the 1995 edition of Osborne's memoir which Thomas himself called *Canada Pioneers*, was not appropriate for the rich and raw story Thomas tells.

Donna Williams knows Thomas Osborne's book very well because reading that earlier edition convinced her to return to university and research Muskoka's land settlement for her master's degree. With much further research and rewriting, her thesis has now been transformed into *Hardscrabble: The High Cost of Muskoka's Free Land*, published this year by Dundurn. It was Donna who suggested this book's apt title, *Reluctant Pioneer*.

To all of them, I am gratefully indebted.

J. Patrick Boyer
Bracebridge, Muskoka
March 4, 2013

OTHER BOOKS
OF INTEREST

Hardscrabble
The High Cost of Free Land
Donna E. Williams
978-1-459708044
$22.99

A tale of deception and adversity, *Hardscrabble* tells how unscrupulous politicians, emigration agents, and philanthropists lured impoverished emigrants to farm the Muskoka backwoods in the 1870s. What these new settlers weren't told was that their land was situated on the rocky Canadian Shield.

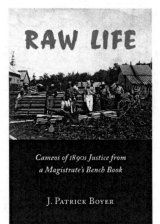

Raw Life
Cameos of 1890s Justice from a Magistrate's Bench Book
J. Patrick Boyer
978-0-978160043
$39.99

In publishing the human stories behind the late-nineteenth-century cases of Magistrate James Boyer in Bracebridge, Ontario, and Muskoka, his great-grandson J. Patrick Boyer shows that Canadian society hasn't changed much whether the focus is on early road rage, the plight of abused women, environmental contamination, or punitive treatment of the poor.

Another Country, Another Life
Calumny, Love, and the Secrets of Isaac Jelfs
J. Patrick Boyer
978-1-459708402
$24.99

Quiet Isaac Jelfs led many hard lives, his escape from each wrapped in deep secrecy. In 1869 he reached Toronto and started his new life with his new wife and his new name. His great-grandson follows that journey, revealing Jelf's well-hidden tracks and the reasons for his double life.

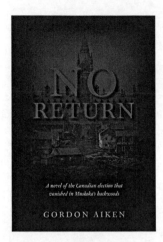

No Return
A Novel of the Canadian Election that Vanished in Muskoka's Backwoods
Gordon Aiken
978-1-926577043
$24.95

A feud that began in the Muskoka's backwoods comes to a dramatic climax with precedent-setting events in the House of Commons at Ottawa after a partisan Tory returning officer uses a technicality to make no return of the Liberal candidate as the district's elected MP in the 1872 general election.

Available at your favourite bookseller.

 DUNDURN

Visit us at
Dundurn.com
Definingcanada.ca
@dundurnpress
Facebook.com/dundurnpress